HE
NEVER
SAID...

HE NEVER SAID...

DISCOVER THE **REAL** MESSAGE OF JESUS

Steve Chalke

Hodder & Stoughton
LONDON SYDNEY AUCKLAND

British Library Cataloguing in Publication Data
A record for this book is available from the British Library

ISBN 0 340 75697 7

Typeset by Avon Dataset Ltd, Bidford-on-Avon, Warks

Printed and bound in Great Britain by
The Guernsey Press Co. Ltd, Channel Isles

Hodder & Stoughton
A Division of Hodder Headline Ltd
338 Euston Road
London NW1 3BH

To my good friend and colleague David McGavin,
who knew the real Jesus and inspired me in my
own relationship with him.

Acknowledgements

A great big 'thanks' to my friend Martyn Joseph, whose song 'He Never Said' provided the inspiration for this book, and to all those people whose hard work and commitment made it a reality, especially Aredi Pitsiaeli, Tina Millen, James Griffin, the team at *Christianity* magazine (John Buckeridge, Andy Peck and Steve Adams) and the team at Hodders (Charles Nettleton, David Moloney and Julie Hatherall). Special thanks to my co-author, Paul, for correcting my grammar over the last six years.

Contents

Acknowledgements   vii
Introduction   1

1   'God helps those who help themselves'   9
2   'The family that prays together stays together'   17
3   'An eye for an eye'   25
4   'You can't take it with you when you die'   34
5   'There's no room for doubt'   43
6   'And now for a time of worship'   53
7   'There's no such thing as a free lunch'   62
8   'Religion and politics don't mix'   72
9   'Success is the key'   84
10   'Accept me into your heart as your personal Lord and Saviour'   95
11   'Better safe than sorry'   105
12   'Touch the screen and you'll be healed'   114
13   'Would you like to apply for church membership?'   124
14   'Pray the little prayer with me'   137
15   'My country, right or wrong'   149
16   'You can't teach an old dog new tricks'   162
17   'If you're a nice guy, nice things happen to you'   175

18 'The Lord laid this on my heart' 184
19 'When in Rome, do as the Romans do' 195
20 'If you've got it, flaunt it' 208

Conclusion 219

Further reading 221
Works cited 224

Introduction

It caused a scandal. In fact, many readers of the USA's leading Catholic newspaper, the *National Catholic Reporter*, must have registered shock levels high on the Richter scale when they saw the cover of the special millennium issue. The paper had earlier launched a competition to find a new painting of Jesus for the new millennium, and the cover featured the winning picture. Picked from 1,700 entries by a panel that included British art critic and nun Sister Wendy Beckett, it was painted by Janet McKenzie, who claimed she had tried to make it 'as inclusive as possible'. But many of the *NCR*'s more conservative readers felt positively *excluded* by the picture, which depicts Jesus not only with what the artist calls 'a subtle feminine dimension' (though the face is male, the model was a woman), but also as being poor and black.

It goes against the grain for most of us. We've become used to seeing Jesus portrayed as a middle-class white man in everything from early Roman and Byzantine icons to Renaissance paintings and big-budget Hollywood movies. Even Agape's much-vaunted *Jesus* film and the famous painting of Jesus standing at the door and knocking ('The Light of the World') by William Holman Hunt, featured in Holy Trinity, Brompton's massively successful *Alpha* course, both picture a white, attractive, respectable, educated,

1

wholesome and middle-class Jesus. In short, the Jesus we normally encounter in art and films is the kind of man you'd feel comfortable with, the kind you'd invite home to meet your mother. He's *not* the kind of person you'd imagine ending up on Death Row. And yet, as the Gospels tell us, the truth is that's exactly where he *did* end up.

Of course, we all know full well that Jesus wasn't white, just as we know that the early first-century culture he lived in – the one that bursts out from the pages of the New Testament – was totally different from our own early twenty-first-century one. We *know* that he was an olive-skinned, Aramaic-speaking, circumcised Palestinian Jew from what's known as the 'classical' period of history. Nevertheless, most of the time we behave and act *as if* he were modern, suburban, Western and well-to-do.

The imitation of Christ

Let our chief endeavour be to meditate on the life of Jesus Christ.
Fifteenth-century German monk Thomas à Kempis

We tend to think of Jesus as being exactly like us . . . so much so, in fact, that it's easy for us to forget just how different his world really was, and to end up imagining that the kind of things *we* do and say are the kind of things *he* did and said. As a result, we often use him to rubber-stamp values and ideas he not only *didn't* believe in, but *wouldn't* have believed in. What's more, most of the time we're not even aware we're doing it.

Tony Campolo remembers being interviewed by the Draft Board for military service back in the 1950s. Finding out that he was a Christian, an Air Force officer asked Tony if he was a 'conscientious objector'. Tony had no idea what that meant, so the officer asked him, 'If you were in a bomber flying over an enemy city, and you knew there were civilians down there, would you still go ahead drop the bombs?'

'I'm not sure,' Tony replied. 'I guess I'd have to pray, and ask Jesus what he'd do.'

'That's ridiculous,' exclaimed the Air Force officer, mentally dismissing Tony as an idiot and marking him unsuitable. 'Everyone knows Jesus wouldn't drop bombs!'

The experience made Tony think. Why, he asked himself, do we naturally assume that the rest of us, even those of us who call ourselves Christian, are allowed to do things that we know, deep down, Jesus would never do?

The last few years have seen a massive craze in Evangelical Christian circles of badges or bracelets bearing the letters WWJD, an abbreviated form of 'What Would Jesus Do?' Some critics have dismissed the initiative as nothing more than a tasteless exercise in making money, but many of those who've supported the idea feel there's a more noble purpose: to encourage young Christians to think about their actions within a moral framework. In a sense, it's a crash course in Christian ethics. But the problem is, many Christians – young and old – don't actually know enough about Jesus to know what he *would* do.

A recent poll revealed that a third of all churchgoers hardly ever read the Bible, and some have never read it at all . . . ever! But tragically, even those of us who read it regularly often do little more than skim the surface. We never really let it *disturb* us. Instead, we tend to scoot over the difficult bits rather than wrestling with their meaning. In fact, not only do most of us have huge gaps in our knowledge of Jesus and the Gospels, but we then unthinkingly tend to fill in these gaps with our own, very modern and Western imagination.

'God created humanity in his own image,' seventeenth-century French mathematician and theologian Blaise Pascal said, wryly adding, 'Unfortunately, humanity decided to return the favour.' Two hundred years later, the German philosopher Ludwig Feuerbach tried to prove him right by arguing that what we call 'God' is really no more than a cosmic projection of what we think the ideal human should be. The famous French sociologist Émile Durkheim picked up on this idea, suggesting that God is a 'collective representation' of the human mind: our beliefs, values and opinions. Every society,

Durkheim argued, unconsciously shapes and develops its concept of God over time, so a particular society's concept of God is really a mirror image of its own core values.

There's more than a grain of truth in this. As Greek philosopher Xenophanes remarked in around 500 BC, 'The Ethiopians say that their gods are snub-nosed and black, the Thracians that theirs have light blue eyes and red hair.' The Greeks' muscle-bound, virile gods and slim, sensual goddesses were part fantasy, part mirror-image of their worshippers' own culture. But tragically, in the last two millennia, Christians have also been guilty of doing the same thing.

Twenty-twenty vision

It's not always easy to see where a legitimate school of thought ends and heresy begins.
German pastor and theologian Dietrich Bonhoeffer

The Willowbank Report from the Lausanne Convention on World Evangelisation defined culture as 'an integrated system of beliefs, values, customs and institutions which bind a society together and give it a sense of identity, dignity, security and continuity'. In his book *Religion and the Rise of Capitalism*, social historian Richard Tawney showed how Christians of all denominations have consistently, but unintentionally, endorsed and even helped create our Western, capitalist culture. Durkheim was blunt in making a similar point: 'Western Christianity is no more than a religionising of capitalist culture.'

Of course, as Christians we know from personal experience that Western Christianity is *far* more than a 'religionising of capitalist culture'. Unfortunately, if we're honest, we have to admit that Christianity has all too often accepted and swallowed huge doses of a culture that is far more capitalist than Christ-like. God is a real, eternal, transcendent being, but the fact remains that our *understanding* of him – and his unique Son, Jesus – is often coloured by the values that lie at the heart of our society. As Lesslie Newbigin noted, 'Our culture issues us with a pair of glasses through which we see and understand the world.' If we're not careful, we only ever see and understand God through these glasses as well.

A few years ago, I had the chance to meet the famous anti-apartheid campaigner Bayers Naudé. Though his work eventually won him the Nobel peace prize, he'd been brought up a firm supporter of apartheid. As a young preacher in the Dutch Reformed Church, he'd positively enjoyed preaching about white superiority and the separation of the races, which he'd considered 'ordained by God'. Apartheid was so much a part of his understanding of God that he couldn't see how it could be wrong. As a result, until the 'scales fell from his eyes' in his mid-thirties, he not only used Jesus and the Bible as a rubber stamp for his racist ideas, but he even attacked as 'anti-Christian' all those who criticised his position. As American theologian Reinhold Niebuhr once put it, 'The tendency to claim God as an ally for our partisan values and ends is . . . the source of all religious fanaticism.'

This may be an extreme example, but the truth is that we all do the same every time we unthinkingly assume that What Jesus Would Do is more or less the same as what we would do in any given situation. Without aiming to, we recreate Jesus in our own image, enlisting him as an ally in whatever we want to justify. If we're not careful, we jump to conclusions about what he'd say, do and think based on a hurried and superficial reading of the Gospels, and perhaps even a rather generous dose of wishful thinking. All too often we merely give a thin 'spiritual' veneer to values and agendas that in reality have little or nothing to do with genuine biblical concerns . . . and may even run entirely contrary to them!

All things to everyone

Christianity was born in Palestine. They took it to Greece and they made it into a philosophy. They took it to Rome and they made it into an institution. They took it to America and they made it into a

***business enterprise. They took it to England and they made it into
a tourist attraction.***

American sociology professor Tony Campolo

When Paul took his Christian gospel to Gentile cultures, he insisted
on adapting his way of expressing that gospel to the surrounding
culture. In fact, he was prepared to use all means at his disposal to
help him explain what a Christian was – even going so far as to
enlist the aid of pagan philosophers, poets and an altar to an
'unknown god' (Acts 17). But while Paul was a contemporary of
Jesus, fully versed in the cultures of both pagan Rome (being a
Roman citizen) and Jewish Palestine (having studied under Rabbi
Gamaliel in Jerusalem), who was concerned to make sure that
'nothing got lost in the translation', many of those who've followed
in his footsteps have been nothing like so well-informed or
conscientious.

When Roman Emperor Constantine converted to Christianity
in AD 312, the Church seized the opportunity to do more than just
communicate the gospel to Roman culture and society, and began
actively trying to *influence* them. Tragically, by this time it was
becoming increasingly difficult to know what was authentically
Christian and what was just Roman. As a result, from the role of
vicars and bishops to the basic view of God, authority and the
kingdom, pagan Roman society left its indelible mark on the
Church.

British missionaries faced an identical problem in the nineteenth
century, when imperial colonial ambitions gave the Church an
unparalleled chance to take the gospel to previously unexplored
parts of the world. Men and women arrived on the 'mission field'
in their thousands, spreading 'the gospel' and starting churches. But
few of them had any real skill in discerning what was genuinely
ungodly in the native traditions and cultures they encountered, and
what was just a different way of doing things. All too often, they
made no real effort to distinguish what was 'Christian' from what
was 'British' – it was something they'd never had to do in the UK.

Instead, they simply assumed that since Britain was a Christian country, British ways were inevitably Christian ways, and vice versa.

Tragically, the legacy of that mistake is still obvious today in a great many churches in what were once British colonies. I've visited churches where congregations are all dressed in suits in sweltering temperatures, where services are in English rather than the people's indigenous language, and where the music seems to have undergone a rhythm bypass operation. Many have hardly changed their format since the day the missionaries left. More than anything else, they're a dull echo of old-fashioned Victorian society half a world away and 100 years on.

In this book, I'm going to be taking my cue from Martyn Joseph's song 'He Never Said', and looking at a number of the popular slogans, sayings and proverbs that reflect some of the core values not only of our society, but also quite often of the Church. I'll be examining a few of the modern myths and philosophies that characterise society, and asking, Did Jesus believe that? *Would* Jesus say that? And to answer these questions, I'll be taking a closer look at some of the things that Jesus not only *would* say, but actually did.

Prepare to be *disturbed*.

1

'God helps those who help themselves'

'Tell me what you want – what you really really want.'

The anthem of a pre-teen generation, the Spice Girls' 'Wannabe' stormed to the top of the 1996 charts, catapulting Sporty, Scary, Posh, Baby and Ginger to instant global fame. But as well as ushering in a pop phenomenon, the song also heralded the arrival of 'girl power' – a potent cocktail of feisty feminism and sassy self-promotion, together with a huge dose of self-help philosophy. If you 'really really want' something – anything – and you're prepared to put in enough hard work and make the necessary sacrifices, you can really really have it. It's a very appealing message, especially to tens of thousands of pre-teenage wannabes. But all the same, it's still nothing but tosh.

Don't get me wrong. I'm not against hard work and I'm definitely not of the view that, if it's 'meant to be', success will just fall into your lap while you do nothing but sit and wait. Nothing of lasting value is ever achieved without hard graft. My experience over the last fifteen years as Founding Director of Oasis Trust has taught me that. But I've also learnt that you sometimes *want* hard and *work* hard and … it still doesn't happen. Call it fate, providence or the way the cookie crumbles – it's just how it is. Sometimes – despite your best efforts, the right contacts, and even the prayerful certainty that you're doing the right thing – it all falls apart. Laziness may be a guarantee of failure, but that doesn't mean that sheer effort – even when you're convinced your cause is a 'righteous' one – will therefore guarantee success.

Doing the 'Lord's work'

They say hard work never hurt anybody, but I figure, why take the chance?

Attributed to former US President Ronald Reagan

In fact, far from being original, the Spice Girls were actually doing no more than buying into a version of the well-worn proverb 'God helps those who help themselves', which dates right back to the Greek playwright Aeschylus in the fifth century BC ('God likes to help those who toil'). However, despite its age, it wasn't really until the eighteenth century that this particular piece of soundbite theology became popular, having first begun to take root in the public imagination during the Reformation.

By the early 1500s, Europe was caught in a ferment of fast-moving, dramatic change, rocked by wave on wave of technological and intellectual innovation. The communications revolution was in full swing, having begun with the invention of the first 'moveable type' printing press by Johannes Gensfleisch zum Gutenberg in Mainz in the 1450s. Suddenly, books and tracts (including the famous 'Gutenberg Bible') could be mass produced, opening up the original information superhighway by taking learning out of the cloister and onto the street. At the same time, the world itself was rapidly expanding: Columbus had discovered the Caribbean in 1492, and the Spanish and Portuguese were exploring the coastline of Africa and unlocking the secrets of the Far East. The impact of all this was a socio-economic revolution – the old medieval way of doing things was breaking down, and a new middle class of merchants and professionals was on the rise. Gone forever were the days when everyone 'knew their place'.

In the midst of this turmoil, on Halloween night 1517, a little-known German monk named Martin Luther nailed a printed placard to the door of Castle Church, Wittenburg. On it, in Latin, was a ninety-five-point 'Disputation on the Power and Efficacy of Indulgences'. The aim of these so-called 'Ninety-Five Theses' was to attack church corruption and kick-start a serious churchwide debate on the nature of repentance, but things quickly spiralled out of Luther's control. In the end, his theological ideas were to have a far-reaching impact not just on the Church's doctrine of repentance, but on *every* aspect of European society, blowing apart the old medieval worldview with all the force of a nuclear explosion.

Nowhere is this more evident than in the spur Luther's reforming theology gave the new middle class. As a result of Luther's emphasis on the 'priesthood of all believers' – which radically redefined the old idea of 'vocation' – secular work came to acquire a new level of dignity. People began to realise that it wasn't just priests, monks and nuns whose daily strivings were 'honouring to God' and who could claim to have a 'holy calling'. Instead, *everyone* had a 'calling'. Everyone's work could be 'honouring to God'.

By the time of the Puritans, a century later, this kind of thinking had developed into a full-blown 'work ethic'. In a nutshell, if you were 'called' to be a trader or butcher, for example, you should work hard to become the very *best* trader or butcher possible. Work was no longer a 'necessary evil' – it was a God-given responsibility and a positive virtue.

Over time, of course, the definition of what it meant to be the 'best possible' trader or butcher became confused and corrupted, as in a game of Chinese whispers. Did they essentially make money or provide a service? It was tempting to see work no longer just in terms of serving people and meeting needs, but as being 'successful' … along with its seeming side-effect of accumulating wealth. As a result, people began to see hard work in the pursuit of success and wealth as a divinely sanctioned activity.

As twentieth-century historian Richard Tawney noted, for many Puritans 'a creed which transformed the acquisition of wealth from a drudgery or a temptation into a moral duty was the milk of lions'. Now 'the good Christian was not wholly dissimilar from the economic man'. Sociologist Max Weber, in his landmark book *The Protestant Ethic and the Spirit of Capitalism*, reached the same conclusion. He showed how the idea of God 'calling' people to 'excellence' in particular professions had helped foster the rapid growth of capitalism and the new breed of self-help economics – despite the fact that most Protestant theology was actually *opposed* to capitalist principles!

Just how far it's possible to take the 'work ethic' idea was demonstrated by 1950s stripper Blaze Starr. In her autobiography, she remembers returning to her small-town US home and admitting to her devout Christian mum that she was an 'exotic dancer' having an affair with state governor Earl Long. She also remembers her mum's reply: 'Well, if that's the gift God gave you, I guess the Christian thing is for you to do it as well as you possibly can!'

With God on our side?

Whenever the Church forgets its call to engage in the task of understanding more and more fully who Jesus actually was, idolatry and ideology lie close at hand.

Canon theologian of Westminster Abbey,
Rev. Tom Wright

One of the great dangers of this 'work ethic', of course, is the way it makes us assume that – because God has given us all talent, and encouraged us to work hard to use it – when we *do* we'll be guaranteed big-time success. From there it's just a short hop, skip and a jump to assuming that – because we're working hard, using our God-given talent, and are successful – God must approve of what we're doing. He must even *help*. And that's how a Protestant 'work ethic' spawns the misinformed saying that 'God helps those who help themselves'.

But the truth is, as virtuous and valuable as they are, neither hard work nor success offer any proof *whatsoever* that what we're doing carries God's official Seal of Approval. It's not for nothing that 'God helps those who help themselves' is dubbed the 'Thief's Charter'. Sometimes, hard work and success accompany the most ungodly ventures, even when those involved convince themselves that God is their helper.

In Nazi Germany, Hitler's infamous National Socialist Party was one of the hardest-working bodies ever to have existed, going from total obscurity to total control of a major world power within ten years. As astonishing as it sounds, most Nazi activists firmly believed they were working with God on their side. In fact, Hitler himself made a number of speeches in which he explicitly claimed divine backing for his cruel brand of ultra-nationalist, racist ideology. 'We tolerate no one in our ranks,' he once remarked of the Nazi party, 'who offends against the ideas of Christianity. In fact, our movement is Christian.'

Tragically, buoyed up by Hitler's phenomenal success – first turning around the country's rock-bottom economy and then pushing ahead with its long-held military ambitions – few Germans seriously doubted the truth of his words. Their success seemed to *prove* God was on their side. The idea that 'God helps those who help themselves' was so ingrained in their thinking that there just didn't seem to be another reasonable explanation. Success and God's support seemed to go hand in hand. Hitler's mistress, Eva Braun, summed up the feelings of many Germans in the closing stages of the war, when it was obvious the Nazi cause was lost, in a letter written from her bunker during the heavy Allied bombing of Berlin: 'I can't understand how all this can happen. It's enough to make one lose one's faith in God!'

It was left to a few brave men to attack this pro-Nazi philosophy . . . and all suffered as a consequence. Of the three most famous church leaders to speak out against Hitler, Karl Barth (one of the twentieth century's greatest theologians) was exiled, Dietrich Bonhoeffer was executed and Martin Niemöller became Hitler's 'personal prisoner'. Most Germans just ignored their cries, sure that Nazi success was confirmation of the 'righteousness' of their ugly cause.

'Insignificant others'

We have made Christianity into a lifestyle of middle-class propriety instead of a call to have one's heart broken by the things that break the heart of Jesus.
American sociologist and Baptist minister Tony Campolo

The truth is, Jesus never said, 'God helps those who help themselves.' In fact, on a number of occasions, in a number of different ways, he said exactly the opposite. As a Jew with a good knowledge of his people's history, and a firm grasp of the writings of the Hebrew Bible, he was only too aware of the well-established Old Testament principle that God helps those who *can't* help themselves ... and expects his people to do the same.

The prophets of Israel and Judah had tirelessly attacked their own people for the heartless way they dealt with the permanent underclass of widows, orphans and 'aliens' – those with 'no visible means of support'. Like the rest of the ancient Near East, Palestinian culture was male-dominated: women and children were totally dependent on men for support, so if a woman or a child had no living male relative, they could end up destitute. Similarly, as the economy was based on land and agriculture, with tight restrictions on foreign ownership, resident 'aliens' had nothing to fall back on if things went wrong and were entirely at the mercy of their Jewish neighbours.

The prophets pulled no punches in their efforts to make it very clear that God judged the people's faithfulness to his covenant 'deal' with them – and the faithfulness of their leaders in particular – at least in part by how they treated these vulnerable members of society. This was a major theme for them. It saturates their writings. The people's treatment of those on the 'underside of history' was more than just a good indicator of their real values or 'litmus test' of their approach to justice. As far as God was concerned, it was a key issue to do with their 'covenant faithfulness' to him, since he saw *himself* as the ultimate 'father of orphans and protector of widows' (Psalm 68:5).

That's why Jesus tells the 'poor in spirit', 'those who mourn', 'the meek' and 'those who hunger and thirst for righteousness' that they're blessed because 'theirs is the kingdom of heaven', 'they will be comforted', 'they will inherit the earth' and 'they will be filled' (Matthew 5:3–6). As American theologian Scot McKnight notes, 'When Jesus says "they will be comforted," he means "God will comfort them"; when he says "they will be filled," he means "God will fill them up".' Why? Not because of anything they've done, but simply because they have *no one else* to comfort them or fill them. God is their only defender.

There's nothing virtuous about being 'poor in spirit' or 'meek'. In fact, these four terms all mean the same thing. They're all ways of describing society's most vulnerable members, using imagery borrowed from the time when the people of Judah were exiles in Babylon – oppressed, needy, mourning the destruction of Jerusalem and longing for God to come and rescue them, restoring the 'honour of his name'. The reason why Jesus chose to use this powerful imagery was to remind people of the foundational truth that God helps those who *can't* help themselves.

This 'bias to the poor', as former Bishop of Liverpool David Sheppard calls it, is a theme that recurs constantly in Jesus' life – forming the backdrop, for example, of what has often been called his 'inaugural speech' in Luke 4:18–19. Taking his cue from the book of Isaiah (61:1–2), Jesus made it clear that he saw his mission fundamentally in terms of helping those who couldn't help themselves. He'd been 'anointed' (the literal meaning of the word 'messiah') to bring 'good news to the oppressed, to bind up the broken-hearted, to proclaim liberty to the captives, and release to the prisoners; to proclaim the [Jubilee] year of the Lord's favour'.

That's why, for me, the Spice Girls' arrival on the world scene *won't* be one of my top ten memories of 1996, but the founding of the Jubilee 2000 campaign *will*. For while girl power promised no more than that 'God helps those who help themselves', Jubilee 2000 helped put the cancellation of unrepayable Third World debt on everyone's agenda for the new millennium. And not only was this a powerful way of saying that God really does help those who *can't* help themselves, but it was also a strong statement of the truth that God expects us to make it a high priority to do exactly the same.

2

'The family that prays together stays together'

The press had a field day. The story was a peach: well-known, well-respected, conservative Evangelical church leader, with a firm reputation for promoting and defending 'family values', leaves his wife and family after resigning his job as a local pastor over issues to do with his sexuality.

The 'fall from grace' in 1999 of Baptist minister Roy Clements provoked a cocktail of emotional reactions from Christians across the UK and beyond: shock, sadness, incredulity, confusion, betrayal. More than just a straight-talking, clear, uncompromising Bible teacher, for many young Christians he was an inspirational role model. While some leaders from his own Reformed, Calvinist background engaged in theological gymnastics to determine whether or not he'd ever been a Christian in the first place, many others from a host of different denominations and groupings simply couldn't believe the news, and some were just at a loss to understand how it could have happened. How *can* a marriage and a family fall apart at the seams when both the husband and wife are 'sincere, Spirit-filled, Bible-believing, born-again Christians'?

But 'Roygate' is far more than just a tragic story of the breakdown of one man's marriage and the collapse of his career. It's a salutary warning to us all of how naïve it is to imagine that if we simply go through the spiritual motions, we'll somehow achieve immunity to the various problems and heartaches that affect the rest of humanity. It just isn't true that, as Christians, we're 'saved' from having to wrestle with our sexuality, resist the temptation of an affair, struggle over problems with the kids, bite back our anger or fight the onset of depression. Faith isn't a kind of fairy godmother that ensures we'll never wake up and wonder where all the passion went in our relationship, or why we and our partner don't seem to talk anymore except on a superficial level. It's the height of folly to imagine that, provided we've had a daily prayer time, we'll live a trouble-free existence, radiating a glow-in-the-dark spirituality that'll attract people in droves.

It's just this kind of warped logic that produced popular American slogans like 'the family that prays together stays together'. It's the worst kind of bumper-sticker theology, still-born and totally incapable of equipping us for the realities of life – as they say, 'For every complex and intractable problem, there's usually a straight-forward and simple answer . . . and it's always wrong!' However, the inadequacy of this logic doesn't stop it fuelling the very kind of Sunday-paper scandalmongering we so deplore (but avidly soak up anyway). Why are the tabloids so keen to find yet another vicar who's run off with the choir mistress? Because so many Christians, both publicly and privately, deny the fact that life is a constant struggle, convinced instead that a 'saving faith in Jesus' and a few basic spiritual laws are all you need to guarantee effortless success in all areas of life. But Roddy Wright – the former Catholic Bishop of Argyll and the Isles, whose 'disappearance' and subsequent resignation to pursue a relationship with a divorcee kept the Sunday press busy for months – hit the nail on the head with the title of his autobiography: we've all got *Feet of Clay*.

No holds barred

No problem is solved when we idly wait for God to undertake full responsibility.

Martin Luther King

A few years ago, I surveyed the Christian twenty-somethings I was in contact with. As part of a project I was involved with at the time, I asked all those whose families had routinely prayed together just how helpful they'd found the experience. The research yielded startling results: those whose parents had imposed praying together as an article of daily dogma almost universally saw it as a negative, manipulative and even divisive experience; by stark contrast, those whose families had taken a more informal, occasional approach tended to view it far more positively.

A friend of mine summarised the survey's findings by joking, 'It's not what you do, it's the way that you do it!' And she's right. There is, of course, absolutely nothing *wrong* with families praying together. In fact, there's a huge amount *right* with it. For starters, it's a great way to help children understand that faith isn't a bolt-on feature, but an integral part of life. But there are three all-too-easy traps to fall into: control, conceit and complacency.

Control
The Anglican *Alternative Service Book* described giving God 'thanks and praise' as 'our duty and our joy, at all times and in all places'. The challenge for every family is to major on the *joy* and minimise the sense of *duty*. If family prayers are allowed to become a mechanical chore slavishly built into a regimented daily routine, there'll be very little joy in them at all. Instead, they'll slowly degenerate into sombre, stifling occasions with little or no room for spontaneity, laughter or (God forbid!) eye contact. If prayer is foisted on children as a lifeless obligation – a meaningless but rigid ritual – they'll come to see faith as blind, unquestioning obedience to a stern, authoritarian 'father' figure. Dogma and

dictatorship dressed up as 'spirituality' always does more harm than good.

Conceit

When I was growing up, 'the family that prays together stays together' was an unwritten rule. Respectable Christian families were expected to go the whole Evangelical nine yards, starting or ending each day with a time of family prayer and Bible study around the kitchen table. Those of us whose parents *didn't* insist on this never dreamt of admitting it in Christian circles: to do so would have risked inviting suggestions that our family was not only 'back-slidden', but probably also teetering on the edge of break-up. It was generally taken for granted that time spent together in fervent prayer was not only a cure-all for any kind of family tension, but a benchmark of any proper, wholesome Christian family.

Many of the young people I surveyed said they'd felt like 'second-class Christians' when they were growing up because their families hadn't regularly prayed together. Some had parents who weren't Christians, so praying together wasn't an option; others came from families where it just wasn't part of the daily routine and ethos. They all felt excluded by the impression, unconsciously given by many of their local churches and the families that *did* 'holy huddle', that praying together somehow made a family spiritually more 'in tune', more godly and therefore better equipped to stay together. Of course, this impression wasn't true then, just as it isn't true today – as amply demonstrated by the fact that the divorce rate among 'born again', 'Bible Belt', Southern Baptists (who invented the slogan 'the family that prays together stays together') is as high as the US as a whole.

Complacency

Of all the things I struggle with in life, my role as a father is one of the most rewarding, but also one of the toughest. If I've learnt one thing in nearly two decades of parenting, it's that *all* parents are learners – we all wear 'L' plates, and we all struggle and make mistakes. There are no mumbled magic words or easy-to-follow three-step plans to a stress-free, carefree, sin-free life. 'Quick fix' solutions tend to be 'quick broke' ones as well. That's why simplistic creeds like 'the family that prays together stays together' are so dangerous: imagining that a single daily dose of eyes-closed praise and intercession will automatically immunise your family from harm is nothing less than naïve daydreaming. There are no instant 'success' formulae for permanently content families, and there never will be. So any soundbite that gives the impression that fifteen minutes of prayer round the breakfast table can be a substitute for loads of constant hard work and effort is at best misleading and at worst fatal.

The slogan 'the family that prays together stays together' may trip off your tongue, but try to live by it and it'll trip you up. Prayer is vital, but on its own will never guarantee family cohesion. The key word in the slogan is *together*, not *prays*. A flower blossoms when it's watered and dies in a drought. Relationships grow when you invest time and love in them, and wither or die when you don't. That's true of our relationship with God, and it's equally true of our family relationships. Praying together is invaluable – though I've actually spent far more time *playing* with my children than *praying* with them over the years – but if it's the only time a family spends together, that family is heading for the rocks. Praying together is something to be done *as well as*, not *instead of*, laughing together, eating together, relaxing together, having days out together, talking together, listening to each other and occasionally even crying together.

All in the family?

What people usually ask for in their prayers is that two and two do not equal four.

Anonymous

From everything the New Testament tells us, far from endorsing 'the family that prays together stays together', Jesus seems to have believed almost the exact reverse: the family that stays together may eventually enjoy the ability to pray together.

Families were at the heart of life in first-century Palestine, but they were far from the modern-day nuclear nest of Mum, Dad, two-point-four kids and a hamster. Up to five generations lived together in a household, and the head man was responsible for the wealth and wellbeing of them all. A family functioned as nursery, school system, employment agency, marital home, religious centre, moral compass and retirement plan for all its many members, providing love, care and support 'from the cradle to the grave'.

By Jesus' time, Jews had also begun to extend their idea of the family beyond the limits of blood and marriage. Both in the bustling cities of pagan Greece and in the towns and villages of occupied Palestine, synagogues had begun to spring up as a kind of 'second family', giving emotional and practical support as well as a place for this wider 'family' to pray and worship together.

But Jesus took this idea even further – *much* further than most Jews, especially Pharisees and other Jewish leaders, were happy with. In fact, according to the Gospels, his innovative reinterpretation of the 'family' unit so scandalised his contemporaries that even his blood relatives thought he'd gone too far and 'lost his senses' (see Mark 3:21).

Home is where the heart is

Home is the place where, when you have to go there, they have to take you in.

US poet Robert Frost

In Mark 3:33, having been told that his mother and brothers have come to see him, Jesus asks rhetorically, 'Who are my mother and my brothers?' Then, in a house crowded with all sorts of different people, he looks around and delivers his shocking answer: 'Whoever does the will of God is my brother and sister and mother.' These words would have struck even some of his most open-minded hearers as nothing less than a breaking of the fifth commandment. But far from breaking it, Jesus was actually *extending* it to cover not just immediate (extended) family but all the 'children of Israel', including the notorious 'outcasts': the tax-collectors, prostitutes and 'sinners'.

This redefinition of the 'family' was so revolutionary that most of Jesus' contemporaries just couldn't cope with it. It was absolutely outrageous for someone of Jesus' influence and authority to eat with tax-collectors and unrepentant 'sinners' (whose wilful neglect of Jewish law isolated them not only from God, but also from their fellow Jews). By doing so, Jesus seemed to be endorsing sinful behaviour and watering down the content of the faith. As far as the Pharisees were concerned, this smacked of the woolly liberalism that was eroding the distinction between God's 'holy nation' and the pagans. For them, Jesus was demonstrating a damaging and treasonous moral laxity just where Jews needed to maintain their distinctiveness if they were to fulfil their God-given vocation as a 'light to the Gentiles' (see Isaiah 42:6).

The truth is, of course, that by placing *acceptance* before *repentance*, Jesus was offering people commonly considered 'beyond redemption' a way back. In essence, he was arguing that belonging precedes believing, which will eventually lead to behaving; that repentance is a *response* to God's love rather than a *precondition* for receiving it.

Some friends of mine, Richard and Kathy, were very committed Christians, so when their daughter Ruth announced she was moving in with her 'non-Christian' boyfriend, David, they were beside themselves. And when she asked if she and David could come and stay for the weekend, Richard was solid as a rock. He reminded her that he and Kathy had standards, and made it perfectly clear that Ruth and David would either have to agree to use separate bedrooms or else stay away for good. Taking it as a personal rejection, they chose to stay away for good. In fact, shortly afterwards they moved away altogether to France.

Fifteen years passed with no contact other than an exchange of

Christmas and birthday cards – fifteen years during which Ruth and David married and had two children that Richard and Kathy never saw. Finally, an ageing Richard, torn apart by the tension between his desire to maintain his moral standards and his aching to see his daughter again – not to mention his grandchildren for the first time – wrote a letter of apology. It took some time to rebuild the relationship, but today David and Ruth and their two daughters regularly holiday with Richard and Kathy. In fact, last year David, who's now a Christian, asked Richard if they could spend some time praying together about the girls' education and his job.

The truth is, Jesus welcomes (back) all sorts of people we're tempted to write off, and he calls us as individuals and the Church to do exactly the same. No one is outside the 'family' or beyond redemption . . . including, of course, Roy Clements. We glibly assert that 'the family that prays together stays together', but Jesus teaches us that the 'family' that casts its net as wide as it can – and refuses to give up on any of its 'members' – may eventually reach the place where it enjoys the experience of finally being able to pray together.

3

'An eye for an eye'

In the wake of Harold Shipman's conviction for multiple murder, a news crew interviewed the daughter of one of the infamous Manchester GP's many victims. Speaking on the day the guilty verdict was handed down, she made it clear that, for her, justice was still far from done. Asked what more she wanted, she delivered a chillingly honest reply: 'I'd like to get my hands on him!'

I remember a few years earlier meeting a couple whose only daughter had been killed by a car while out riding her bike. The driver responsible was driving without a licence – his licence had been revoked as a result of a prior conviction! The judge sent him to prison for manslaughter. But for the girl's parents, Roger and Cathy, this just wasn't enough. When he was released from prison after just a couple of years, Roger borrowed a friend's shotgun and shot the driver, fully intending to kill him. Amazingly, the man survived, and Roger was tried for attempted murder. Even more amazingly, he was acquitted. The jury found the driver – who'd never once shown the slightest sign of remorse – so repulsive they delivered a unanimous verdict of 'not guilty'. But for Roger and Cathy, it was still far from over. All they could think of was exacting their own brand of 'justice' on their daughter's killer. In fact, when I asked Cathy if she wished Roger had been successful in his attempt at murder, her reply sent shivers down my spine. 'No,' she said. 'I need to pull that trigger myself. I need to see him dead, and know *I'm* responsible.'

Making the punishment fit the crime

Real forgiveness means looking steadily at the sin, the sin that is left over without any excuse, after all allowances have been made, and seeing it in all its horror, dirt, meanness and malice, and nevertheless being wholly reconciled to the person who has done it. That, and only that, is forgiveness.

Cambridge medievalist and writer C. S. Lewis

Not everyone takes things as far as Roger and Cathy, of course, but behind their extremist attitude is the ever-popular, ancient approach to justice known as retaliation – a principle most clearly and famously expressed in the line from the Lord High Executioner's song in Gilbert and Sullivan's celebrated Victorian operetta *The Mikado*: 'Let the punishment fit the crime.'

'Retaliation' comes from the Latin word *talis*, meaning 'like' or 'such'. In other words, by its very definition it's the practice of matching like for like: punishment for crime. As Deuteronomy 19:21 defines it, 'Life for life, eye for eye, tooth for tooth, hand for hand, foot for foot.' Retaliation is built into justice systems for a number of reasons, but two of them take pride of place: *deterrence* and, to an even greater degree, *retribution*.

First, retaliation is meant to be an effective *deterrent*, convincing at least some potential criminals of the truth of the maxim that 'crime doesn't pay', dissuading them from future criminal activity. Crippling fines, stiff custodial sentences, other harsh penalties and the ultimate deterrent – the death penalty – are all designed to send the message that crime isn't worth it because the cost of getting caught is too high. In medieval times, the deterrent element of the death penalty, in particular, was emphasised by the *means* of execution ordered by the courts. England may have considered the continental practices of crucifixion and breaking on the wheel to be too barbaric to use, but it was still standard practice to burn heretics, hang common criminals and behead nobles. For traitors, the end was the even more grisly fate of being hanged, drawn and quartered: those found guilty were partially hanged, then taken down and killed by disembowelling and castration, and finally, after death, chopped into quarters to be displayed around the town.

But in fact, there's little evidence that tough sentences *are*, or ever *were*, an effective deterrent. Rather than reflecting solemnly on the possible outcome if they *do* get caught, most criminals focus instead on the probable outcome that they *won't* get caught. Research done in New York City in the 1970s still basically holds true, even in the UK: for every thousand felonies committed there are just thirty-six convictions, and only three offenders go to prison for over a year.

The failure of deterrence is especially true of capital crimes like murder, where extensive investigations in Europe and North America reveal that having the death penalty makes little or no difference to the murder rate. Most murders are committed *within* the family in a time of emotional crisis; those that aren't are done by cold-blooded killers who can't imagine, or don't care about, getting caught. As Stanford law professor Lawrence Friedman explains, 'Most people start out already deterred; they do not rob, rape, and kill because they think it is dead wrong to rob, rape, and kill . . . The few who are left are the toughest cases.' And the toughest cases aren't deterred, even by the death penalty.

Ironically, the US Supreme Court acknowledged this when it upheld the constitutional right of individual states to execute prisoners, in 1976. The Court's reason for keeping state execution on the statute books – and retaliation as an integral part of the justice system – wasn't deterrence, but instead to allow for the far more familiar and important element of *retribution*. The Court wanted to make sure that criminals got their 'just deserts'.

There seems to be something basically 'right' about someone paying back exactly what they took – like for like. A court in

Pakistan recently doled out this kind of 'poetic justice' to two serial killers found guilty of over a hundred murders. Since the men had disposed of their victims' bodies by dismembering them and then dissolving them in acid, the court put its own novel twist on the old-fashioned punishment of hanging, drawing and quartering: after death at the end of a rope, the men were to be chopped up and their body parts dumped in a vat of acid!

Of course, though retribution has always been part of the justice system, it's never been an exact like-for-like match. For example, when someone is caught stealing, we don't send in the bailiffs to take something of equal value from them – although fines *are* imposed for some offences, magistrates and judges also routinely use custodial sentences or community service as alternative forms of punishment. Rather than demanding an exact like-for-like sentence, we tend to insist instead on a sentence that *represents the seriousness* of the crime: fairly light community sentences for minor offences, but tough custodial sentences for serious crimes.

That's why we're so outraged when people whose criminal behaviour has caused a great deal of harm and distress seem to 'get off lightly'. The punishment just doesn't seem to fit the crime. Instead, it seems to belittle its severity, giving no more than a half-hearted rap on the knuckles for what is in effect a major offence. Overly *light* sentences like those given to the killer of Roger and Cathy's daughter or white-collar criminals like former Guinness boss Ernest Saunders seem very unjust. And judges who impose inappropriately light sentences – like the judge who hit the headlines a couple of years ago for giving a teenage date-rapist a derisively light (non-custodial) sentence – soon find themselves at the receiving end of the public's anger.

Just how central retribution is within the justice system became clear in February 2000, when Moors murderer Ian Brady petitioned the courts for what amounted to the right to die. Doctors had started force-feeding him in order to end his self-imposed hunger strike, but after more than thirty years in custody, the sixty-year-old Brady wanted to end it all. Unlike his seemingly reformed partner-in-crime, Myra Hindley, Brady was being held in the secure ward of a mental hospital, not prison, and the courts had to decide if he was *sane* enough to have the legal right to die. In the end, they decided he wasn't, and ordered the doctors to continue force-feeding. The case divided not just public opinion, but the relatives of Brady's victims. Half wanted to see him dead; the other half agreed with the father of one of the victims: 'His body doesn't belong to him; it belongs to us. He shouldn't have a right to die. We want him to keep on suffering for the rest of his life!'

A mark of restraint

An eye for an eye leaves everyone blind.

Martin Luther King

The interesting thing is that both parties were motivated by the desire for retribution, and a form of justice that included retaliation. Both those who wanted to see Brady dead and those who wanted to see him continue to suffer, convinced that his death would cheat them of any real justice, would probably have entirely agreed with the sentiments of Deuteronomy 19:21: 'Show no pity: life for life, eye for eye, tooth for tooth, hand for hand, foot for foot.'

So it's rather ironic to discover that, as Old Testament ethicist Chris Wright remarks, the eye-for-eye ruling was designed to be 'a very limiting law, preventing excessive or vengeful punishment'. Rather than legislating a *mandatory* sentence, it was there – like other legal codes in ancient Near Eastern cultures – to set the *maximum* penalty, beyond which it was considered unjust to go. 'This far, no further' was the idea behind it. Since punishment was often enacted by the victim or their relatives, rather than the court, a firm hand was essential to ensure that what prevailed was justice, not vengeance, and to stop things descending into a deadly spiral of violence: retribution and counter-retribution, tit for tat.

'Possibly no other Old Testament text has been the victim of more misunderstanding and exaggeration than this one,' Chris

29

Wright continues. Victims and their families weren't *obliged* to demand exact like-for-like punishment; in fact, they were encouraged to show mercy. The eye-for-eye rule occurs in Exodus 21:24 and Leviticus 24:20, where it's *clearly* a maximum punishment, and Deuteronomy 19:21. Only in Deuteronomy – where the offence is deliberately attempting to corrupt the justice system by being a *false witness* (breaking the ninth commandment) – are people told to 'show no pity', but even here retaliation is a *maximum* not a *mandatory* sentence, as Leviticus 6:1–7 makes clear. 'Contrary to the popular view,' Wright concludes, 'the law does not condone rampant physical vengeance . . . [This popular misconception] totally ignores the ethos of compassion, generosity, concern for the weak, and restraint of the powerful that pervades the book.'

It's this same ethos of compassion, generosity, concern for the weak and restraint of the powerful that pushes Jesus to declare, in the Sermon on the Mount, 'You have heard that it was said, "An eye for an eye and a tooth for a tooth." But I say to you, Do not resist an evildoer. But if anyone strikes you on the right cheek, turn the other also; and if anyone wants to sue you and take your coat, give your cloak as well; and if anyone forces you to go one mile, go also the second mile' (Matthew 5:38–41).

It's tempting to see this as contradicting the law of the Old Testament, but the truth is that, far from being a contradiction, it's actually a *clarification* of its teaching. That's why Jesus said, 'Do not think that I have come to abolish the law or the prophets; I have come not to abolish but to fulfil' (Matthew 5:17). Over the years, people had lost sight of the fact that 'an eye for an eye' was the *maximum* penalty, and had mistakenly started to think of it as a *mandatory* one. The letter of the law remained, but its spirit had been lost. So by putting even stronger limits on vengeance, Jesus wasn't aiming to abolish the eye-for-eye ruling, but to explain the thinking behind it by recreating the shocking sense of restraint it once carried.

The quality of mercy

The act of forgiveness carries a lot of power. It is an assertion of one's dignity to have the means and ability to forgive.

Palestinian human rights lawyer Raja Shehadeh

In Shakespeare's famous play *The Merchant of Venice*, shipping magnate Antonio borrows money from Shylock. He's so confident he can repay the loan that he foolishly agrees to put up a pound of his own flesh as collateral. So when he hears that his fleet has been wrecked at sea, he's understandably beside himself. Shylock demands payment – he wants his promised pound of flesh. When the case is referred to Portia for judgment, she agrees that Shylock is entitled to a pound of Antonio's flesh – but not an ounce more or less, and not if it means taking his life – but she nevertheless encourages him to be merciful. 'The quality of mercy,' she remarks, 'is not strained . . . It is twice blessed.' It blesses both the person who gives mercy and the person who receives mercy.

It's this kind of thinking that lies behind not only Jesus' words in the Sermon on the Mount, but also his insistence in Matthew 18:22 that people forgive each other not seven but *seventy*-seven times. Though people were entitled to take an eye for an eye, he encouraged them instead to be merciful. Though they had a right to retaliation, he encouraged them *not* to use it. Why? Because mercy and forgiveness, unlike exacting vengeance to the strict letter of the law, are attitudes and actions that 'bless' both the person forgiving and the person forgiven.

When Debbie Morris was raped and beaten – and her boyfriend shot in the head – the last thing on her mind was forgiving her attackers. But when one of them, Robert Lee Willie, was sentenced to death, she knew she couldn't go on feeling bitter. For Debbie the issue was never about Willie. It was about her. 'It took a long time for me to accept the fact that my life would never be the same – and it was in that process that I encountered the need to forgive,' she told US magazine *Youthworker*. 'That's the only thing that takes away the anger and pain and restores the peace . . . People ask, "Why do you even have a need to forgive Robert Willie? He doesn't deserve your forgiveness." But what he deserves is not the problem I'm trying to solve . . . When I forgive, I'm the one who benefits.'

It's tempting to look at advice like 'go the extra mile' and wonder how it benefits anyone. What's served by behaving like a carpet, inviting others to walk over you? But this is *not* what going 'the second mile' is all about. Roman soldiers (and probably Herod's soldiers, too) were entitled to force anyone they liked to carry their pack for one mile, and most used it as a power game. By forcing someone to carry their pack, they were underlining the legal and physical power they had over them. It signalled to all faithful Jews that they were, in effect, still slaves and second-class citizens in their 'promised land'. But by volunteering to go the second mile, a person could set things on an equal footing and make it clear they were carrying the pack because they *chose* to, not because they *had* to. It was an act which *brought* dignity and equality, not *robbed* it.

The same is true of turning the other cheek. In Jesus' day, as now, the *safe* thing to do if someone hit you in the face was to keep your head down in submission, while the *natural* thing to do was hit back. Jesus urged his followers not to do either, but instead to *offer* the other cheek. It was a way of retaking the initiative, of refusing to submit or acknowledge an attacker's power. But at the same time it was also a refusal to play by the attacker's rules. It was a moral slap in the face rather than a physical one, and a very deliberate and positive 'pre-emptive' attempt at peace and reconciliation.

Turning the other cheek may sound somewhat other-worldly and unrealistic in our culture, but in fact it was a positive approach designed for the cut and thrust of everyday life under the yoke of a brutal Roman oppression. Its aim was to maintain dignity and defiance without resorting to violence or the weapons of war. And most importantly, rather than killing the enemy, it was concerned to *transform* them.

The practical, down-to-earth value of this turn-the-other-cheek policy, on both a personal and a political level, is powerfully demonstrated in the life of Martin Luther King. At a time of enormous racial tension and violence, daily beatings and discrimination, and in the face of huge oppression and provocation, King refused either to submit or to strike back with violence. Though he and his followers may have been morally entitled to an eye for an eye – and blacks in northern cities were more than happy to assert that right – King knew that 'non-violent resistance' (turning the other cheek) was the only way forward. Consciously modelling his approach on Jesus' teaching, he was convinced that it was the only solution capable of creating a lasting peace. In his book *Stride Toward Freedom* – written after his successful Montgomery campaign but before the bigger, more challenging campaigns of the early 1960s that would earn him a Nobel peace prize – he wrote,

> The non-violent approach does not immediately change the heart of the oppressor. It first does something to the hearts and souls of those committed to it. It gives them new self-respect; it calls up resources of strength and courage that they did not know they had. Finally it reaches the opponent and so stirs [their] conscience that reconciliation becomes a reality.

The question that Jesus and Martin Luther King confront us with is a tough one. The temptation to demand retaliation – an eye for an eye – is always strong. But while no one is suggesting that people like Shipman and Brady be released, the challenge to forgive them is still there. Perhaps being forgiven will change them; perhaps it won't. But one thing is certain: the act of forgiving those who do us wrong, whoever they are, will change *us*.

4

'You can't take it with you when you die'

'I'm sure the Almighty will be very, very pleased with the finished article ... After all, what is one supposed to do with one's riches?'

At a cost of over £32 million, Hamilton Palace in East Sussex is one of the most expensive mansions ever built. The brainchild of wealthy property magnate Nicholas Van Hoogstraten, it's intended to last a thousand years, serving as both a personal mausoleum and a showcase for his own precious hoard of furniture and paintings, valued at well over £200 million. 'The whole purpose of this,' he explained in the BBC Two documentary *Money, Money, Money,* 'is to take my money with me . . . to make sure nobody else gets their hands on it.'

Van Hoogstraten seems to have gone to extraordinary lengths to try to disprove the old adage, 'You can't take it with you when you die.' But to most of us, the idea is so watertight, we wonder why anyone would even *attempt* to discredit it. From childhood, we have it ingrained in us that the division between this life and the next is hard and fast – the things of heaven belong in heaven and the things of earth belong on earth. You can't trade commodities between the two.

So it may come as something of a shock for us to learn that Jesus, for one, wouldn't have agreed. Not only did he see heaven and earth as much closer than most of us would dare to imagine, but he was also a firm believer in there being a healthy import-export relationship between them. In fact, he was adamant there were some things you *could*, and *should*, take with you when you died. What? Read on ...

Pyramid. Reasonable condition. One former owner

I used to think, when I was a child, that Christ might have been exaggerating when he warned about the dangers of wealth. Today I know better. I know how very hard it is to be rich and still keep the milk of human kindness. Money has a dangerous way of putting scales on one's eyes, a dangerous way of freezing people's hands, eyes, lips and hearts.

Former Brazilian Archbishop Helder Câmara

The idea that you *can* take it with you has a very long history. Van Hoogstraten's mausoleum – decorated in 'Egyptian-French Empire taste' and containing a lead-lined sarcophagus for his embalmed body – seems deliberately designed to remind future visitors of the handiwork of another wealthy élite who firmly believed they could take it all with them into the afterlife: the ancient Egyptians. The great pyramids of Giza and extravagant underground tombs of the Valley of the Kings, built between 3,500 and 4,500 years ago, stand as a monument to the seriousness with which they held their beliefs.

Determined to enjoy both this life and the next, the Egyptians made detailed preparations for death and developed elaborate burial rituals (including the removal and preservation of all the body's vital organs except the heart, and a sophisticated embalming technique that took two weeks to complete). The tombs of the rich, as well as kings and queens, were filled with everything they were thought to need in the 'Field of Reeds', their version of 'heaven'. Beside the biggest of the pyramids, built for King Khufu in 2500 BC, was a covered trench containing the ultimate in 'flat pack' furniture: a 43m royal yacht, ready to be put together by the king's servants in his posthumous existence! Buried for 4,500 years before being unearthed in 1954, it now serves as a graphic reminder of just how wrong Khufu was – he *couldn't* take it with him when he died, which is why it's still here!

How, then, could Jesus have believed you really *could* take it with you? Was he really teaching that it was possible to pack up all your creature comforts and move them lock, stock and barrel through the pearly gates into your waiting heavenly 'mansion'? Of course not! But those weren't the kind of 'valuables' he was referring to. Your *real* treasure in life is where your heart is, he insisted. What drives you? What matters most to you? Where do your priorities lie? If money is the big 'it' for you, then of course you won't be able to take it with you when you die. But if that's the case, your problems are a good deal bigger than just furnishing your mansion in the afterlife.

At the dawn of the new century, Archbishop of Canterbury George Carey struck out at what he saw as a pervasive spirit of greed and acquisitiveness in British society, characterising it in the form of a parody of the Beatitudes: 'Blessed are the famous,' he lamented, 'for they will receive the praise of men. Blessed are the rich, for they will inherit the earth. Blessed are the mighty, for they will become more powerful yet.' Despite the 1990s having been a 'Decade of Evangelism', and all our talk about the depth of the 'great British pocket', all the indications are that this analysis is right on target. At heart, we've allowed ourselves to become a money-driven people.

When I was growing up, in the 1950s and 1960s, money was something most Christians didn't have and, in public at least, didn't want. There was something suspect about it. Money, we were told (wrongly, of course: see 1 Timothy 6:10) was 'the root of all evil'. Now all of that's changed: like the rest of society, the Church is increasingly middle-class, middle-income and middle-of-the-road. In a world where the pace of life is constantly accelerating and where gratification is instant, it's very tempting to imagine that if something can't be packed into a soundbite it's not worth hearing, if it isn't immediately practical and relevant it's not worth knowing, and if it doesn't make life even faster and more luxurious it's not worth having. At the end of the day, even Christians tend to calculate something's basic worth in terms of cash and convenience.

All this is a long way away from the moral universe of Jesus, who – while he had nothing against money per se – warned his disciples against the dangers of trying to 'serve two masters'. Money has a nasty habit of restructuring our priorities and reordering our values. It 'morphs' itself from servant into master with astonishing speed. 'You cannot serve God and wealth,' Jesus told his followers. 'Do not store up for yourselves treasures on earth, where moth and rust consume and where thieves break in and steal; but store up for yourselves treasures in heaven, where neither moth nor rust consumes and where thieves do not break in and steal. For where your treasure is, there your heart will be also' (Matthew 6:24, 19–21). In other words, there are things you can take with you when you die. There are treasures you can 'store up' in heaven. What's more, you can start right now.

Who wants to be a millionaire?

To be clever enough to get all that money, one must be stupid enough to want it.

G. K. Chesterton, *The Innocence of Father Brown*

Asked to settle a family dispute over land and money, Jesus told a story about a rich man whose bumper crop was so big that he ran out of room to store it all (Luke 12:13–21). The man resolved to build bigger barns to hold his massive harvest, and looked forward to a life of luxury for years to come. But God chastised him: 'Fool! This very night your life is being demanded of you. And the things you have prepared, whose will they be?'

The parable of the rich fool is often held up as a prime exponent of the lesson that 'you can't take it with you when you die'. What good are material possessions, we ask, when death comes knocking? Christians have usually seen the parable as a warning against enjoying the 'fruits of the harvest' and treating material things as any more than a 'necessary evil'. But in fact, this is a misunderstanding, for two reasons. First, the fool of the story had no intention of taking *anything* with him when he died – on the contrary, his aim was to enjoy it all while he was still alive! And second, Jesus *didn't* criticise him for *having* wealth, or even *enjoying* it – the story portrays his wealth as a gift from God, there to *be* enjoyed. Instead, his offence was that, in enjoying his wealth, he left God and his local community out of the equation.

In Old Testament thinking, the whole of life was considered a gift from God. Even the 'promised land' of Israel was seen as *God's* land, 'on loan' to his chosen people. Rather than being owners, the people saw themselves as *stewards*. That's why lease laws, for example, were governed by the 'Jubilee' principle (Leviticus 25): no one could buy land permanently, as it belonged to God. This idea also lay behind the sacrifices of praise and thanksgiving (of crops, not just animals) offered at harvest times throughout the Jewish year. It was essential to thank God for his generosity, giving him back in gratitude the *best* of what he'd given you.

So Jesus' audience, listening to his story about a rich man, would have been very aware of what *wasn't* in it – the man never thanked God for his goodness. In fact, he talked as if God didn't even exist – as if his crop, barns, land and life were permanently *his*, rather than 'on loan' from God. So it's not surprising God called him a 'fool' – the kind of 'fool' condemned in Psalm 14:1 (Luke spells out this connection by using exactly the same word that was used in the Greek translation of Psalm 14 around in his day). But Psalm 14 also provides a key for understanding the *second* thing the rich man left out of his thinking: his community. As well as failing to 'call upon the LORD', the 'fool' of Psalm 14 exploited the poor and forgot that 'the LORD is their refuge'. For the psalmist, this was a 'double whammy' – ignore God and trample on the people he's sworn to protect. It could only end badly. The fool of Jesus' story acted in the same irresponsible, self-centred way.

As Joel Green notes, though he was already rich, he didn't sell his grain – in such a bumper year, the price would have been very low. Instead, he built bigger, higher barns so he could 'hold his harvest back in order to achieve a higher price when the market [was] not glutted'. But this selfish decision not to sell – to withhold his crop – would have pushed up the price of everyone else's grain. Though this would have been good news for middle-income farmers, it would effectively have stopped the poorest people – who didn't own land and so had nothing to sell – from sharing in the blessings of a bumper harvest. In other words, not only was the rich man *not* using his wealth to *benefit* the poorer members of his community, he was actually using it to boost his own wealth *at their expense*.

As far as Jesus was concerned, the rich man had lost an *eternal* perspective. He'd not only ignored death, he'd also forgotten that both his land and life belonged ultimately to God, and would be 'demanded back' (the economic term used by God in the story, suggesting the repayment of a loan). The Old Testament prophets had constantly taken a hard line against those rich, powerful members of society who'd lived in luxury while others around them went hungry. They'd spoken out against those wealthy individuals who'd lined their own pockets while widows and orphans starved, and they'd condemned those kings who'd built fine palaces for themselves while poor people saw even the little they had taken away.

In a similar way, the fool in Jesus' story assumed that his land and life were his to do with as he pleased, unaccountable to anyone. He was to find out they weren't. It was payback time! In the end, despite all his wealth, he had nothing to show for his time on earth. His crime wasn't that he had money; it was that he used it for his own self-aggrandisement rather than for helping out his fellow human beings. Had he poured more of his resources into loving his neighbours, he would have possessed a 'treasure' worth more than all his wealth.

Now and then

It is well to remember that the mark of sacrificial giving in the New Testament is not how much is given, but, rather, how much is left over after the giving is finished.

American church and Sojourners Community leader
Jim Wallis

After telling this story, Jesus presented his audience with a stern warning: 'So it is with those who store up treasures for themselves but are not rich toward God' (Luke 12:29). But what does it mean to be 'rich toward God'? For too many Christians, storing up 'treasures in heaven' or being 'rich toward God' are basically a matter of doing some form of 'good deed' – anything from acts of charity to daily Bible study – in order to rack up spiritual Brownie points. In other words, our time on earth is best spent making the heavenly 'mansion' we'll live in after death as comfortable as possible by doing the kind of thing that'll put us in God's good books. But the truth is, this view is not only wrong, it's also an absolute travesty of 'heaven'.

Heaven has lost its appeal these days. The generations that lived through two World Wars, a global economic depression and the Cold War threat of nuclear holocaust constantly and fervently prayed and preached about heaven and hell, death and eternity. Today, such sermons are not only out of fashion, they're more or less out of bounds! It's hardly surprising. The African slaves of eighteenth- and nineteenth-century America sang about the 'sweet chariot' of death that would 'swing low', bringing release from the bonds of oppression. But if you're the proud owner of a sleek, black 'sweet chariot' marked BMW, and comfortable with what it says about you as a success in life, the last thing you're looking for is the arrival of another one called death! Most of us aren't concerned about trying to 'take it with us' when we die – we're too busy trying to keep it all down here! A hundred years ago, Salvation Army founder William Booth remarked, 'We like the thought of heaven, but not the thought of hell.' Today, most of us don't much care for either.

But the truth is, of course, that most of us have got entirely the wrong idea about heaven. For one thing, it's not really about an *afterlife*. It's about *eternal life*, and it begins right here and now. For another, it's nothing like as far away as most of us tend to imagine. As Jesus put it, 'the kingdom of God is *among you*' (Luke 17:21). ('Heaven' is short for 'the kingdom of heaven', which is just another way of saying 'the kingdom of God'.) Celtic Christians used to reflect this idea in their belief that in some places the dividing line between heaven and earth was very 'thin'. Today, one of our main aims as Christians has to be to make our whole lives that 'thin' and transparent, enabling us to shine 'as a light to the nations' (Isaiah 49:6).

It's a goal we'll never achieve as long as we reduce 'heaven' to the single dimension of the afterlife – and keep that clearly out of our thinking on a whole range of personal, moral and social issues. Storing up 'treasures in heaven' isn't a case of setting up a spiritual endowment plan – one where we save now through good works and then collect on our investment in a lump sum when we die – because heaven is as much 'now' as 'then'. When we think through our beliefs and actions from an eternal perspective, we reap the benefits both now and later.

In other words, 'treasures in heaven' are things we can take with us when we die because they're things we can take with us absolutely *anywhere*. They're the emotions and actions, attitudes and convictions that spring spontaneously from committing ourselves to 'love the Lord your God with all your heart, and with all your soul, and with all your mind', and to 'love your neighbour as yourself' (Matthew 22:37–9, quoting Deuteronomy 6:5 and Leviticus 19:18). They're the things we do to serve and reflect God, and to help other people, not because we *have* to but because we *want* to. They're the selfless acts we perform for other people, not to get anything in return but simply because we know they're the *right* things to do, the *Christ-like* things to do. Above all, they're the things we do not *in order to* be loved and accepted by God, but as a natural response to knowing that we *are already* loved and accepted by God. They're the occasions by which we allow the Holy Spirit, through us, to bring a little 'heaven on earth'. As Charles Spurgeon once said, 'A little faith will take you to heaven, but I pray for the kind of faith that will bring heaven to earth.'

In contrast to the false riches of the fool in Jesus' story, an example of 'treasures in heaven' was graphically illustrated by Andrew and Linda Southwood, also featured in BBC Two's *Money, Money, Money* documentary. When Andrew was given a pay rise over and above what he and Linda felt they needed, they chose to give the extra money away. In the end, they found themselves giving away such a large proportion of their growing income that they had to set up a charitable trust to help them do it.

'We've redefined "millionaire",' Andrew told BBC Two viewers. 'You become one when you've given a million pounds away. It'll give me a tremendous thrill when we reach that position because I know that we'll have been able to have been a benefit to a huge number of people. I feel that we're doing no more and no less than Scripture asks us to do. This is the way we've worked out what the Bible talks about in terms of living generously.'

Rich? Certainly! Enjoying it? Absolutely! Foolish? I think not. The Southwoods have found the only treasures worth having – the kind you can enjoy 'now' and also take with you into the 'not yet' of the afterlife. Are the rest of us prepared to settle for less?

5

'There's no room for doubt'

Thunder. Lightning. Falling masonry. Inferno. Judgment Day.

That's what some Evangelicals believe happened (albeit on a micro scale) at York Minster on Sunday 8 July 1984, after David Jenkins was consecrated Bishop of Durham. Jenkins had caused a storm of protest after voicing doubts about whether Jesus' 'virgin birth' and resurrection actually happened. So when the Minster was struck by lightning two days after his official consecration, many of those who'd strongly opposed his appointment felt God was clearly demonstrating divine displeasure at the dubious doctrines of a doubting doctor.

In the months that followed, senior church figures of all denominations, ordinary church members and all sections of the media debated the seemingly vital question: should Jenkins resign? Was the Church of England right to tolerate such doubt and uncertainty in its higher echelons? Wasn't there a need for church leaders to present a traditional, unified, doctrinally sound voice of authority and guidance? Some senior church figures felt Jenkins was wrong to voice his doubts in public; it's one thing for a bishop to harbour personal doubts, they argued, but quite another for them to air those doubts in a public forum. Others felt that, while shadows of doubt were acceptable – perhaps inevitable – in *ordinary* Christians, the Church's leadership had to be cut from a different cloth, carefully sewing up their views *before* accepting the job.

But running alongside this dispute over leadership was another, far more fundamental question about the very nature of faith and doubt. From their public pronouncements, it was clear that huge numbers of Christians saw serious doubts of *any* kind as totally antithetical to faith — *true* Christians couldn't have misgivings of the type shown by Jenkins. As one of the placards protesting Jenkins' appointment starkly put it: 'No bodily resurrection, no Christian faith.'

Are they right? Is doubt a no-go area for Christians? Has our faith left us and gone in search of more fertile ground the moment we feel a twinge of uncertainty, or struggle to accept a troublesome doctrine, or grapple with the loose ends of a Bible passage?

'Houston, we have a problem . . .'

Evangelicals are party people. They easily divide the world into those who are 'for' or 'against' what they stand for . . . [They] were early practitioners of political correctness in expecting their adherents and especially spokespeople to be ideologically pure.

Baptist minister Nigel Wright

A decade after the Jenkins débâcle, the publication of Dave Tomlinson's hugely controversial book *The Post-Evangelical* made it clear that doubt is a significantly bigger 'problem' for the Church than just 'a handful of woolly C of E liberals'. Tomlinson wrote his book out of an experience of ministering to people 'who were either on the edges of evangelical and charismatic churches or who had fallen off the edge altogether'.

Having been a charismatic (in both senses) New Church leader for twenty years, Tomlinson had slowly come to see another side of Evangelicalism. Working on the premise that the real test of a society is how it treats those on its margins, he'd come to believe that all was not well with 'high street' Evangelicalism. He and his wife had felt themselves 'called' to work with those people who, try as they might, couldn't fit themselves into the Evangelical/charismatic mould. In the process, Tomlinson had not only seen aspects of Evangelical culture and belief that filled him with dread and despair; he'd also come to share some of his flock's doubts.

The Post-Evangelical sought to give a voice not only to Tomlinson's own concerns, but also to the concerns of those Christians who felt they'd either 'outgrown' Evangelicalism or been chewed up and spat out by Evangelical churches. Few Evangelical leaders welcomed its release. Most judged that Tomlinson had sold out and 'gone liberal'. They strenuously objected to both his beliefs (or, as they saw it, lack of them) and the term 'post-evangelical'. Many challenged him to come clean and admit that he was really an *ex*-Evangelical' – by which some clearly meant 'ex-Christian'. As far as they were concerned, what was true of Jenkins was equally true of Tomlinson – you couldn't struggle with real faith-shaking doubts and still call yourself a genuine Christian.

Culture guru and Ridley Hall theological college principal Graham Cray praised Tomlinson's book for addressing vital issues, but his was almost a lone voice. Most conservative Evangelical leaders avoided getting drawn into debate on the subject, perhaps because they felt that it was irrelevant to their congregation. Many seemed unaware of the pastoral needs of the growing number of people hurt by their experience of ordinary Evangelicalism – people Murray Watts calls 'the wounded pilgrim souls who refuse to settle in the halfway houses of cosy reassurance or bland sentiments which many of our churches have become'. Some battened down the hatches and prepared to weather the storm by ignoring the problems and dismissing Tomlinson as a closet liberal. Instead of facing his criticisms head-on, they attacked him for daring to step out of line. Even Alister McGrath, who rightly highlighted the shallowness of some of the theological views expressed in *The Post-Evangelical*, seemed to overlook the pain and experience of those who no longer felt comfortable with the label 'Evangelical'.

The truth is, we Evangelicals aren't good at dealing with mess.

We like things to be cut and dried. We like to know just where we stand – a confident faith in 'sound' doctrine. This is a great strength: the danger with liberalism is that its doctrinal content can be so dilute that it has nothing distinctive to say. But our strength is also our weakness: we've tended to put so much value on confidence and soundness that we've lost the ability to handle mess and doubt. All too often, we respond to people's sincere problems and crises of faith, not by reaching out to help them slowly work through the issues, but by expecting them just to 'snap out of it'. As Evangelical Alliance General Secretary Joel Edwards says, 'We're only interested in having a conversation if we know all the answers in advance.'

That's why, as Nigel Wright warns in his book *The Radical Evangelical*, 'Large numbers of liberals are refugee fundamentalists.' If someone doesn't feel able to sign on the dotted line of a kosher Evangelical 'statement of faith', we tend to view them with suspicion, if not outright hostility. Rather than asking what the problem is, and thinking it all through with them – over a long period of time, humbly and on an equal footing – we arrogantly tend to assert that the statement *must* be true and that their faith *must* be defective. Then we chastise them and tell them they'd better shape up or ship out. Occasionally we do this explicitly, but more often it's something we do unconsciously in the way we act toward those who dare to voice any kind of doubt and uncertainty. However, the effect is the same: by giving them the cold shoulder, we more or less force them either to give up thinking or to take refuge in the crumbling edifice of liberalism.

The huge personal cost of all this hit me recently when a seventeen-year-old girl explained how hard she found it to fit into her church youth group now she'd started doing RE A Level. 'I can't be honest with people any more,' she admitted. 'In class we learn to think, to ask questions, to dig a bit deeper into the Bible, not just to take everything at face value. Our teacher's a really committed Evangelical, and he's helping us see just how brilliant the Bible is. But every time I try to bring what I've learnt into a youth group Bible study, I get really suspicious looks from everyone.

People used to be interested in what I had to say, but now the leaders have stopped even asking me what I think. It's like they don't want to know that there might be more than one way of looking at something, or that things aren't always quite as clear cut.'

It's tough to go against the flow, holding on to what you think is right in the face of heated opposition. It's tough, also, to respect other people's opinions when you're utterly convinced they're wrong. When the 'Toronto Blessing' first hit the UK, for example, churches up and down the country polarised between the advocates and the adversaries – those on the one hand who believed that 'this is from God' and that all opposition was tantamount to 'resisting the Holy Spirit', and those on the other who felt that it was demonically inspired and that all those who supported it were bowing down to Beelzebub. There tended to be little tolerance for those of a different persuasion . . . or even for those who hadn't made up their minds. A heavy 'three-line whip' was imposed, and all dissenters were rapidly expelled from the party. God, it seemed, wasn't big enough to accommodate more than one approach.

The challenge, as Rudyard Kipling famously put it, is to 'trust yourself when all men doubt you, but make allowance for their doubting too'. At heart, most of us feel threatened by those whose views are different ... especially if they claim to have found a chink in our breastplate of theological self-righteousness. As a kind of defence mechanism, we tend to act as if the weakness is theirs, and chastise them for their 'error' or their 'lack of faith'. But the truth is far more disturbing. The truth is, the weakness is ours. We're afraid to give people the right to be wrong. We shy away from doubt and insist on *certainty* and strict party lines because our *faith* isn't strong enough to get by without certainty and strict party lines.

Enter the Grand Inquisitor

Lots of us would be in sympathy with evangelicalism if there were more open debate, if instead of being shielded from the disturbing discussions which lie just around the corner, people were facilitated

in the task of rethinking and reinterpreting the Christian faith.
Post-Evangelical author and Anglican clergyman Dave Tomlinson

It's all a long way from the approach taken by Jesus in the Gospels. Even the briefest of looks at the character and track record of his disciples makes it clear that, if he expected doubt-free faith from those in his inner circle of friends, Jesus was in for a big disappointment. But in fact, he never demanded absolute certainty or doctrinal orthodoxy from his followers. We only have to notice the disciples' surprise and disbelief on Easter morning, when the women told them about the empty tomb, to realise that there were a great many things about Jesus they hadn't even *begun* to understand ... despite three years spent constantly at his side.

In all four Gospels, the disciples are shown making mistake after mistake – as alternating between intense faith and crippling doubt, great insight and gobsmacking stupidity. But how does Jesus respond? By cracking down hard?

The harsh realities of this hardline, intolerant approach – which we Evangelicals are often quick to condemn in others, but slow to perceive in ourselves – is powerfully shown by Fyodor Dostoevsky in his great novel *The Brothers Karamazov*, the story of three brothers torn apart by guilt after the murder of their father. In the best-known chapter, atheist intellectual Ivan tells younger brother Alyosha a tale he's dreamt about Jesus' return. Making it clear this isn't the 'Second Coming', Ivan explains that the return takes place in sixteenth-century Seville during the time of the infamous Spanish Inquisition.

Appearing with no fanfare, Jesus travels on foot to Seville Cathedral ... and promptly finds himself being arrested by the ninety-year-old Cardinal Grand Inquisitor! The Inquisitor visits Jesus in prison, calmly telling him he'll be burnt at the stake the next day. Jesus says nothing as the old man details the charge against him. He'll be killed, the Inquisitor explains, because he jeopardises people's salvation. He gives them too much freedom. People may all have been *born* with freedom, the Inquisitor goes on, but only a tiny élite actually have the moral strength and courage to *cope* with it – to handle the complexities of distinguishing right from wrong, and to *believe* in the face of doubt and uncertainty. The majority of folk just aren't up to the demands of the task.

'I tell you,' the Grand Inquisitor continues, 'humans are pathetic creatures, with no more urgent need than to find someone to whom they can surrender the gift of freedom they were born with.' This, he explains, is what Jesus failed to understand the first time. By refusing to give in to the temptations in the wilderness, or come down from the cross – actions that would have *proved* his power and identity *beyond all doubt* – he saddled people with the crippling burden of having to think for themselves. 'We've corrected your mighty achievement,' the old man boasts, defending the brutal way in which the Inquisition forces people to believe the Church's doctrines. 'They'll accept whatever we tell them with joy, because they'll have been spared the anguish and torment of having to make their own, free and independent choices.'

This is the terrible danger we face. Like the people in Ivan's dream, we crave certainty. We want things to be absolutely beyond doubt – black or white, right or wrong. We want to know 'the truth, the whole truth and nothing but the truth'. We want science to give us clear-cut, objective facts and preachers to give us the pure, unadulterated 'word of God'. We don't want to have to think, agonise or grapple with life's difficult questions. Instead we want guaranteed answers. We want shoot-from-the-hip certainty.

But that's the problem, because Jesus doesn't give us *certainty*. He invites us to have *faith*. And that's very different. He accepted that even his closest and most loyal followers (the Church's future leaders) would have their doubts and their misunderstandings. But rather than adopting a policy of 'zero tolerance', he encouraged them to *explore* their doubts as a way of learning to deepen their faith.

'I believe; help my unbelief!'

A perfect faith is nowhere to be found, so it follows that all of us are partly unbelievers. Yet in his kindness, God pardons us and reckons us to be believers on account of our small portion of faith.

French Reformer John Calvin

'If a man will begin with certainties, he shall end in doubts,' wrote Francis Bacon, 'but if he will be content to begin with doubts, he shall end in certainties.' From the temptation to throw himself from the highest point of the Temple in plain view of the crowds (Matthew 4:5–6), and the constant demands for him to produce a 'sign' to *prove* who he was, right down to the final taunts for him to come down from the cross, Jesus consistently refused to do things that would provide certainties and *force* people into believing in him. Instead, he always allowed room for doubt, but presented people with the opportunity to deepen their faith.

Jesus never pushed, forced, bludgeoned, beat, coerced, cajoled, manhandled or manipulated people into faith – he never threatened them with the kind of 'offer they couldn't refuse'. In contrast to the high-handed 'interventionist' approach we so often adopt, his efforts to bring the people he encountered into a closer relationship with God were characterised by what Philip Yancey calls 'the slow, steady undertow of grace'. He had what we often lack – the maturity to see that faith isn't something you either have or don't have, but something that grows slowly over the course of a lifetime from small to big, from shallow to profound, as we grow in our relationship with God. As Scots theologian Robert Davidson puts it, 'Faith does not depend on our grasp of God, but on God's grasp of us.'

Jesus responded to his people's doubt by offering them something – or more particularly some*one* – to believe in. When a father brought his demon-possessed son to him for healing, the man begged, 'If you are able to do anything, have pity on us and help us' (Mark 9:22). The disciples had already tried – and failed – to exorcise the boy themselves, which must have dented the father's initial confidence in bringing him to Jesus. But rather than rebuking him for his lack of faith – 'I believe; help my unbelief!' – Jesus healed the boy there and then. He didn't wait for the father's faith to be 100 per cent . . . or anything near it.

In the same way, rather than rebuking Thomas for his doubts about the resurrection, Jesus invited him to deepen his faith: 'Put your finger here and see my hands. Reach out your hand and put it in my side. Do not doubt but believe' (John 20:27). And for those who're tempted to hear in these words a tone of impatience and frustration – of *demand* rather than *gentle invitation* – it's worth noticing that the encouragement for Thomas not to doubt comes *after* the invitation to explore these doubts for himself with the kind of in-depth probing (literally putting his hands into Jesus's wounds) most of us would find deeply disrespectful. In fact, Jesus was prepared to give Thomas far more space than he needed – it seems he never did take Jesus up on his offer. A rebuke might have pulled Thomas into line, but an invitation to explore his doubt deepened his faith considerably. As F. F. Bruce put it, 'Thomas might have been slower than his fellow-disciples to come to faith in the risen Christ, but when he did so, his faith was expressed in language which went beyond any that they had used . . . "My Lord and my God!" '

Jesus *invites* but never *compels* us to believe. As a result, we'd do well to avoid making snap judgments about whether someone is 'in' or 'out' of the Christian community based on their ability to sign up to this or that established statement of faith, and instead learn how to create the opportunities for them gradually to deepen their faith and relationship with God. Whatever we may make of his theology, David Jenkins' definition of faith was actually a lot truer than that of many of his critics, who seemed to think that any chink in the armour of certainty would put 'real' faith in jeopardy. But faith, Jenkins insisted, *isn't* certainty. It's a 'risky commitment to a glimpsed possibility in the face of reasonable human hesitation about whether it is really possible'. We're so keen for things to be cut-and-dried, we often fail to see that faith and doubt aren't mutually exclusive. As the German-born theologian Paul Tillich wrote, 'Doubt isn't the opposite of faith. It is an element of faith.' Where there's *absolute* certainty, there can be no room for faith.

6

'And now for a time of worship'

To be honest, I'd had it. I was at the end of my rag. The previous week had been rough. I was under intense pressure, and felt I was failing in all departments. There wasn't a single area of my life where chaos didn't have the upper hand. Everywhere I looked, things seemed to be falling apart. I was fast losing the battle to be a sensitive and loving husband. And as for being a wise and compassionate father, an inspiring and understanding boss, or a loyal and generous friend . . . well, as far as I could see, the battle was well and truly over. Now here I was, sat in church for the Sunday morning service, desperately hoping for a line to be thrown to a drowning man.

But I was in for bitter disappointment. Instead of offering comfort or help, in *any* area, what followed only compounded the sense of frustration and despair I felt welling up inside. It all seemed so unrelated to my troubled life. In his sermon the preacher had, for reasons known only to himself and God, chosen to deal at length with the three Hebrew words for 'worship' used in one of the psalms. Like someone picking apart a carcass, he'd painstakingly dissected the biblical text to leave it exposed and in pieces for display. But he'd made almost no effort to put it back together again afterwards, and his two sorry lines of 'application' did nothing to stem my anguish. Worse, despite his insistence that worship was an integral part of life in Old Testament times, neither his sermon nor anything else in the service seemed even remotely connected to, let alone *helpful* to, anything in my life or any aspect of contemporary culture.

'Well, thanks a lot,' I prayed, with all the sarcasm I could muster as we left after the service. 'I can't say I've been helped with any of the major issues I'm facing by coming to church this morning, but at least I have a far better grasp of a few of the more obscure Hebrew words for worship! I'm sure that'll come in handy one day soon!' What struck me again that morning was just how far-removed from everyday life so much of what we call 'worship' really is – all shades and varieties, from sober traditional to flamboyant charismatic. And I couldn't help feeling Jesus would have shared my frustration. For him, worship and life were never far apart.

All aglow

For many, the Church is 'irrelevant' because it is no longer central to their needs or interests.

Archbishop of Canterbury George Carey

I was reminded of this incident a few months ago, when some friends were discussing the story in Matthew 14 where Jesus walks on the water and reaches out to stop Peter from drowning. One friend, who's been a Christian longer than I can remember, remarked on how Matthew 14:33 records that the disciples in the boat 'worshipped' Jesus and joked that one of them must have smuggled a guitar on board and then suddenly whipped it out to lead a round of 'My Jesus, My Saviour' at the appropriate moment. I laughed, but at the same time I realised that that's just the problem. When most of us think about the word 'worship', our first thought is to reach for a guitar and sing a chorus (or, for some, incense and sing a choral evensong). But not only is this our *first* thought, it's often our *last* as well! It's a sad fact that, when we say things like, 'And now for a time of worship', we generally mean nothing more (or less) than, 'And now let's sing some songs . . .'

For Jesus, Peter and Paul, however, 'worship' had a much more expansive meaning. From the Bible's perspective, not only is 'worship' far more than that 'eyes-closed-hands-up guitar-strumming magic moment', but its heart is nothing to do with music or songs at all. The most common New Testament word for worship initially referred to a kneel-and-kiss gesture. But its use wasn't confined to worshipping God – the same word, for example, is used in the Greek translation of the Old Testament to describe Joseph's eleven brothers bowing before him in his dream (Genesis 37:9) and Moses bowing down to God (Exodus 34:8). As New Testament scholar Larry Hurtado explains, worship 'seems always to express reverence or respect', but exactly how much or what type 'varies with the nature and claims of the figure to whom the reverence is given'.

Though it may strike us as odd – even blasphemous – to 'worship' a human being, in fact this shows just how far we've come from the biblical idea. The use of the word 'worship' in the marriage service gives us a more accurate steer than does the phrase, 'And now for a time of worship'. In the traditional form of the wedding vows contained in the Book of Common Prayer, for instance, written in the time of Elizabeth I, the man gives his bride the ring with the words, 'With my body I thee worship.' Clearly, he wasn't expected to whip out a lute and sing eyes-closed heart-felt choruses to his wife, or process solemnly round her with candles and incense. Within this context, 'worship' means paying her the respect she deserves and living a life *worthy* of her. It's worth noting that the modern version of these vows updates the words without robbing them of the depth of their basic meaning: 'With my body I *honour* you.'

The English word 'worship' is actually derived from the Old English *weorpscipe* ('worth-ship'), meaning *any* kind of 'worthy' activity, but especially those that show the 'worthiness' of God. Similarly, 'liturgy' comes from a Greek word literally meaning 'the people's work'; in classical Greek it referred to a person's 'civic duties', but the New Testament writers used it to describe a range of activities from the priestly duties of Zechariah (Luke 1:23) to the 'works of service' of the entire Corinthian church (2 Corinthians 9:12). Even the fact that we traditionally refer to our Sunday meeting as a 'service' clearly points to the whole mission of the Church over the entire week, not just a couple of hours of prayers, readings and songs on a Sunday morning!

Worship is an integral part of everyday life. It's not really about fuzzy feelings or pomp and circumstance, but about how we live the *whole* of life. It's not that worship shouldn't include musical expression; it's just that we usually end up with a case of the tail wagging the dog. Our huge overemphasis on 'worship services' has cost us dearly in our understanding, and more importantly our practice, of real integrated daily worship. Tragically, just like Peter at the time of the transfiguration, most of us are so keen to enjoy and cling to the obvious beauty and benefit of the 'mountain top' experience that rather than treating it as a kind of *fuel* for the rest of life, we tend to want to build 'dwellings' to prolong it as long as we can. We begin to see it as a 'sacred' event, isolated from and unsullied by the crime and grime of the 'secular' world. But this isn't how Jesus saw it. In fact, he made no distinctions at all between 'secular' and 'sacred', and wouldn't have seen the point of them. Instead, he saw the whole of life as being of-a-piece.

In Matthew, Mark and Luke, the ecstasy of the transfiguration follows hot on the heels of Jesus' first attempts to explain to his disciples about his impending execution, and provides a temporary breathing space before he throws himself back into the fray. It's a 'moment of truth', in which Jesus receives the acclaim and recognition that are his by right, but which the disciples, in their ignorance, aren't able to give him. Moses and Elijah, the two undisputed heavyweight champions of the prophetic world, validate not only the *fact* of his messiahship but its *style* as well, less than a week after his inner circle of friends and disciples have told him off for imagining that death could be on the cards for God's 'anointed'.

But ironically, the fact and style of his messiahship only hold true *if he comes back down* the mountain and continues on to his death. A messiah who doesn't save is no messiah at all (whoever he may have been in his pre-existence). So the worship of the transfiguration acts as a kind of *anticipation* of the worship of Jesus once his mission is over. It's what's called an 'eschatological' moment – one in which the end result breaks into the present, not as an end in itself, but *in order to put things in their true perspective and give us the strength and energy to carry on*. Like all authentic worship – musical or otherwise – the transfiguration doesn't stand apart from life as distinctly 'sacred'; it stands in the midst of it.

'The heart of worship'

Worship and the Christian's daily life of obedience are not two separate spheres, but two concentric circles, of which worship is the inner and gives to the outer its content and character.

American church and Sojourners
Community leader Jim Wallis

The Iona Community have found a particularly graphic way of highlighting the relationship between worship and everyday life. When they gather for morning prayer each day, their conventional service has an unconventional ending. In fact, to be precise, it has no ending at all. Unlike most worship services, there's no blessing or 'benediction' . . . until the end of the *evening* service. Instead, community members go about their daily tasks as if these were in themselves a continuation of the worship service – which they are! There's no hard distinction between 'worship' and work, 'liturgy' and life. Nor should there be. The community's 200 members (and to some extent its 1,500 associates) are as committed to real hands-on action in pursuit of justice and peace as they are to a life of daily prayer and Bible reading, sharing time and money, but they don't see one as 'secular' and the other 'sacred'. Instead, they see everything they do in life – politics or prayer – as a form of 'worship' and 'service'.

In 1999 a national newspaper reported that the island has become so popular as a modern-day pilgrimage and tourist site that the jetty used for the ferry is falling to bits. People are prepared to travel hundreds of miles to visit the remote community – so many, in fact, that its leader recently suggested Iona would have to work hard to avoid becoming 'a theme park for privatised middle-class spirituality'. But what visitors find when they arrive often comes as something of a shock: rather than hordes of cassocked and cloistered monks, there's just a skeleton crew of men and women swamped by visitors. The rest of the community lives in mainland Britain, and sometimes overseas, rebuilding 'the common life'. Its head-quarters, far from the peaceful island, are in the run-down Glasgow district of Govan. 'The community will only succeed,' its leader has stated, 'if it energizes its visitors to go back to the everyday world to bring about change.'

Iona's pattern is, at least in part, modelled on the first-century Jerusalem church. As Luke shows in Acts, this was a community not only of *spiritual* unity, but of *material* unity as well. They 'were of one heart and soul . . . everything they owned was held in common' (Acts 4:32). Their worship wasn't just concerned with people's 'spiritual' needs; it was concerned with *all* their needs. This is the model Paul had in mind when he attacked Corinthian church members for the way they treated the communion (1 Corinthians 11:17–34). He was angry *not* because of some knotty, immediate theological problem – a poorly defined doctrine of the atonement, perhaps, or the wrong ideas about the 'real presence' of Jesus in the bread and wine – but because, unlike the Jerusalem church, the Corinthians were acting with no consideration for one another. The 'Lord's Supper' was meant to be a powerful and effective reminder of their *comm*union, but it was in fact a stark indicator of their *dis*union! 'Do you show contempt for the church of God and humiliate those who have nothing?' Paul asked rhetorically.

It was a lesson he'd learnt, indirectly, from Jesus himself. 'When you are offering your gift at the altar, if you remember that your brother or sister has something against you, leave your gift there before the altar and go; first be reconciled to your brother or sister, and then come and offer your gift' (Matthew 5:23–4). In turn, this was a principle both Paul and Jesus understood from the Old Testament prophets, as well as passages such as Psalm 51:16–17: 'You have no delight in sacrifice; if I were to give a burnt-offering, you would not be pleased. The sacrifice acceptable to God is a broken spirit; a broken and contrite heart, O God, you will not despise.'

Worship, in other words, isn't primarily about singing songs, chanting anthems, getting a warm fuzzy feeling or being over-whelmed by the mystique and mystery of the Eucharist. It's about *how we live our lives.* It's not a case of 'God turning up' in our services every Sunday; it's about us following him out to serve in places where perhaps we've never been but he's never left. So the kind of sung and acted worship we have in our meetings each Sunday is just the tip of the iceberg, and certainly not an end in itself. As James might have said, ' "Worship" by itself, if it has no works, is dead' (see James 2:17).

Eat in, take away

With whatever needs we come to worship, whatever the hopes or fears we bring with us, worship should lift us from the shifting sands of our ever-changing moods, to the bedrock of a faith which has nothing to do with what we are or how we feel.

Former Moderator of the Church of Scotland
Professor Robert Davidson

When I was growing up in the 1960s, my brothers and sisters and I – like most children of our generation – would be carefully dressed up in our 'Sunday best' for going to church. 'After all,' my mother would say, 'you'd want to look your best if you were going to see the Queen. Well, you're going to see the King of Kings.' I make no such insistence for my own children, not because I have no respect for the King of Kings, but because I don't want to send them the message that Jesus is only there when you're ushered 'into his presence' on Sunday morning. It's vital for them to grasp that he's with them wherever they are and whatever they're wearing (or not), every second of every day. He's not someone who waits for us to come to him, but one who comes to be with us and to help us in every area of our everyday lives.

In his book, *Struggling to Belong*, Simon Jones tells the story of a friend who was a youth leader on Sundays but worked as an advertising executive in the week. 'His two worlds were separated by a long train ride,' he writes, in which 'he underwent a spiritual metamorphosis' from Jekyll to Hyde – from erudite Evangelical to happy heathen. 'This man was an extreme example of something that is not unusual,' he concludes. This 'spiritual schizophrenia' is also present in the language we use, and in the way we contrast 'ministers' or 'full-time Christian workers' with 'the laity' (by which we often disparagingly mean 'the hoi polloi'). It's there in the way we think that an engineer working with a mission agency in Dubai is a 'missionary', while someone doing the same job with Railtrack in Derby *isn't*. And it's there in the way we assume that 'Christian music' or 'worship songs', however banal their lyrics or bad their musical content, are somehow more spiritually uplifting and superior to a Mozart concerto or a Motown CD.

As 'split personalities', we struggle to keep a unity between the kind of people we want to be – and to some extent *are* on Sundays – and the kind of people we find ourselves being the rest of the time. That's why it's so vital for us not to reduce worship to just hum-and-strum – personal penitence or private praise. It's about living 'a life worthy of the calling to which you have been called, with all humility and gentleness, with patience, bearing with one another in love, making every effort to maintain the unity of the Spirit in the bond of peace' (Ephesians 4:1–3; see also Philippians 1:27; Colossians 1:10; 1 Thessalonians 2:12).

'Sadly,' explains Robert Davidson, what we usually see as worship is rarely 'a real sharing experience. Instead we come, we sit consumer-like in the pew; we take in, we seldom give.' Rather than being players, we're spectators – an attitude that's reinforced by the architecture in so many of our churches. Old Anglican-type buildings tend to be arranged like a Number 57 bus, with everyone facing the front and the altar, trusting the priest as 'driver' to get them where they're meant to go. By the nineteenth century, many nonconformists were unhappy with this emphasis on the Eucharist, and chose to highlight instead the importance of biblical preaching. They tended to design buildings more like music halls, with a spectators' gallery and a raised pulpit where the stage/altar would have been. In the twentieth century, church buildings tended to resemble school assembly halls more than anything else, often with a raised platform at the front. But in each case, members are arranged in a face-the-front way, with their gaze directed at goings-on ahead of them rather than at their fellow congregants. (One or two churches even arranged their pews as individual, isolated cubicles; the idea was that, once you were in your own seat, you were totally cut off from the rest of the congregation. The only things you could see were the preacher and the pulpit!)

'We need new patterns and forms of worship which will help us to see worship as a sharing experience,' concludes Davidson. Simon Jones recalls the first time he encountered this form of worship, in an architecturally in-the-round building:

> I remember standing in the modern amphitheatre of the university church of Brunswick in Manchester, aware of the other people worshipping with me, and able to see their faces rather than just the backs of their necks. I found myself laughing out loud. It wasn't funny. The preacher wasn't cracking jokes; the worship leader's trousers hadn't fallen down . . . I was laughing for joy because I realised in my heart what I had been wrestling with in my mind: God has given me all these people to help me live my life in the world. I am not alone. I do not have to make my way to the pearly gates as a solitary traveller, a sort of spiritual Ranulph Fiennes, pulling my sled solo through the wilderness, frost-bitten, existing on survival rations, with only an unreliable satellite link to an unseen mission control for company.

7

'There's no such thing as a free lunch'

The phone rang. I picked it up. The girl at the other end was extremely warm and charming. 'Congratulations,' she beamed, 'you've won a holiday!'

But of course there was a catch. There's always a catch. In order to claim my 'prize', I'd have to endure several hours of audio-visual presentation while doing my best to resist the 'high pressure' temptation to spend money I don't have on a timeshare I probably don't even want. It just goes to show, there's no such thing as a free lunch. If someone gives you something for 'free', you can be pretty sure they have some kind of eventual payback in mind.

It's a basic, universal rule. You don't get something for nothing in this world. It's even enshrined in two of science's most fundamental 'laws': Newton's Third Law of Motion (for every action there's an equal and opposite reaction) and the anonymous First Law of Thermodynamics (energy can't be created or destroyed, merely passed on from one object to another). It's there in every 'buy one, get one free' promotion, 'free gift' and 'huge discount' enticing you to shop with one company rather than its rivals. And it's only thinly disguised in the 'charitable' corporate sports sponsorship offered by multinationals in return for the right kind of branding in the right kind of places. In the end, you get what you pay for and pay for what you get.

The truth is, it's a tit-for-tat, dog-eat-dog world. It's a world where what looks like a 'free lunch' is often no more than a disguised investment – one on which the investor eventually aims to make a handsome return. It's no wonder we've grown suspicious. Experience has taught us that what initially looks like a simple act of generosity often turns out in the end to be nothing less than a covert attempt by someone to exploit us for their own ends.

The warriors of ancient Troy, of course, learnt this lesson the hard way. They woke one morning to find that the Greek army that had besieged them for ten years had vanished and, in their place, outside the city, they'd left the 'free gift' of a massive wooden horse. The Trojans realised their mistake too late, after they'd dragged the horse inside the city gates and found to their cost that there was a regiment of fully-armed Greek soldiers hidden inside waiting to attack! The story of the 'Trojan horse' ended in disaster for the people of Troy, and has acted as a warning to 'beware Greeks bearing gifts' ever since the Greek poet Homer first recounted it in his epic poem *The Odyssey* in around 800 BC.

There's a streak of suspicion in us all – a healthy dose of the kind of cynicism we say makes us 'worldly wise'. We're wary when something looks 'too good to be true', and so assume it almost certainly *isn't* true. The problem is this suspicion becomes so deeply ingrained that most of us end up applying it *universally*. We assume, for instance, that other people are only interested in us because of what we can deliver – our looks, wealth, status, skills, contacts – and what we can offer them. But as a result, we can end up finding it hard to believe that *anyone* is interested in us for *us*. And sometimes we even adopt the same mercenary approach in our friendships with others. After all, only the naïve are gullible enough to fall for the 'free lunch' theory.

Amazing grace?

Grace is, by definition, freely given. Yet both materially and spiritually, Christians act as if we had to earn our way in.

Australian biker minister John Smith

How often do people who aren't card-carrying members of the Church suggest that they're not really 'good enough' to be a Christian? How often have you heard church members of long-standing admit that, a lot of the time, they don't feel like they're a 'real' Christian? At heart, these opinions are born out of the idea that there's a baseline standard – like a minimum height measurement for admission to a theme park ride – that people have to reach before they can qualify as 'Christian'. For some people, it's a moral standard they feel they've failed to achieve, which disqualifies them from being 'pure' enough to be a *proper* Christian. For others, it's a feeling that they'll never be more than 'second-class' because they're not smart enough to understand all the ins and outs of degree-level doctrine.

In one of his hugely successful *Alpha* course talks, Nicky Gumbel explains how he once asked course members to fill in a questionnaire. One of the questions was, 'Would you have described yourself as a Christian at the beginning of the course?' Among the many different answers he got were 'sort of', 'probably' and '-ish'. It's more than likely that many people at the start of the course imagined that becoming a Christian, let alone *continuing* as a Christian, required a certain level of commitment, moral fibre and spiritual integrity . . . not to mention theological nous. It couldn't be as simple as accepting the free gift of forgiveness and 'salvation'. After all, there's no such thing as a 'free lunch'. Is there?

In the Robert Bolt scripted film *The Mission*, Robert de Niro plays Rodrigo Mendoza, a slave trader who kills his brother in a fit of jealous rage. Overwhelmed with grief at having done such a terrible thing, he locks himself in a monastery cell, point-blank refusing all offers of forgiveness and absolution. In his own mind, what he's done is too awful – he simply doesn't *deserve* forgiveness. Eventually he's persuaded, as an act of penance, to accompany a small group of Jesuit missionaries to a mission station in the upper reaches of the Amazon, among the very Guarani Indians he's spent years enslaving.

Still consumed with guilt, he insists on dragging a full suit of armour with him the whole way. Trussed up in a rope bag and tied to his back, the armour symbolises everything that's wrong with his life – all his sins – and though he desperately wants to be rid of them, he just can't bring himself to accept the 'free gift' of God's forgiveness and sever the cord. In fact, when one of the Jesuits cuts it off him during a particularly treacherous ascent up a waterfall, Mendoza insists on climbing all the way back down to tie the armour bag back on.

Our churches are full of people who have equal difficulty accepting God's 'free gift' of a new start and a new life. They may have been through all the right moves of 'conversion', but they still hold on to some of the weight of their guilt because, like Mendoza, they feel that just being forgiven is too easy. It seems to make light of their sins. There has to be a catch. But the truth is the exact reverse. It's the *refusing* to let go of sins and accept forgiveness that makes light of their importance.

We often refuse to accept God's free gift of forgiveness in the mistaken belief that there's something we ourselves can do to atone, at least in part, for all we've done wrong. This, of course, vastly underestimates the severity of our wrongdoing. As Paul suggests (Romans 6:23), 'The wages of sin is death.' It's that serious. Our sins are so grave that even thinking about *trying* to atone for them ourselves is a waste of time. Nothing we can do can even begin to make up for the havoc we wreak in other people's lives, and the pain this causes God as a loving Father. So if we're offered forgiveness – and by God's undeserved, unconditional love we *are* – the only thing we can do is accept it gratefully as a genuine free gift, with no strings attached.

Anything goes?

The realisation that the Lord loves us and the acceptance of the unmerited gift of the Lord's love are the deepest source of the joy of those who live by God's word.

Peruvian theologian Gustavo Gutiérrez

Of course, just because grateful acceptance is the only appropriate response we can make to God's free gift of 'eternal life' doesn't mean that actually *making* this response is easy. In fact, just how hard it is to accept the idea that forgiveness and salvation are real free gifts – given not because we deserve them but because we can *never* deserve them – is indicated by the sheer frequency with which the Church itself, in its long and chequered history, has shied away from daring to accept the idea of what Paul called 'justification by faith' and has opted instead for some variation of what has often been called 'justification by works'.

The most famous occasion of this was the debate and conflict that surrounded the radical ideas of the sixteenth-century German theologian Martin Luther. It's easy to forget now that when Luther made his protest, he had absolutely no intention of starting a full-blown breakaway movement of 'Reformation'. Instead, his aim was purely and simply to fire the opening salvo in what he hoped would be a serious churchwide debate on the nature of authentic repentance and the abusive way in which 'indulgences' were being sold.

Originally conceived as a symbol of God's forgiveness and grace, an 'indulgence' was a kind of pardon. When a person confessed their sins to a priest, they were required to do an act of penance (a prayer or deed) as a spiritual exercise: a way of focussing on God's grace and thanking him for his totally unearned forgiveness. It was a chance for them to 'present [their] bodies as a living sacrifice, holy and acceptable to God' in order to 'be transformed by the renewing of [their] minds' (Romans 12:1–2). But slowly, over the years, the concept became twisted until people came to see penance not as a *response* to God's gracious forgiveness, but as a means to *earn* it. They behaved as if it were basically a *quid pro quo*: provided they did *x, y* or *z*, they'd automatically qualify for God's forgiveness. Indulgences were a way of writing off some or all of this penance, originally intended to remind people of the *unearned* nature of God's forgiveness. But they also slowly became corrupt until, by the sixteenth century, people had come to see them as a way of reducing the amount of time they or a relative spent in the 'refining fire' of purgatory (a kind of clearing house between heaven and hell). More importantly, by then 'certificates of indulgence' were for sale, which effectively turned them into a way of *bribing* God for forgiveness.

It was this scandalous situation that pushed Luther to develop his radical 'Reformed' ideas of 'justification by faith'. He didn't initially condemn either the *bona fide* use of indulgences or the doctrine of purgatory, but he did insist that people could do nothing to *deserve* the forgiveness of sins or the 'eternal life' God offers. If they thought there was anything they could do, or any price they could pay, in any way to offset or 'justify' their sins, they were kidding themselves. All they could really do was accept undeserved 'justification' by faith. Of course, Luther still believed in moral behaviour and good 'works' – like Paul in Romans 6:1, he strongly disagreed with the idea that, if God's grace (not our behaviour) is the deciding factor, we can do what we like. But while Luther was a firm believer in 'works', he saw them as the *result* of 'justification', not the *cause* of it.

For Luther, as for Paul, this was the heart of the gospel: God saves us *gratuitously* through Jesus' death and resurrection, which we accept in faith. It isn't a matter of living a moral life – doing some things, not doing others – in order to remain faithful and deserve 'justification'. On the contrary: it's a matter of remaining faithful and accepting undeserved 'justification' in order to live a moral life.

A pastor friend of mine once took the funeral of Barry, a member of his congregation who'd died in his thirties leaving behind a wife, Rachel, and two children. They'd both been pillars of the church, though at the end there had been obvious problems in the marriage. As he tried to comfort Rachel and prepare the funeral, he discovered just how bad things had been. 'We even lived apart last summer,' Rachel admitted. 'I took the kids to stay with my mother for the holidays. You know – absence makes the heart grow fonder and all that. But it didn't, and in the end we only came back for their school.'

After the funeral, she and the children went back to live with her mother, but five years on my friend saw Rachel again. This time she seemed radiant, as if she'd been given a new lease of life. 'I'm happier than I've ever been,' she explained to him. 'I got married again a couple of years ago, to Greg, and to tell you the truth things just couldn't be better.

'You know,' she went on, 'I found Barry's old letters a few weeks back, in a box in the attic – the ones he sent when I was staying with my mum that last summer. It was so odd reading them. So sad. He just spent the whole time listing what was wrong with me as a wife – where he felt I'd failed. I mean, literally listing! But do you know what's really strange? All those 'wife' type things he wanted me to do – all those things I point-blank refused – I do them *all* now! But the funniest thing is, Greg doesn't *ask* me to do them. He's never asked me to do them. And he certainly doesn't *expect* them. I just do them because I *want* to do them, because I love him and I know he loves me.'

Generous to a fault

Christ died for our sins. Dare we make his martyrdom meaningless by not committing them?

US cartoonist Jules Feiffer

This tension between 'faith' and 'works' has run constantly through the Church's history. We may be clear *in theory* that our 'salvation' isn't something we can earn, yet all too often we allow ourselves *in practice* to make the mistake of placing so much emphasis on behaviour that we end up putting the cart before the horse and imagining that our actions in some way contribute to our place in God's favour.

This was something Jesus actively warned against in his parable of the workers in the vineyard (Matthew 20:1–16): the deciding factor isn't our work, but God's unmerited grace. In the story, a man hires casual labourers – men who're gathered in the town because they *need* the work – to bring in his grape harvest. Then four more times during the course of the day he hires more labourers, the last lot just before dusk. At the end of the day he pays each worker exactly the same wage, a fair amount for a whole day's work. However, those who've worked all day complain, expecting to earn more than the late-comers. But the vineyard owner refuses to be trapped into playing by their rules – it's his money, he argues, and he'll do as he pleases. If he wants to be generous, that's his right.

The day-long workers have, of course, forgotten that they wouldn't have had a job *at all* if it weren't for the vineyard owner – they need the work and the payment he offers just as much as the late-comers. The economic situation is such that there's a surplus of workers – the late-comers make it clear that there's no other work available. So the vineyard owner can actually get away with paying whatever he wants, just or unjust, knowing that the labourers will have to take it because they need the money and have no alternative. That he chooses to pay them a fair wage is a mark of his generosity. In fact, as the story makes clear, the workers are saved entirely by the vineyard owner's generosity, not their own work. It may be difficult to accept, but it's just the way it is.

The same challenge faces us. We can all too easily fall into the trap of imagining that *our* moral behaviour, daily Bible study, selfless acts of compassion and dedicated service to God are anything more than our heartfelt response to his love. But when we do that, we start to replace faith in God with faith in our own competence and commitment. We start to think we can somehow earn our way into

God's good books. We start trying to pay for a free lunch. The truth is, all we can do is accept the offer . . . and tuck in!

In the middle of the nineteenth century, the minister and core members of a large church in a prosperous American city became very concerned about the moral and doctrinal laxity of some of the church's more 'fringe' members. One night, as he was praying for all the church members by name (a lifelong habit), the minister felt God clearly telling him to call together the leadership team and 'purify' the membership – everyone whose beliefs or behaviour failed to live up to the mark would be expelled from the church. The following night, they met and, after long discussion, agreed to disbar almost half the church's signed-up members.

A week later, as he was again praying for all the members of the church (a shorter process now), the minister once more felt God telling him to call together the leaders and 'purify' the membership still further. Again they met, and again they resolved to excommunicate around half of the existing members. A few weeks later, the minister felt the same leading and the leadership culled the membership once more. Eventually, the concern for purity had reached such heights, and the standard of excellence had become so strict, that only the minister and two very old ladies were left on the membership list. The following month, the ladies sacked the minister for having 'impure thoughts' and confidently declared that the church was finally and entirely 'pure'. But that winter was a severe one, and the two saintly old ladies both caught a chill and . . . died. The minister later admitted that the whole experience had taught him two invaluable lessons: first, never try to 'exclude' people from God's love or from church membership on the grounds that they don't deserve that love, or your church will soon be entirely empty; and second, always dress up warm in the winter!

If the core message of the Christian faith – the one we're called to shout from the rooftops – is 'God is love', why have so many people in our society got the wrong end of the stick? Why do they seem to think that Christianity is basically all about rules and regulations and 'thou shalt nots'? The answer to this question, I think, is that our churches are full of people who've never really grasped the depths of God's grace and love themselves. We haven't expressed it properly because we haven't understood it properly. We're so convinced that 'there's no such thing as a free lunch' that we can't bring ourselves to dare believe that, as Philip Yancey puts it, 'There is nothing you can do to make God love you more, and nothing you can do to make God love you less.'

It may be a very hard message to accept, but as Martyn Lloyd-Jones wrote in his famous commentary on Romans, God's grace is scandalous and outrageous: if you preach on it and *don't* get attacked afterwards by most members of your congregation for sailing perilously close to universalism, then you probably haven't understood it properly yourself!

8

'Religion and politics don't mix'

'When I feed the hungry, they call me a saint. When I ask why the hungry have no food, they call me a communist' – the now famous words of Helder Câmara, former Archbishop of Olinda and Recife on Brazil's poverty-stricken north-east coast. Though branded a 'communist subversive' by the military regimes that governed Brazil between 1964 and 1985, Câmara was no left-wing political fire-brand. In fact, as a young priest he'd even flirted briefly with fascism! It was only when a visiting French cardinal remarked that his God-given organisational skills should be used to help those in Rio's fast-growing *favelas* (slums) that Câmara found himself reluctantly re-entering the political fray. 'I'm making the most of a certain clerical advantage,' he admitted, 'because in this country today, in present conditions, a bishop can say what a student or worker, even a professor, could not risk saying.'

It's often claimed that 'religion and politics don't mix' – that they're two entirely separate spheres of life. In the well-known words of Jesus from the Authorised Version, our task is to 'render to Caesar the things that are Caesar's, and to God the things that are God's' (Mark 12:17). In other words, the argument goes, interfering church leaders like Câmara should stick to saving *souls* and leave politics to the professionals – as Jesus himself made clear to Pilate, 'My kingdom is not from this world' (John 18:36). But the million-dollar question is, is that what he really meant?

The sound of silence

God's involvement with the world in Christ places upon every Christian the burden of care for the world at all its [levels] – including politics.

Anglican theologian Brian Horne

The maxim 'religion and politics don't mix' is a perennially popular one. It's wheeled out time after time by governments right across the political spectrum to quash any criticism of them and their policies by the Church. In the 1980s, for example, it was used in such diverse places as Poland, where the communist regime warned Catholics not to support Solidarity (the free trade union that kicked off Eastern Europe's anti-communist 'velvet revolution'), and Great Britain, where Tory MPs attacked the Church of England (the *state* church) for what they saw as the 'meddling' political overtones of its controversial 1985 *Faith in the City* report.

Of course, criticism by the Church sometimes amounts to little more than an uncomfortable stone in a government's shoe, but in other situations the Church's willingness to stand up and speak out can literally make the difference between life and death. Helder Câmara is a case in point. The situation he faced in Brazil was extreme, with both priests and people being arrested, tortured and murdered. The Church was the only national body *not* controlled by the army, and one with a lot of influence. The choice was stark: to denounce a brutal regime that was prepared to flout international law and use murder and intimidation to keep a grip on power, or to remain silent and wash its hands of responsibility in the belief that 'religion and politics don't mix'. What would Jesus have done? Helder Câmara reluctantly came to the conclusion that Jesus would have spoken out, and that he must do exactly the same (unlike many fellow Brazilian bishops, some of whom even weighed in for the other side).

Thirty years earlier in Europe, the German Church, Protestant and Catholic, had adopted the opposite, 'silence is golden' approach. In July 1933, Hitler signed a concordat with Rome, agreeing to respect the Catholic Church and its affiliated organisations. In return, the Vatican committed German Catholics to respecting Nazi authority, abstaining from political criticism and disbanding all Catholic organisations that crossed over into the political arena. As Cambridge research fellow John Cornwell explains in his contro-versial bestseller *Hitler's Pope*, the deal had disastrous consequences. As he did with all agreements, Hitler broke the terms of the concordat whenever he liked, but Germany's Catholic bishops – determined to honour their side of the deal – remained silent. Even when priests were beaten, 'non-Aryan' Catholics were deprived of jobs, and Jews were herded into ghettos and finally, from 1942, sent to gas chambers, the bishops and the Vatican refused to make an unequivocal denunciation of Hitler's 'ethnic cleansing' programme. In the beginning they wouldn't speak out; in the end they couldn't.

But Germany's Protestants were no less to blame. The state Lutheran Church, unwilling to go against 400 years of submission to their secular rulers and convinced that 'religion and politics don't mix', swallowed Hitler's German nationalist ideology hook, line and sinker. More honourably, a few isolated Protestant leaders, including Karl Barth and Martin Niemöller, *did* resist – on 31 May 1934, they signed the 'Barmen Declaration', and split to form the 'Confessing Church'. But the truth is that even this wasn't a full excursion into politics. The Barmen leaders were just as convinced as anyone else that 'religion and politics don't mix', and ironically it was this very belief that spurred them into action. They were outraged at the totalitarian and quasi-religious claims being made by the Nazis, who weren't content to leave Christianity to the clergy but seemed intent on encroaching into the Church's 'sacred' ground and controlling everything from doctrine to personnel.

Specifically, Barmen's leaders objected to the April 1933 law dismissing all state officials (including Lutheran pastors) who were either 'non-Aryan' or married to a 'non-Aryan'. They saw this as state meddling, and fought to maintain church autonomy. But in doing so they were very careful never to stray outside their home ground of 'religion' into the world of 'politics', or denounce Hitler's policy on the 'Jewish problem'. Some even endorsed it, while others downplayed its scale and importance. Niemöller didn't realise it entailed *extermination* until 1938, by which time his attack on Hitler's messianic claims had already landed him in a concentration camp. As he later admitted, 'We acted as if we had only to sustain the Church. Afterward, from the experience of those bygone years, we learned we had a responsibility for the whole nation.'

At the time, only Dietrich Bonhoeffer was prepared to launch a full *political* denunciation of Nazi ideology. It involved a decisive break with his earlier thinking. 'The Church . . . has no right to address the state directly in its specifically political actions,' he'd written in 1933. 'Thus even today in the Jewish question it cannot address the state directly and demand of it some definite action of a different nature.' By the next year, however, his views had changed dramatically. He even refused to sign the Barmen Declaration because he felt it was too soft on the evils of Hitler's platform. Instead, he tackled the anti-Semitism and political oppression head-on. As far as he was concerned, the 'Jewish question' had become the exception to prove (that is, test) the rule, and the rule – 'religion and politics don't mix' – had failed.

A taxing question

In first-century Palestine religion and politics cannot be separated: prophetic calls for religious renewal had sufficiently strong political overtones to account for the downfall of both John and Jesus.

Graham Stanton, Lady Margaret's Professor of Divinity,
Cambridge

Most of us have no real problem with the idea of Christians as private individuals expressing political opinions or belonging to political parties, but a strong nervousness surfaces as soon as we're faced with the prospect of expressing political views or forming temporary alliances with political parties as the Church per se. We've grown up to be very wary of the Church having political 'entanglements'. We're willing to campaign in the political arena on what we see as 'moral' issues. And we're happy to get involved in social action, treating the symptoms of poverty, loneliness, disease and exploitation with charitable work aimed at demonstrating and communicating God's love and compassion. But we're uncomfortable with the concept of getting involved in the struggle for social justice which works to minimise or eliminate the *causes* of these symptoms. Not only are we worried about compromising our neutrality, we're also deeply concerned about selling out – turning a message of radical spiritual transformation and personal reconciliation with God into nothing more than an ineffective, pseudo-political 'social gospel'. But this nervousness is misplaced, born of a disjointed and compartmentalised theology and worldview.

We're so used to seeing 'religion' and 'politics' as two mutually exclusive spheres of life that we've even come to imagine that the Bible endorses this view. Though we trace it back in particular to Jesus' command to 'render to Caesar' and Paul's opinion that 'those authorities that exist have been instituted by God' (Romans 13:1), the truth is that these two well-known passages don't make the case we imagine when taken in context, and sit beside a considerable amount of less well-known material, throughout the Bible, that flatly contradicts the idea of a sacred/secular dualism.

For example, until the time of the kings (a development only reluctantly allowed by God in 1 Samuel 8), Israel's leaders were simultaneously religious *and* political figures. In fact, the nearest thing to a religious/political split known before the kings was the distinction between Aaron the priest and Moses, but even Moses was as much a 'religious' as a 'political' leader – he was a prophet, not a 'secular' ruler. And even when the 'secular' kings *did* reign, neither the prophets nor their pro-regime counterparts (the 'Yes-men' of 1 Kings 22:12, for example) ever thought of retreating to the safe haven of 'religious' issues. They considered *all* issues religious. Prophets like Isaiah, Micah, Amos, Hosea and Jeremiah consistently spoke out, in both private audience and public forum, against what they saw as the moral and strategic errors of the king's political programme. 'The ordering of social relationships and structures, locally, nationally and globally, is of direct concern to our Creator God,' notes Chris Wright. 'That is precisely the stuff of politics. The Bible, therefore, makes no unnatural separation between "politics" and "religion".'

But what about Jesus' famous line about rendering unto Caesar? On the face of it, this does seem to endorse a clear divide between 'sacred' and 'secular'. The truth, however, is that while this division is *there* in Mark 12, it *wasn't* created by Jesus. Instead, it was *already implied* in the loaded question – should Jews pay tax to the 'divine' Caesar? – asked jointly by the Herodians (who had a stake in Rome's occupation and felt you could be loyal both to God in the 'sacred' realm and to Caesar in the 'secular' one) and the Pharisees (who wanted the Romans gone, considered *everything* to be in the 'sacred' realm and insisted that being loyal to Caesar was nothing short of idolatry).

Jesus' brilliant response was designed to challenge the thinking of both groups. Inspired by Psalm 24:1 – 'The earth is the LORD's and all that is in it, the world, and those who live in it' – he urged people to ask, what exactly *are* 'the things that are the emperor's'? Mark tells us that his answer left his questioners completely 'amazed'. The Herodians saw it as a direct assault on Rome and their own secular/sacred division. (Luke 23:2 notes that it was used at Jesus' trial as evidence that he resisted Caesar and his tax.) But at the same time, the Pharisees were totally gobsmacked by the brilliance of Jesus' response. Luke adds that they 'became silent' – quite literally lost for words!

The same thinking underlies Romans 13:1–2: 'There is no authority except from God, and those authorities that exist have been instituted by God. Therefore whoever resists authority resists what God has appointed.' Because of our assumption that Paul saw politics as a no-go area, generations of Christians have mis-understood this passage, seeing it as a prohibition against 'meddling' in politics. At first, the logic of this argument seems almost inescapable:

- God is the ultimate source of all authority; therefore
- All authorities that exist do so by appointment of God; therefore
- Rebelling against an authority is rebelling against God.

But however impeccable it seems at first glance, this logic is nevertheless flawed. Two years before writing Romans, Paul boasted 'foolishly' to the Christians of Corinth that he'd been flogged by the Jewish authorities five times and beaten with rods by Roman magistrates three times (2 Corinthians 11:24–5), and all for doing nothing more 'subversive' than preaching the gospel. His persistence speaks volumes. As Oscar Wilde might have put it, to be punished by the existing 'authorities' *once* may perhaps be regarded as a misfortune; to be punished *twice* looks like carelessness; but to be punished *eight* times is nothing less than out-and-out, calculated rebellion.

Was Paul a hypocrite, telling the Roman church to do one thing while himself doing the exact opposite? This question begs another – what happens when an 'authority' persecutes Christians? This isn't a purely academic issue: a decade after Paul wrote Romans, Emperor Nero blamed and persecuted Christians for burning the city of Rome. Nor is it an extinct question: the twentieth century saw more Christian martyrs than all the previous nineteen combined! In Mexico in the 1920s, for example, it was a death-penalty offence just to be a priest. So clearly, when a state orders its citizens to stop preaching or to abandon faith in God, obedience is not an option. Some form of 'political' resistance is mandatory.

But is this the only condition in which political action and resistance are acceptable? Like many church leaders, John Stott, in his commentary on Romans, thinks not. 'He cannot be taken to mean that all the Caligulas, Herods, Neros and Domitians of New Testament times, and all the Hitlers, Stalins, Amins and Saddams of our times, were personally appointed by God, that God is responsible for their behaviour, or that their authority is in no circumstances to be resisted.' There are, he argues, times when faith and conscience combine to make it *immoral*, even *heretical*, for Christians to stay silent. As Niemöller put it, explaining his (albeit limited) opposition to Hitler, 'The question became:"What do I do when the state tells me something different to what Jesus Christ, or my Christian conscience, tells me is just?" In the face of this conflict, some gave the political demands of the day priority, and others said, "No, as a Christian I will not do that."'

However, Paul's argument actually goes a great deal deeper than even this. In the Roman world, religion and politics were so totally fused that the emperor himself was seen as a god, with his own innate authority. Paul undermined that authority completely by maintaining the traditional Jewish view – frequently voiced by the prophets – that the only *real* 'authority' to govern came from God (the true King) and was recognisably benign. A *true* ruler, therefore – Jewish or Roman – was 'not a terror to good conduct, but to bad', since authority is 'God's servant for your good' (Romans 13:3–4). This being the case, rulers were entitled to people's tax simply in order to let them fulfil their roles as servants, and because workers deserved their pay (but no more). Paul was no revolutionary and didn't want to rock the boat, but he'd lived through the excesses of the notorious Emperor Gaius 'Caligula' and the unfair expulsion of Jews and Christians from Rome by Emperor Claudius, so he harboured no illusions that the Romans were sheep in wolves' clothing. Instead, he subjected them to exactly the same critique and power limitations as the Israelite kings of old and the Jewish leaders of his own day. As long as a ruler acted as 'God's servant for your good', their authority was *real* and they were to be obeyed. But if they stopped acting as God's servant, they'd overstepped the limits of their legitimate authority and were now acting as *false* authorities. And for Paul, obeying a false authority rather than God was nothing short of idolatry – an unthinkable course of action for a Christian.

An idle, selfish neglect of duty

If we are to say that religion cannot be concerned with politics, then we are really saying that there is a substantial part of human life in which God's will does not run. If it is not God's, then whose is it?
Former Archbishop of Cape Town Desmond Tutu

Of course, if the whole world is God's and all *true* 'authority' comes from him, then in *no* area of life are we unaccountable to him. This means that *nothing* is out-of-bounds for either individual Christians or the Church. There's *no* area of life that is beyond our responsibility as stewards and as prophets – no area where we can legitimately wash our hands and say, 'That's not my problem!'

'When St Paul says, "Come out and be separate," he did not mean that Christians ought to take no interest in anything on earth except religion,' wrote the nineteenth-century Evangelical bishop of Liverpool J. C. Ryle. 'To care nothing about the government of one's own country, and to be utterly indifferent to the persons who guide its counsels and make its laws – all this may seem very right and proper in the eyes of some people. But I take leave to think that it is an idle, selfish neglect of duty.'

The Church has grown comfortable with the idea of responding to the world *pastorally*, but much of it is distinctly squeamish when it comes to responding *prophetically*, as this usually seems to entail some form of political involvement. Prophecy has been more or less privatised in our day and age, reduced to comfortable pictures of trees planted by rivers or eagles soaring in the sky. It's as if God were no longer interested in mainstream society, as he was in the Old Testament, but has narrowed his focus and is content with nothing more than having a private conversation with the Church. As Karl Barth said, 'How distressingly correct and friendly the

Church manages to make itself. Were an Amos or an Elijah to appear as a modern preacher, he would be rendered perfectly harmless.'

'Politics is the discourse of our public life,' writes Jim Wallis. 'There are real limits to what politics can provide to better the human condition. But politics *can* make a great difference, for good or for evil, in the ways that we live together.' Like it or not, entering the political arena is one of the most effective ways for the Church to be 'salt' and 'light'. It's our job to speak and act prophetically to ensure that our political involvement makes a difference for *good*, not evil, on a wide range of issues. Church bodies have often been keen to speak out politically on what they consider 'non-political' subjects – abortion in the 1980s, for example, or the gay age of consent in the 1990s – but the truth is that if *no* area is outside God's love, then *no* area is outside our remit. Education, the environment, transport, poverty, crime, racism, working conditions, immigration, taxation, defence, health . . . are we really prepared to say that God has no sovereignty or interest in any of these vital human areas?

But words alone are rarely enough. If we, like God, 'so love the world', we also have to roll up our sleeves and get involved on an activist, and often a *party*, level. This idea sends shivers down the spines of many church leaders. However, while *no* leader or organisation can ever claim our total allegiance, there's no reason why we shouldn't actively partner specific political parties over specific political issues. What's more, there's no reason why a political party's co-operation with us in one area should be bought at the cost of our silence in another. We have a responsibility to speak out, and mustn't allow that to be muzzled.

Two outstanding examples, one from the nineteenth century and one from the twentieth, point the way forward for political involvement by both the Church and individual Christians. William Wilberforce became an MP in 1780 at the age of twenty-one. On becoming an Evangelical Christian five years later, he briefly considered abandoning his political career, but changed his mind when he saw he could, as historian Asa Briggs puts it, 'save souls through the medium of political action'. In 1787 he started a lifelong campaign against slavery and a range of other social problems – from promoting Bible knowledge and keeping Sunday 'holy' to preventing cruelty to children or animals and eradicating poverty. Through a complex web of joined-up strategies and working partnerships, both religious and political, he laboured tirelessly to turn his dream into a reality.

In his fight against slavery, for example, he found himself working alongside people with very different agendas, united only in their desire to see an end to the slave trade – Quakers, whose social platform was otherwise far more radical than his; free-market capitalists, who considered the overheads involved in owning slaves a huge waste of money; and nationalists, whose only interest in abolition was the pressure it would put on France (with whom Britain was at war) to abandon its plans to recapture its valuable West Indian slave colony of Haiti, which won its independence in 1804. Wilberforce's ideals were a major force in the drive for abolition, but without his hard-nosed political realism and willing-ness to work alongside those who were often his opponents in other areas, his plans would have come to nothing.

In the twentieth century, Martin Luther King adopted the same kind of approach to politics and partnership. The Church was a major player in the political battle to end segregation in the Southern states of the USA, thanks in no small part to King's energy, wisdom and leadership. Had he and other church leaders, black and white, balked at the idea of 'mixing religion and politics' in a fully fledged civil rights campaign, racial bigotry and legal discrimination would have continued for decades. Similarly, if he'd been unwilling to form temporary alliances with both radical groups and the Kennedy and Johnson governments, nothing would have come about. But at the same time, King never felt so tied to any of his network of contacts and supporters that he couldn't speak out on issues that were close to his heart – his decision in 1967 to break silence and denounce the Vietnam War, for example, lost him many of the friends and allies he'd carefully won during the decade-long fight for civil rights.

The real problem facing the 'body of Christ' isn't so much the secularisation of society as the secularisation and privatisation of the Church, removing Christian witness and truth from the mainstream. We have to get beyond the image of an insipid and apolitical Christ to rediscover a message that speaks not just to the spiritual side of life, but also to the social, economic and political realm with 'disturbing' effect. Would Jesus have remained silent while millions of Jews were led to the gas chambers in the interests of political neutrality? No. Of course not! So what makes us so different?

9

'Success is the key'

Pride, as they say, comes before a fall. Gordon MacDonald – then President of the Inter-Varsity Christian Fellowship and one of America's most influential Evangelical leaders – once asked Billy Graham what advice he could give to avoid 'trouble at the top'. The veteran evangelist suggested he took careful stock of his weaknesses. 'If you know your weak spots,' Graham explained, 'you know where temptation is likely to strike.' Having had success and influence on both sides of the Atlantic with two acclaimed books on spiritual discipline – *Ordering Your Private World* and *Restoring Your Spiritual Passion* – MacDonald felt he knew both his strengths and his weaknesses. 'Well,' he replied confidently, 'it won't be sex.'

Sadly, history records otherwise. MacDonald's career crashed as news of his affair leaked out. In Evangelical circles, he moved instantly from hero to zero. For me, however, the most depressing aspect of his affair wasn't the fall of a respected Church leader, the near-collapse of his marriage, or even the media muck-raking as another 'model' Evangelical got caught with his pants down in the scandal-set 1980s. As tragic as this was, what concerned me most was what the episode revealed about Church culture.

When MacDonald fell, many of his harshest critics were those who'd been the most vocal in their praise of his book. As Ian

Coffey noted, 'It's sad, but true, that the Christian army often shoots its wounded.' Rightly or not, *Ordering Your Private World* struck a powerful chord in a macho Evangelical culture that blindly assumed 'success' was an essential spiritual quality, without seriously questioning *what kind* of success, or *why*. For all its undoubted virtues, the book bought heavily into the self-centred success ethic of 1980s Evangelicalism. It contains a lot of genuine insight and wisdom, but it's also thoroughly infused with a spirit of clean-cut, individualistic 'successful living' that, in my view, owes more to management theory and Reaganism than the New Testament. As a result, those who'd seen in MacDonald's life and work a reflection of the kind of all-American 'Lone Ranger' spirituality that told them they could climb any mountain and conquer any foe, provided they had the right faith-boosting cassette series and Filofax inserts, felt the most betrayed.

Of course, the reasons for wanting, and even promoting, an orderly private world and a self-evidently 'successful' life are for the most part extremely healthy and sincere. 'To bring order to one's personal life,' wrote MacDonald, 'is to invite [Christ's] control over every segment of one's life.' Who can argue with that? All of us, deep down, want Jesus to be at the heart of our lives. We want to be 'successful' not just for our own benefit, but also so our lives can be an example of the power of the gospel. But *that's* actually the problem. As extraordinary as it seems, *that's* where we part company with the New Testament. Why? Two reasons.

'A victim of your own success'

Success has always been a great liar.

German philosopher Friedrich Nietzsche

The first reason is very practical: 'successful', 'triumphant', entirely God-ordered lives are neither realistic nor truthful. MacDonald's critics were keen to point out that if he'd only followed his own private-world-ordering advice, he'd never have landed himself in such deep water. But they were wrong – their assessment was facile. It represents a serious misdiagnosis of the situation. The problem wasn't that he'd failed to practise what he'd preached – it was that what he preached was basically *impracticable*. It couldn't deliver what it promised.

Let's be honest: if Gordon MacDonald – a man with a first-class spiritual pedigree, great insight, strict discipline, top mentors, a *bona fide* support network and a loving family, not to mention a great deal to lose – still couldn't manage to keep his private world permanently in order, what hope is there for the rest of us? Most of the time, we just *aren't* that together. In fact, most of the time, if we're honest, we're just one or two steps away from the brink of total chaos. Our lives are watermarked by stress and disorder, and what we see as 'triumphant' or 'successful' Christian living is really no more than the calm between inevitable storms. We delude ourselves when we imagine that this rare *exception* is actually the rule. We convince ourselves that life *should* be all plain sailing, with just the occasional patch of rough seas. We tell ourselves that everyone else is on an even keel, and we're the only ones having trouble at the helm. But the truth is far more messy, and the effects of our self-delusion are disastrous.

Over the years, I've seen too many friends tragically crash and burn because they've compounded the natural stress of their jobs with the myth that their lives are supposed to be constantly ordered, 'successful' and under control. Statistics across all denominations confirm that overly high expectations, stress and burnout are huge problems for church leaders, and exactly the same is true in industry and other employment sectors. A MORI poll of the top 500 UK companies of the 1990s revealed that 65 per cent of employers were concerned about the effects of ill health in the workplace, and saw stress as far and away the biggest cause.

The severity of our response to excess stress can vary enormously: physical exhaustion or illness, nervous exhaustion or breakdown, mistakes or misdemeanours, clinical depression, suicide, adultery, alcoholism, substance abuse, domestic violence ... the list is almost endless. But these 'symptoms' all have one factor in common: *our performance never measures up to our expectations*. And make no mistake: the problem isn't our performance – the problem is our expectations.

Twenty years ago, when I was ordained as a Baptist minister, I promised 'to execute [my] charge with all fidelity, to preach and teach the word of God from the Holy Scriptures, to lead the congregation in worship and administer the gospel sacraments, to tend the flock of Christ and to do the work of an evangelist', as well as personally 'to be faithful in prayer and in the reading and study of the Holy Scriptures, and to lead a life worthy of the calling to which [I had] been called'. Taken individually, none of these tasks seems overly demanding, but taken together they add up to a pretty tall order. So tall, in fact, that I knew even as I solemnly made the promise that I would never really be able to live up to it. There was no way I could be on target in every area – it wasn't just an *enormous* challenge, it was an *impossible* one.

The truth of this situation seems to be reflected in the latest version of the Baptist ordination vows. Rather than being asked to make rash promises they can't possibly keep, ordinands are now only required to '*seek* to ensure that the gospel . . . is proclaimed', '*play [their] part* in the nourishment of the flock', '*do [their] best* to ensure that the welcome and help of the church are available for all' and be '*determined* to walk this path' of faith. The fact is, if we expect any more than this from our church leaders, or members, we'll be demanding an equilibrium that escaped even two of the Church's 'founding fathers', Peter and Paul. Peter constantly vacillated between faith and doubt, hope and despair, insight and misunderstanding, big-heartedness and narrow-mindedness, and the New Testament is littered with his blunders. And Paul, a far more stable character, still went through a bitter bust-up with his former mentor, Barnabas, when he refused to let Mark go with them on their travels (Acts 15:36–9) – a rash decision that with hindsight Paul came to regret deeply (for example, Colossians 4:10).

Sustained individual 'success', whatever our motives, is quite simply a figment of our fallen imagination. If we don't expect to fail some of the time, we're just not being realistic. And if we build up an image of Christian living – and Christian leadership – that makes no allowance for human frailty, but demands constant superhuman effort and success, then we're not only setting ourselves up for personal disappointment, we're also virtually ensuring that we run our leaders (and ourselves) into the ground.

The wounded healer

Adversity introduces a person to themselves.

Anonymous

But there's a second reason why our well-intentioned desire to live a 'successful' Christian life as a witness to the power of the gospel is *not* in line with biblical thinking, and it's more theological. It assumes God can use us as effective witnesses only in our times of strength. We *admit*, for example, that Peter and Paul had weaknesses, but tend to think that only their 'greatest moments' – Paul's church planting, Peter's Pentecost speech, etc. – were powerful instruments for communicating the gospel of peace, justice and reconciliation that lies at the heart of the Christian message. And that's not only wrong, it's *dangerously* wrong.

There's a tendency for us to imagine that our weaknesses are best kept hidden, or protected – that they're nothing more than a gateway to sin, as in the case of Gordon MacDonald. But the truth is that, while our weaknesses frequently *are* battlefields for temptation, they're also crucial areas through which God chooses to work. As Graham Kendrick put it, God frequently turns *our* weaknesses into *his* opportunities.

It's not that sin doesn't matter – in fact, it's precisely because it *does* matter that it's such a mistake for us to keep our weaknesses and our areas of temptation hidden, pretending to other people (and often even to ourselves) that they're not really there. Self-denial of this kind just sets us up for a fall. Nor should we deliberately lead ourselves into areas where we know we'll be tempted just in order to allow God the opportunity to work through our weakness and sin (cf. Romans 6:1–2). It's just that we need to be a lot more transparent, open and honest with people about our struggles as well as our successes, our weaknesses as well as our strengths.

My friend Nick remembers once returning home for a family occasion. He'd been depressed and despondent about a number of things that were going on his life, and wasn't relishing the thought of seeing his family in such an obviously 'unsuccessful' state. As a Baptist minister with sound Evangelical credentials, he knew he'd be closely scrutinised by his six brothers and sisters, not all of whom were Christians. One sister in particular had always had difficulty dealing with his faith and his job as a 'professional Christian'. Nevertheless, as his sister she loved him, and she knew him well enough to realise as they talked that something was wrong.

'Are you all right?' she asked him.

Nick knew that the real answer was 'no', but that he'd have to reply with the expected and obligatory 'yes'. He didn't want to give anything but the best impression of what it meant to be a Christian – and that meant 'joyful victorious living', not depression and despondency. But as he opened his mouth to reply, to his amazement he found himself being completely honest. 'No,' he told her. 'I'm not. Things aren't going particularly well in my job, and I'm really struggling with my faith.' He waited for his sister to recoil in shock or make snide I-told-you-so remarks, but instead she opened up and Nick found they were sharing on a deeper level than ever before. But what really surprised him was her positive reaction to his faith.

'I always thought your Christianity was too good to be true,' she told him. 'This is the first time it's ever seemed real.'

Like Nick and so many other kids of my generation, I was taught at Sunday school that God blesses only those who pray regularly and consistently, and are spiritually dynamic. But I'm now forty-five, and I'm living proof that that kind of thinking is wrong. I know I've only survived as a Christian person – let alone a Christian leader – because of grace. As Paul wrote, under arrest in Rome, 'Everything I *can* do, I do only in the strength of the one who empowers me [Christ]' (Philippians 4:13). I'm aware he *has* used (and I pray will *continue* to use) my failures and weaknesses as much as, and at times even *more than*, my successes and strengths.

My friend Karen says the best thing her dad ever did for her was crash the car! It's not that he was a bad father. In fact, if he hadn't been such a good dad, the crash wouldn't have had such an impact on her. He was kind, loving and *very* clever, but all this just made her aware of the huge mountain she had to climb to be like him. And then, when she was fourteen, he crashed the car. No one was hurt, but Karen was never the same again. She'd seen the accident coming but hadn't said anything, assuming he'd seen it coming too. As the other car ploughed into the side of them, Karen's shock gave way to a sudden understanding of her own strengths and her dad's weaknesses. He might be 'Brain of Britain', but there were still things *she* could see that *he* couldn't. And ironically, their relationship took a quantum leap forward. For the first time, she saw him as a frail, fallible human being, just like her . . . and loved him for it!

The truth is, none of us is perfect. We all have our Achilles' heels. So when people present a perfect profile to us – clean-cut and minty-fresh – we *know* it isn't real. And we don't connect with it. It doesn't carry the stamp of authenticity. We *know* they must be hiding something, or being less than honest (perhaps especially with themselves). If we're smart we won't fall for the deception. But that's why it's such a mistake for us to think that other people – Christian or not – will only respond positively to a cleaned-up, air-brushed image of the Christian life. In fact, the book MacDonald wrote after his tragic affair, *Rebuilding Your Broken World*, has connected more deeply with more people than *Ordering Your Private World* ever could – not because there's anything laudable about having an affair, but because people find it easier to identify with a book that is, in the words of Jim Packer, 'written with gut-wrenching honesty by one who knows what he is talking about'.

If we insist on feeding people a squeaky-clean and unrealistic illusion of what it means to be a Christian – one that leaves no room for the kind of human frailty all of us readily identify with and know from our own experience – they won't identify with it. By contrast, if we let them see how God loves us as whole individuals, fully accepting us not just where we think we're up to the mark but also in our areas of weakness, they'll begin to see that there's hope for us *all*. As Bono once wrote, 'That the Scriptures are brim full of husslers, murderers, cowards, adulterers and mercenaries used to shock me. Now it's a source of great comfort.'

'We preach Christ crucified'

If a thing is worth doing, it is worth doing badly.

G. K. Chesterton

In his story about a Pharisee and a tax-collector (Luke 18:9–14), Jesus explicitly warned against this kind of unreal, hard-to-identify-with 'successful' approach to faith. We're used to seeing the Pharisees as people who felt they could *earn* their way into God's good books, but this view doesn't actually fit the facts. The Pharisees were firm believers in God's grace. So when the Pharisee in Jesus' story prays, 'God, I thank you I'm not like other people: thieves, rogues, adulterers, like this tax-collector,' he's utterly sincere in his gratitude, convinced that he's unlike the tax-collector because God, out of the depths of his love, has *made* him unlike the tax-collector. As an ancient prayer put it, 'Blessed are you, Lord our God, King of the Universe, who didn't make me a Gentile. Blessed are you . . . who didn't make me a slave. Blessed are you . . . who didn't make me a woman.' As 'un-PC' as it seems today, this prayer began as a Jewish man's thanks to God for totally undeservedly making him one of the 'elect' chosen people (and a free male, the 'elect' of the 'elect'). But slowly and insidiously it acquired the dangerous side-effect of promoting an 'us and them' mentality. The Pharisees were so glad that God had saved them through his ongoing 'special relationship' with them that they gradually came to see themselves as being morally superior to the rest of humanity.

The Pharisee in Jesus' story has bought into this 'us and them' approach completely. That's why he stands alone to make himself distinct when he prays (out loud for all to hear). He's proud that God, in his mercy, has made him not only righteous but enthusiastically faithful (hence the tithes and fasts). He 'exalts himself' not by imagining that his own 'works' can save him, but by becoming so proudly confident in his own God-given righteousness and purity as one of 'us' that he begins to despise anyone who seems like one of 'them'. He lets himself become so focussed on what God has done for *him*, and all the things he's done in *his* life – how his lifestyle is deliberately and painstakingly ordered to be a 'successful' reflection of God's purity and holiness, a powerful witness to his glory – that he loses sight of the fact that God doesn't wait for people's lives to be this 'worthy' before graciously saving them.

Were the Pharisees, in effect, the conservative Evangelicals of their day? Many deliberately 'exalted themselves' out of a genuine desire to *evangelise*. Whole-heartedly committed to their God-given task of being a 'light to the Gentiles' (Isaiah 42:6, 49:6), they wanted their own pure spotless lives to serve as a powerful witness for God. Their strict faithfulness to the Law was meant to be a walking advertisement for 'eternal life'. So as he stands in the Temple praying, the Pharisee in Jesus' parable exaggerates the 'clear blue water' between himself and the tax-collector, consciously parading his 'successful' and holy lifestyle in the hope that it will either shame or attract the tax-collector to repent. But tragically, all his 'power evangelism' attitude does is stop him from seeing that the 'strength' of his hardline holy lifestyle *isn't* the key component in the tax-collector's change of heart. In fact, if anything, this self-righteousness makes faith seem totally unattainable. Instead, what produces a turnabout in the tax-collector is the outrageous mercy and un-earned forgiveness of God, graphically demonstrated in the twice-daily atonement sacrifices in the Temple which form the backdrop to the parable.

We shouldn't be surprised. After all, at the heart of our faith is the crucifixion, which Paul describes as 'a stumbling block to Jews and foolishness to Gentiles' (1 Corinthians 1:23). The cross is the ultimate sign of weakness, but the means through which God saved the whole world. So when we think that God can't use our weaknesses and failures as much as – or at times perhaps even more than – our strengths and successes, we're basically calling the cross into question. It's as if we're telling God, 'You may already have opted for weakness as a way to save the world and reveal yourself, but there's still time to correct that mistake. The smart option is power and strength.'

In C. S. Lewis' classic allegorical novel *The Lion, the Witch and the Wardrobe*, Aslan the lion comes back to life after offering himself to be killed by the Witch in exchange for Edmund's life. 'Though the Witch knew the Deep Magic,' he tells Edmund's sisters, Lucy and Susan, 'there is a magic deeper still which she did not know.' The Witch opted for power, and Aslan for weakness, but there was a wisdom and strength to the 'weak' option which, like the Pharisee and sometimes the Church, the Witch had failed to grasp.

The wisdom of God's weakness is as powerful now as ever. In 1979, Harvard professor and Catholic priest Henri Nouwen wrote a book called *The Wounded Healer*. In it he argued that pastoral strategies based on the types of professional technique used by psychotherapists weren't working. His advice bucked a trend toward 'professionalisation' among priests and ministers that had grown during the 1970s and would grow even more in the success–driven 1980s. Rather than duplicating the work of 'secular' colleagues, Nouwen felt that pastors should offer something uniquely 'Christian'. In short, they should stop trying to minister to people primarily out of their strengths and success, and learn to see their own weaknesses and failure as a more effective and Christ-like way to identify with people's suffering and help them cope with it. In 1985, he followed his own advice. He quit his Harvard job to spend the last eleven years of his life ministering to people with learning disabilities in L'Arche communities first in France and then in Canada. Harvard represented the peak of his professional success, fully allowing God to use his strengths. But L'Arche gave him a chance to live with and allow God to use his weaknesses. He never regretted it.

Success is the key? Only if your god is very small-minded. And only if you've opted for Christianity without the cross.

10

'Accept me into your heart as your personal Lord and Saviour'

Prince Otto von Bismarck was a master tactician and a smooth political operator. Germany's 'Iron Chancellor' from 1871 to 1890, second only to the kaiser, he was the real power behind the throne. As Prussian Prime Minister, he'd deliberately engineered successful 'defensive' wars against Denmark, Austria and France. He'd intentionally provoked conflict just in order to strengthen Prussia's power and achieve his goal of 'unification' of the numerous semi-independent states that now make up Germany. By 1871, through a mixture of guile and gore, he'd succeeded in making Germany one nation for the first time in its long history.

Chancellor Bismarck was aristocratic, autocratic, militaristic, nationalistic, manipulative and totally ruthless. But he was also a very sincere and active Christian who'd have had no trouble affirming, in the words of the modern creed, that Jesus was his 'personal Lord and Saviour'. Most of us probably find that a bit hard to believe, but the truth is that Bismarck merely achieved in an extreme way what *all* of us do to some extent or other – he compartmentalised his life. As one critic joked, there was an invisible sign on his office door in Berlin that read, '*Jesus Christus Verboten!*' ('Jesus Christ forbidden here!'); Bismarck wouldn't have put it that way, but it was true nonetheless.

'Accept Jesus into your heart as your personal Lord and Saviour' may be a time-honoured evangelistic maxim, but consciously or not it encourages just the kind of compartmentalised and privatised understanding of faith that stamped out Bismarck's approach. Faith is faith, politics is politics, business is business, sex is sex, family is family – each sphere of life is totally separate, watertight and distinct. Like children insisting that the different foods on their plate mustn't touch or intermingle, we try to keep the different strands of our lives segregated from one another, each with its own set of moral standards. And though this distinction is sometimes acknowledged, most of the time it's well hidden beneath the surface . . . even, or perhaps especially, from those like Bismarck who maintain it.

> Lieutenant Dan Taylor: 'Have you found Jesus yet, Gump?'
> Forrest Gump: 'I didn't know I was supposed to be looking for him, sir.'

It's a personal thing
Of course, it's easy to see the potential benefits of a phrase like 'personal Lord and Saviour', and to understand why it's entered popular usage. You only have to look at the nineteenth-century world of Jane Austen, for example, to see how Christianity can sometimes slide into the background and end up as little more than part of the cultural furniture. Though almost all the characters in her novels would call themselves Christian, few if any are 'serious' about it – even among the clergy! From the odious and obsequious Mr Collins in *Pride and Prejudice* to the charming and affable Edward Farrars in *Sense and Sensibility*, her clergymen enter the profession more out of a sense of social ambition or vague suitability than real commitment or passionate faith.

In fact, many clergy in the early 1800s believed that faith should be anything *but* personal or seriously life-changing. Christianity was at the time basically seen as a social and moral code (and a good excuse for dressing up on Sundays!), not a vibrant faith. It was said that, for most Anglican clergymen, faith came a poor third after farming and fox-hunting! In circumstances like this, the idea that Jesus wasn't an automatic redeemer or a distant social superior, but a *personal Saviour* and *Lord*, was an extremely challenging one.

In many ways, not a lot seems to have changed. An American preacher visiting the UK a few years ago couldn't resist taking the opportunity to 'share his faith' in a shopping centre. He made his way to the main piazza and began striking up conversations with the passers-by. Most people either scurried quickly away or, trapped by their own politeness, talked with him cautiously for a few minutes before eventually finding some pretext to escape. But one blue-rinsed old lady gave him a reply he never forgot – when he asked her politely, 'Excuse me, madam, are you a Christian?' she shot back, 'Oh no, young man. I'm Church of England!'

According to the most recent statistics, while 65 per cent of the English population consider themselves Christian, just under 8 per cent is actually in church on a Sunday morning (and the situation isn't likely to be much better for the rest of the UK). In other words, over half the population see themselves as having a Christian faith but don't really appreciate the full value of taking it seriously. However, unlike most of polite society in Jane Austen's day, people now tend to have at best only a casual connection with the Church – Christmas and Easter, perhaps, or just 'hatches, matches and despatches'. Now more than ever, it seems, there's a real need for them to know that Christianity isn't just a cultural trait or some kind of inherited genetic attribute – it's a personal, life-changing journey of forgiveness and reconciliation with God. Jesus wasn't just a good bloke – he was, and *is*, the Lord and Saviour of the world, knowable in a personal way.

The problem is, of course, that in our genuine desire to put right one problem, we've created another. And tragically, it's one of those instances where the 'cure' is every bit as deadly as the 'disease'. In seeking to address the issue of Jesus being seen as an *im*personal Lord and Saviour – part of our cultural baggage – we've allowed things to swing too far the other way, and unwittingly portrayed him as a *purely* personal Lord and Saviour.

It's become fashionable to accept him into our 'hearts' as our privately effective Saviour and as 'Lord' of our very narrowly defined 'personal lives', but often that's as far as it goes. Rather than granting him a mandate to 'access all areas', we essentially bar him from all other parts of our lives. We compartmentalise ourselves – ensuring 'private and personal' is totally separate from 'public, corporate and communal' – and confine Jesus to quarters, keeping him in his 'proper' place in the 'spiritual' realm. He is, after all, the Lord of our 'hearts'. And this isn't just an Evangelical thing: people in every sector of society, and across the religious spectrum, constantly insist that their faith is 'private and personal', totally disconnected from their public life. The result is that they keep Jesus politely but firmly caged.

Beauty and the Beast

> *I'm devout, I'm sincere and I'm proud to say*
> *That it's had exactly no effect on who I am today.*
> American singer/songwriter Steve Taylor,
> 'It's a Personal Thing'

In Robert Louis Stevenson's famous novel *The Strange Case of Dr Jekyll and Mr Hyde*, well-respected London doctor Henry Jekyll experiments with drugs to turn himself into his alter ego, Edward Hyde. Physically unrecognisable, Hyde is every bit as bad as Jekyll is good, and his evil ways soon lead to a grisly murder and the eventual death of Jekyll/Hyde. The story is well known, but what's *less* well known is just *why* Dr Jekyll begins his eerie pharmaceutical experiments in the first place. The truth is, Jekyll has been living a life of 'profound duplicity' for a long time before Mr Hyde arrives on the scene. His public persona and his private wants and needs pull him in completely opposite directions. In fact, it's precisely *because* his hidden personal life is so sharply different to his desires and aspirations as a Victorian doctor that he starts to concoct his strange potions, determined to allow himself to express the darker side of his personality entirely without constraint. But, as he explains, 'I was in no sense a hypocrite; both sides of me were in dead earnest.'

The Strange Case of Dr Jekyll and Mr Hyde was an instant commercial and critical success when it was first published in 1886, and has continued to capture the public imagination ever since. Perhaps one of the reasons we identify with it so strongly is because, for most of us, it represents merely an extreme form of the kind of compartmentalised life we all tend to lead.

My friend Bill, a highly successful businessman, recently bought an old, established family firm that had once been a dominant force in the marketplace and a virtual household name. Its heyday was well and truly over, and its owners no longer had the massive amounts of capital needed to keep it afloat, but Bill could see that it still had potential in the much smaller 'niche market' . . . provided the right management changes were made and the whole operation was radically 'downsized'. I'd met him years before through church, and I knew he was a caring and sensitive man, so when I had lunch with him a few days after he'd personally had to inform over two hundred staff that they were now 'surplus to requirements', I asked him how he was holding up. Both of us knew it was an economic necessity – the company had been on its last legs, and it was more a case of *saving* sixty jobs than *losing* two hundred. Nevertheless, his stark reply really startled me. 'That's business,' he remarked, shrugging the whole thing off with a grin and a wave of his hand. 'If you swim with the sharks, you either learn to swim fast or you get eaten!' The look in his eyes as he spoke told me that he really hadn't given it another thought. But knowing him well, I knew that if he'd encountered one of those employees in his 'other world' at home or church, he'd have felt the full pain of their predicament and moved heaven and earth to ensure they were given all the pastoral support and understanding they needed. However, this was work, and he felt nothing. 'That's business.'

It's important to realise, however, that this 'double standard' – like that of Dr Jekyll – is *not* hypocrisy. It's not that Bill is *pretending* to be one person when the truth is that he's really someone completely different. Nor is he suggesting that people should have one consistent moral standard, but then failing to live up to that himself. Instead, like so many of us – not just high-profile politicians such as Clinton and an endless procession of British MPs – he's created *different* standards for different 'compartments' within his life. Business is business, church is church, family is family, public is public, private is private.

Our ability to hold these conflicting worlds together – or perhaps more accurately *apart* – is reminiscent of the process of mental gymnastics known as 'doublethink' in George Orwell's futuristic novel *Nineteen Eighty-Four*. In the nightmare world of Oceania, a totalitarian state watched over by the all-powerful 'Big Brother', the government tries to control every aspect of people's lives, right down to their thoughts. Through a mixture of relentless propaganda, absolute control of the media, blatant spin-doctoring and the dreaded 'thought police', Big Brother manipulates people into totally compartmentalising their thinking. As a result, they swallow the party's lies hook, line and sinker. For most of Oceania's population, doublethink – defined as 'the power of holding two contradictory beliefs in one's mind simultaneously, and accepting both of them' – is simply a way of life. Of course, while none of us would ever engage in doublethink in the same kind of blatant way that the characters in Orwell's book do, the truth is that our compartmentalising creates a kind of doublethink of its own. We hold two contradictory lifestyles in our minds simultaneously, and accept both of them!

That's why a phrase like 'personal Lord and Saviour' can be so dangerous. It allows us to compartmentalise. Jesus becomes our *personal* Lord and Saviour, not the *absolute* Lord and Saviour. His efficacy and authority covers our 'spiritual' and 'personal' lives, but it rarely spills over into the other areas, where we never even think to invite him in. However, like it or not, as the cliché goes, if Jesus isn't Lord *of* all, he isn't Lord *at* all.

See! Hear!

The greatest tragedy of modern evangelism is in calling many to belief, but few to obedience.

> American church and Sojourners Community
> leader Jim Wallis

Given the frequency with which it's bandied about in Evangelical circles, it may surprise you to learn that the phrase 'accept me/Jesus into your heart as your personal Lord and Saviour' doesn't appear *once* in the pages of the New Testament. In fact, even if it did, it would carry a very different meaning to the one we generally give it.

For a start, when the Bible talks about the 'heart', it doesn't use the term in the same way we do. It never refers just to the emotions, which are usually symbolised by the guts. (When Jesus stepped off the boat to encounter a crowd of over five thousand hungry people, Matthew 14:14 tells us he 'had compassion for them'. A more literal translation would be, 'His guts wrenched for them.') Instead, in Hebrew and Greek thinking, the term 'heart' embraced the *whole* of life, reflecting their holistic, every-aspect approach. So when the 'fool' of Psalm 14:1 says 'in their heart' there's no God, they're effectively denying God's existence in *every* area of their lives, especially (as the rest of the Psalm makes clear) their wallet, their 'wisdom' and their attitude to others, not just their emotions.

The same unbiblical skew is seen in our modern-day understanding of the word 'personal'. In fact, there's not even a word for 'personal' *anywhere* in the Hebrew and Greek manuscripts of the Bible. Despite the fact that the Bible's ancient culture was far more community-oriented and less individualistic than ours, no biblical writer ever felt the need to describe their faith as private and 'personal'. And none of them considered their salvation a purely 'spiritual' matter.

The word 'saviour' had very specific – and very public – connotations to Jews and Gentiles in the first century. Jews would initially have thought of the kind of redeemer figure typified by Boaz in the book of Ruth – a close relative who 'saved' them from social and financial ruin. There was nothing exclusively private and 'personal' about this: Ruth and Naomi were refugees (what we'd now call 'economic migrants') and Ruth wasn't even a natural-born Jew. Their grinding poverty was gritty and real, and Boaz' gratuitous rescue was a community action, done in front of the whole council of elders. By extension, then, 'saviour' became a word Jews used to describe God – a father figure who'd 'saved' them from the brink of disaster time after time, and would do so again in the future. They didn't see him in purely personal terms, as the saviour of mere *individuals*, but as the saviour of the *entire nation*. Gentiles, too, would have had something distinctly public in mind when they heard the word 'saviour'. Roman emperors from Octavian 'Augustus' onwards were routinely called 'saviour', and an inscription found in the ancient Greek city of Priene (near Ephesus) refers to Augustus as 'a saviour for us and those who come after us'. This wasn't a 'spiritual' title, and nor was it a purely private and 'personal' one – it was a solemn pledge of absolute loyalty and devotion by a whole city to a military dictator frequently dubbed 'lord' and 'saviour'.

However, the phrase 'Lord and Saviour' by itself does occur in the Bible on four occasions, all in 2 Peter (1:11; 2:20; 3:2, 18). But though Paul comes close (referring to 'a Saviour, the Lord Jesus Christ', Philippians 3:20), no other New Testament author even links 'Lord' and 'Saviour' together. In fact, 'Saviour' is rarely used in the New Testament as a title for Jesus. Paul explicitly calls him 'Saviour' just six times in his letters (the same number of times he calls God 'Saviour'), preferring to describe Jesus as 'Lord', something he does around 200 times. Like all New Testament authors, Paul discusses Jesus' *lordship* far more frequently and deeply than his *saviourhood*. Of course, it's more a question of emphasis than content, but Paul puts the emphasis firmly on Jesus as Lord, in sharp contrast to our emphasis on Jesus' role as a 'personal' Saviour.

Besides not being a biblical injunction, therefore, the real danger with a phrase like 'accept Jesus into your heart as your personal Lord and Saviour' is that while it *contains* the word 'Lord', its meaning and impact is considerably diluted – if not decimated – by adding the words 'heart', 'personal' and 'saviour', all of which now carry a highly unbiblical, overly individualistic and self-centred flavour. To put it bluntly, we use the phrase to reinforce our tendency to treat the Lord of the Cosmos as our 'best buddy'.

This overfamiliarity is something Jesus warned his disciples about. 'Not everyone who says to me, "Lord, Lord,"' he cautioned them, 'will enter the kingdom of heaven, but only the one who does the will of my Father in heaven' (Matthew 7:21). And what kind of master, he asked, hires a servant to do a job and then waits on them hand and foot in sheer gratitude because they're actually doing it (Luke 17:7–10)? What kind of servant expects such red carpet treatment for doing no more than they've been paid to do? 'In the Middle East the traditional roles of master and servant are well-defined,' notes Lebanese-based biblical scholar Kenneth Bailey. 'For a master to serve his own servants is unheard of.'

The problem is, as Christians we've now become so used to seeing Jesus as the 'suffering servant' that we've lost the ability to understand the culture in which he lived – one in which not just the super-rich but even people of modest means hired servants, and in which servants knew what was expected of them. What's more, we've become so ingrained with the belief that 'all men are created equal', as the American Declaration of Independence puts it, that we tend to read our modern-day egalitarianism back into the text and get very uncomfortable with the idea, commonplace at the time of Jesus, that a servant should serve their master, not the other way round. We've come to expect that masters *should* be servants – humble enablers rather than despotic tyrants. But as true as this is, there are two crucial factors that we need to bear in mind.

First, no one in first-century Palestine – except Jesus – would have shared our way of thinking. Every servant would instead have 'known their place'. In fact, it's *because* servants knew their place that Jesus' washing of his disciples' feet on his last night (a very menial task) was so shocking, and why Peter recoiled from the idea in total horror (John 13:6–8). If masters behaving like servants had been common, there'd have been no significance in Jesus' action. It wouldn't have symbolised his upcoming 'suffering servant' death at all. Second, linked to this, just because masters should behave more like servants, that *doesn't* mean that servants therefore have a right to lord it over their masters. The concept of the 'servant king' is *mutual service*, not a turning of the tables so that former servants now become the new tyrants. 'You call me Teacher and Lord – and you are right, for that is what I am,' Jesus told his disciples. 'So if I, your Lord and Teacher, have washed your feet, you also ought to wash one another's feet. For I have set you an example, that you also should do as I have done to you.' But then he warned them against complacency and overfamiliarity, 'Very truly, I tell you, servants are not greater than their master' (John 13:13–16). Being served by Jesus wasn't an invitation to lord it over him or become too buddy-buddy. Instead, it was an invitation, like him, to 'humble' ourselves, 'taking the form of a slave'. (Philippians 2:7–8).

The truth is, the phrase 'personal Lord and Saviour' comes far too close to sounding like 'personal assistant' or 'personal valet' to be anything even remotely like an adequate or appropriate way of describing our relationship with the Lord of the Cosmos – the person Paul preferred to call 'our Lord Jesus Christ'. For all his humility, Jesus is still our *master*, not our puppet on a string. 'An arrogant attitude views God as fortunate for having people like us in his service,' writes North American New Testament theologian Craig Evans. 'The proper attitude, however, is thankfulness for having the privilege and opportunity to serve God.'

'Accept me into your heart as your personal Lord and Saviour, sir'?

'More sugar in your tea, madam?'

Perhaps not.

11

'Better safe than sorry'

Having finished his impassioned speech, the pastor sits down. For a few seconds no one says a word. Then the church secretary gets to his feet. 'I'm sorry,' he tells his fellow members of the leadership council. 'I've sat and listened to the arguments, and I can see their merit. I can understand what you're trying to achieve, and in principle I'm behind you 100 per cent. But in all honesty I can't support this venture. I just don't think it's a responsible use of the resources God has given us to steward.'

A familiar scene, re-enacted week-in, week-out up and down the country. It doesn't really matter what the venture is. It could be diverting church funds to open a hostel for homeless teenagers; or creating a suite of user-friendly rooms in the church's old Victorian building for use by the church and groups from the local community; or buying a set of the latest hymn books. The specific project itself isn't the deciding factor. Instead, the salient facts are these: it represents something the church hasn't done before; there's an element of risk involved; and it's going to cost money.

That's when we get cold feet. Most of us personally have some form of standard long-term financial commitment or risk: mortgages on our houses, finance deals on our cars, unpaid bills on our credit cards, outstanding student loans or perhaps even a few shares or an investment fund. We don't consider these things reckless. We see them as necessary, even prudent. But when it comes to the prospect of spending *church* money, even the biggest spenders among us tend to go ultra-conservative. It may be a project we whole-heartedly support in theory, but when it actually comes to 'stepping out boldly in faith' and confidently expecting that God will 'honour our faith', we have a habit of squeezing the purse strings so tight we're in danger of cutting off our *own* circulation. Even those who firmly believe that Christians ought to 'pray the money in' (rather than making use of fundraising events) stop asking if it's the *right* thing to do and ask instead if it's the *prudent* thing to do. After all, everybody knows that it's far better to be safe than sorry.

Well, I've got bad news for you. The hard evidence suggests that Jesus almost *never* did the prudent or cautious thing. Instead of being ultra-careful, he took constant risks. Rather than always walking 'on the safe side', he stepped out in faith, doing things that often made no sense to those around him . . . and, what's worse, that didn't always succeed. The Jesus of Nazareth Discipleship School, for example, got off to a shaky start in its first few years: even a casual glance through Luke 9 reveals the disciples' very poor performance in the mission 'block placement' scheme (verses 1–9), the faith expectation course (verses 10–17), the suffering messiah module (verses 18–27), the practical holiness class (verses 28–36), and various sessions in healing (verses 37–43a), basic comprehension (verses 43b–5), humility (verses 46–8), exorcism (verses 49–50) and forgiveness (verses 51–6). What's more, in their 'final exam', eleven students abandoned him and the other one betrayed him.

Hole in the ground

The choice is never between a risk and a sure thing. It's always a choice between risks.
American Presbyterian theologian Robert McAfee Brown

In his book *Ship of Gold in the Deep Blue Sea*, bestselling author

Gary Kinder tells the true story of the search for the treasure ship SS *Central America*, a side-wheel steamer that sank in a hurricane off the coast of South Carolina in 1857. Laden with gold from the California gold rush, it remained undiscovered 160 miles off the US coast for 130 years until finally being located by hi-tech salvage expert Thomas Thompson in 1988. The costs of finding the wreck, 8,000 ft beneath the ocean's surface, and recovering the gold eventually came to a staggering $12 million. Most of the money came from private investors who were willing to put capital into the high-risk venture because the potential rewards were massive. They invested in uncertainty, taking a long-term gamble, but the return on their investment was definitely worth it. The discovery of the wreck hit the headlines around the world, not just because it used state-of-the-art robotic technology, but also because it was the highest-yielding gold salvage operation ever mounted. The total worth of the coins and bullion recovered is conservatively estimated at over $100 million.

But this kind of 'speculate to accumulate' principle isn't confined to treasure seekers and venture capitalists. It's a basic rule of life. It's even found in the Bible, on the lips of Jesus himself. In the run-up to his death, Jesus told a story about a rich man going on a journey who gave three of his servants differing amounts of 'venture capital' to invest during his absence, each according to their ability (Matthew 25:14–30). The first, given five talents, used the money to make another five; the second, given two talents, made another two; but the last, given just one talent, hid it safely in the ground. Afraid to take a risk with his investment and lose even his seed money, he chose to play it safe. After all, there was too much at stake – a talent (from which we get the English word) was a sizable sum.

According to the conventional wisdom of the time, burying money in a hole in the ground was the safest thing you could do with it, so the ultra-cautious servant probably expected to be praised for his prudence. He may have made nothing, but he'd also *lost* nothing – as such he'd been a good steward. Given the options available to him, he'd chosen the most sensible, low-risk approach.

However, his master saw things rather differently. He was used to making his (and other people's) money work hard for him. He'd taken a calculated risk in giving the money to the servant – if he'd wanted to play safe and guarantee getting it all back, he could have hidden it in the ground himself! Instead he'd entrusted it to a servant who'd failed to repay that trust. As a result, the master did what any wise investor would do – he took his account away from so bad a fund manager and gave it to someone from whom he could expect a higher yield.

Of course, Jesus didn't tell this parable in order to give people financial advice. Nor did he tell it primarily about individuals. Instead, it's a parable about the failure of the *entire people*, and the religious leadership in particular, to follow God's risk-taking lead. Unwilling to do anything that might just turn out to be less than entirely honouring to God, they chose to bury their treasure in the ground. But if a double-dealing landowner has a right to expect his servants to make good on his investment – which is, after all, just money – how much more does God have a right to expect *his* chosen servants to make good on *his* investment – the salvation of the entire world? As the late Oxford theologian George Caird put it, religious leaders like the Pharisees 'believed that their whole duty was to preserve intact what God had entrusted to them, not realising that God expected his capital to be invested in a world mission for the redemption of the outcast and sinful'.

We (and in particular those of us who're leaders) are in exactly the same position. We've been entrusted with something of ultimate value – the gospel of Jesus and his kingdom. We need to ensure that we're not guilty of just burying it in a hole in the ground. When the 'father of modern missions', William Carey, first stood up to talk to a group of Christian leaders about the need to be actively engaged in mission, he was told, 'Sit down, young man! When God chooses to save the heathen, he'll do so without your help!' But Carey *didn't* sit down. He *couldn't* sit down. And in time, his enthusiasm led not only to the founding of the Baptist Missionary Society, but also indirectly became an inspiration to the founders of many other mission organisations. Like him, we need to be prepared to step out in faith and do *something* – even if it later turns out to be the *wrong* thing – rather than *nothing*, because most of the time doing nothing – 'risking nothing' – actually means taking the biggest risk of all.

'Wait for it, wait for it . . .'

In order to act wisely, it is not enough to be wise.

Russian novelist Fyodor Dostoevsky

Not everything, of course, has to be high-risk, high-return – there's all the difference in the world between a *calculated* risk and a *careless* one. Faith isn't the same thing as stupidity. In fact, adequate thought and risk-analysis are *part* of faith, not the opposite of it. After all, it was Jesus himself who warned about making unwise commitments – the kind you can't complete. 'Who among you, intent on building a tower, doesn't first sit down and figure out the cost to see if you've got enough to complete it? Otherwise, everyone who sees that you've laid a foundation but aren't able to finish will begin to ridicule you, saying, "This person began to build but couldn't finish!" Or what king, going to war against another king, doesn't first sit down and carefully consider if with ten thousand troops he can oppose one coming against him with twenty thousand? If not, he'll send ambassadors while the other is still far off and negotiate for peace' (Luke 14:28–32).

The wisdom of this advice seems glaringly obvious. It's not too hard to think of ambitious building projects that ran into major financial difficulties midway through construction. The British Library, Tate Modern, the Millennium Dome – all were massively over budget and would never have seen the light of day without huge financial bail-outs at crucial stages. Even military examples aren't hard to find: in 1961, French President Charles de Gaulle told newly elected US President John F. Kennedy that 'intervention' in Vietnam (from which the French had withdrawn six years before) would be 'an entanglement without end' – a war the USA could never win. Unwisely, successive presidents Kennedy, Johnson and Nixon ignored this advice and committed increasing numbers of American troops and resources to defend what Kennedy called 'the cornerstone of the Free World'. Eventual US disgrace, and even the Vietnam War itself, could have been avoided with better advance planning and risk-analysis.

Any project will run far more smoothly if it's been carefully planned, costed and thought through in advance. The problem is, however, that we very easily get bogged down in what Martin Luther King called 'the paralysis of analysis'. A friend of mine recently joined the national leadership council of his denomination, a body that had just taken the decision to 'modernise' the denomination's antiquated administration and personnel structures. 'They've been discussing these changes for years – I mean, for more than a decade,' he explained. 'They wanted to be absolutely sure it was the right way to go, and just before I joined they finally made the decision to move ahead. But I've got friends in management consultancy, and when I told them what we were planning – and how it would revolutionise everything and bring the church bang up to date – they looked at me in disbelief. "Congratulations on joining the 1980s at last," they joked. "But we're now advising our clients to move on from those kind of outdated structures. They're better than what you've got at the moment, of course, but people and culture change. It's like you're finally upgrading to colour TV just when everyone else is going digital." ' As the Canadian theologian and philosopher Bernard Lonergan once remarked, 'The Church always arrives on the scene a little breathless and a little late.'

Sometimes, of course, our slowness and hesitancy means that we're more than just behind the times. The truth is, many things in life have sell-by dates – narrow windows of opportunity during which a decision has to be made about whether or not to move forward. From marriage proposals to investment opportunities, we can't always afford to wait forever. Even the cost-counting king in Jesus' story couldn't afford to dither – he had to choose fast between going to war and negotiating for peace. The longer he put off making a decision, the closer the opposing king's army would be to his borders and the more expensive it would be to buy them off (which is what, in the political reality of the day, 'negotiating for peace' actually meant). It's a reality reflected in Shakespeare's play *Julius Caesar*, when Brutus tells Cassius that if they don't act soon, they'll lose the support they need to defeat the combined armies of Octavian and Mark Anthony. 'There is a tide in the affairs of men which, taken at the flood, leads on to fortune; omitted, all the voyage of their life is bound in shallows and in miseries. On such a full sea are we now afloat; and we must take the current when it serves, or lose our ventures.'

*Ana*lysis doesn't equal *para*lysis – waiting too long can be just as disastrous a policy as jumping in too soon. And nor can we afford to wait until a course of action is essentially risk-free: by the time the risks are gone, the opportunities are usually gone as well. As George Caird said, 'They also serve who have the courage to be mistaken.' There comes a time when we have to put our money (or whatever else we're proposing to risk) where our *faith* is. There comes a time when we have to act. And if we decide *not* to act, it should be because we're convinced that *in*activity is the *right* activity – not because we let our fears get in the way of our dreams. After all, God is constantly taking risks with us – why aren't we prepared to take risks with him?

The book of heroic failures

A church will never learn from its mistakes unless it is ready to risk making some.

Former Archbishop of Canterbury Robert Runcie

'The opposite of success is not failure,' writes Hilary Brand. 'The opposite of success is never trying. The only *real* failure is not trying.' This is a lesson we desperately need to learn. We remember Peter's walk on the water (Matthew 14:30) as a 'failure' because he quickly sank, but the truth is that to this day he's second only to Jesus in the world record stakes. What's more, we don't seem to notice that everyone else in the boat failed even to *enter* the contest. They just sat there in the boat.

Most of the time, we don't act not so much because we're cautious as because we're afraid. We don't want to fail, convinced that failure isn't 'honouring to God'. But Jesus' parable makes it clear that the gospel and the kingdom of God aren't things we 'honour' by burying them in the backyard. As Lesslie Newbigin used to say, the gospel is something to be *risked*, not protected. It's all right to be afraid, and it's all right to fail. Both fear and failure are not only natural, but virtually inevitable. The two servants in the story who managed to double their original investment must at times have seen the value of their portfolio go down as well as up, but by staying the course they developed the courage to confront their fears and reverse their failures. There was no guarantee of a happy ending, of course, but that's what made it a risk. Faith and success are far from identical – in fact, those of us who're unwilling to make a move until we're sure it'll succeed are actually attempting to avoid the path of *faith* altogether, striving instead for one of *certainty*.

The Church in the West is currently haemorrhaging thousands of people a week and rapidly losing what little social influence we still have. If we just keep on doing what we're doing, rather than embarking on new and risky ventures that require genuine faith to sustain them, then we can confidently expect to become nothing more than a piece of first- and second-millennium memorabilia. Actual extinction may not be on the cards, but what we're left with won't be much practical use for anything other than survival. I don't know about you, but that's a risk I think we just can't afford to take.

A friend of mine, a city banker, always talks about the need when choosing an investment to pick the one you think will give you 'more bang for your buck'. It's a principle we need to incorporate into both our church and our personal planning . . . and not just when it comes to money. Rather than always playing it safe, we need to weigh up all the options as carefully as possible, consciously trying to match opportunities to resources. But above all, we need to be courageous and inspired, allowing our dreams to conquer our fears rather than the other way round. As James might have said, *faith without risk is dead*. We need to commit ourselves to stepping out in faith, even when failure seems all too possible an outcome, confident that failure isn't the end of the story but a part of the learning curve. And we need to learn to see God's opportunities wherever they present themselves.

There's an old joke. A torrential downpour in the American Midwest leads to very serious floods, and as the floodwater rises, the emergency services launch an all-out effort to evacuate people from their homes. One pious man, however, refuses to leave his house, insisting that divine intervention will save him. 'The Lord will rescue me,' he tells the emergency crew as it arrives to pick him up in an off-road vehicle. 'I'll wait on him and pray,' he adds, turning down their offers of help. A few hours later, when the floodwater has risen several feet, the emergency crew tries again, this time in a boat. 'The Lord will rescue me,' the man insists from the safety of his upstairs window. 'I'll wait on him and pray,' he adds, returning to his devotions. By nightfall, the waters have risen so high that they're now up to the roof of the man's house, where he sits alone and prays fervently for deliverance. The police again try to pick him up, this time in a helicopter. 'The Lord will rescue me,' he shouts back to the helicopter crew. 'I'll wait on him and pray,' he adds, resisting all attempts to winch him to safety. By the next morning, the floodwater covers the man's house completely and the man, now quite dead, stands before the pearly gates.

'I don't understand,' he complains to St Peter. 'Why didn't the Lord save me?'

'Well,' Peter replies, 'we tried. We sent a car, a boat and a helicopter. What more did you want?'

God's opportunities are all around us, if we're willing to take the risk. Sometimes being *safe* now only guarantees that we'll be *sorry* later.

12

'Touch the screen and you'll be healed'

'It's not over till it's over!' Standing on the courthouse steps, bravely facing the news cameras after a US court had found husband Jim guilty of massive fraud and embezzlement, Tammy Faye Bakker refused to give up. The Bakkers – presenters of the successful *Praise the Lord Club* TV evangelism show – were no strangers to notoriety. They'd previously made headlines in the mid-1980s when it was revealed that prominent televangelist Jim had had an affair. At that time they'd managed to bounce back, proving – together with Jimmy Swaggart, the preacher who'd blown the lid on Bakker's adultery and then faltered with an affair of his own – that if confession is good for the soul, it's also good for the ratings. Now, however, it was obvious to all but Tammy that it was definitely over – the fat lady had well and truly sung! Jim had lost his career, his reputation, his fortune and his liberty. At forty-eight, he'd just been handed down a forty-five-year jail sentence.

But if Bakker's high-flying career was over, the 'health and wealth' type of theology that had propelled him to fame in the first place was still fighting fit. Perhaps Bakker himself is now a reformed character, but a great many other pastors and punters remain convinced that the 'name it and claim it' approach to Christianity is totally biblical and thoroughly orthodox. The public and legal controversy surrounding Bakker's downfall was naturally focussed on his criminal duplicity – fraud and betrayal – but what of the basic morality of his underlying, self-centred 'believe and receive' attitude, the overall greed creed that had helped foster his PTL empire? As Tony Campolo remarked, 'Nobody raises questions about the lifestyle of this man with Rolls-Royces and Mercedes and expensive houses and a theme park. This whole extravagant value system is the thing that ought to be raising questions. What right does somebody have to assemble a $172 million empire in the name of the one who was rich but for our sakes became poor?'

Being rich and healthy and Christian is one thing, but claiming that health and wealth are *hallmarks* of authentic Christianity is a different ballgame altogether.

'Oh Lord, won't you buy me a Mercedes Benz . . .'

'Put your hand on the TV screen' makes God look like a slot machine.

Singer/songwriter Garth Hewitt

The Bible, of course, has nothing against being rich per se. (According to 1 Timothy 6:10, it's 'the *love* of money', not money itself, that's 'a root of all kinds of evil'.) In fact, the biblical authors not only see life as something to be enjoyed, they present riches as a blessing to be thankful to God for. None of the Genesis 'patriarchs' – Abraham, Isaac, Jacob and Esau, Joseph and his brothers – were short of a bob or two, and Moses, for a time, lived in the lap of luxury. Solomon's wealth reached literally monumental proportions.

The trouble is, those who adhere to a 'prosperity gospel' tend to interpret this 'blessing' not as a kind of 'windfall', but as the automatic and basic right of all those with 'true faith'. The size of your bank balance, in effect, becomes the measure of your faith. 'Blessing', they argue, is both the right and the reward of faith, and riches are an obvious sign of that blessing. So those with real faith can expect to be richly blessed by God, while those whose faith is shallow or insincere will reap nothing.

In part, supporters of this name–it–and–claim–it approach draw their ideas from the covenant with Abraham, whom God 'greatly blessed' and made wealthy:'he has given him flocks and herds, silver and gold, male and female slaves, camels and donkeys' (Genesis 24:35). They then back up their ideas with texts like Deuteronomy 8:18 ('Remember the Lord your God, for it is he who gives you power to get wealth, so that he may confirm his covenant that he swore to your ancestors'), Proverbs 13:21 ('prosperity rewards the righteous'), and Psalm 112:3 (which states that those who fear the Lord will find that 'wealth and riches are in their houses, and their righteousness endures for ever').

But there are two major problems with this kind of biblical approach. The first is that it relies not so much on an *understanding of the text* as on a complete *ignoring of the context*. So prosperity theologians suggest that God made Abraham rich as a reward for his faith, for example, conveniently ignoring the fact that he was *already* very wealthy to begin with. Similarly, Psalm 1, which states that 'those who do not follow the advice of the wicked' are to be blessed, is quoted out of context to support a prosperity gospel view. The psalm does indeed suggest that,'They are like trees planted by streams of water, which yield their fruit in its season, and their leaves do not wither. In all that they do, they prosper' (Psalm 1:1–3). But you should, as they say, always read the small print.

For one thing, prosperity preachers interpret Psalm 1 to mean that God punishes the wicked and gives believers material prosperity. But if that's true, why are so many wicked people prosperous (the issue at the heart of Habakkuk)? In fact, as Canadian scholar Craig Broyles notes, the psalm doesn't 'describe a present, visible reality,' but 'what will transpire at some unspecified time in the future'. In addition, believe–and–receivers automatically assume that the prosperity on offer in Psalm 1 is for *individuals*, but the psalms were actually a crucial musical and liturgical part of Israel's *worship*, and worship was (and is) a *collective* activity. The truth is, Psalm 1 isn't so much about *faith-filled individuals* as about a *faithful nation*. Its canvas is broad, and its subject isn't the prosperity of individuals but the sovereignty of God.

But the second mistake made by health-and-wealth preachers – even more dangerous than their tendency to *distort* texts – is their habit of completely *disregarding* vast amounts of the biblical record. The interpretation of those passages *used* by name-it-and-claim-it advocates needs to be weighed alongside (rather than in isolation from) the biblical passages they *don't use* that teach something quite different to their get-rich-quick gospel. If Jesus really believed, for example, that material prosperity was the reward of true faith, why did he warn his followers about the *costs* of discipleship? Why did he send his disciples out as prophets of the kingdom of God with strict instructions to go with *nothing* – none of the signs of 'blessing' and faith so important to prosperity teaching – and be totally reliant on people's hospitality: 'Take no gold, or silver, or copper in your belts, no bag for your journey, or two tunics, or sandals, or a staff' (Matthew 10:9–10)? And if wealth is the reward for faith and poverty is, as many health-and-wealthers imply, the fate of those who stand condemned for their *lack* of faith, what are we to make of the Bible's obsession with helping society's 'widows and orphans'? What are we to make of the prophets' insistence that *God himself* is their protector and redeemer?

In his book *The Soul of Politics*, Jim Wallis – founder of the Sojourners Community in Washington DC's poor inner city – recalls once being part of a study group with some theological students in Chicago. 'We decided to do a study to find every biblical reference to one particular subject – the poor and oppressed,' he explains, 'and found, to our astonishment, that there are thousands of verses about the poor in the Bible.' But one student, he remembers, took the experiment a stage further. 'He found an old Bible, took a pair of scissors, and then proceeded to cut out every single reference to the poor. It took him a very long time.' When at last he'd finished, Wallis recalls, 'That old Bible hung in threads. It wouldn't hold together; it fell apart in our hands ... I used to take that holey old Bible out with me to preach. I would hold it high above American congregations and say, "My friends, this *is* the American Bible – full of holes from all that we have cut out." ' As he concludes, 'In America and throughout the Western world, we have responded to all that the Scriptures say about the poor by pretending it just isn't there. We have cut the poor out of the Bible.'

The coldest night of the year

In a small house, God has his corner. In a big house, he has to stand in the hall.

Swedish proverb

Contrary to popular opinion, health-and-wealth isn't a new phenomenon – a twentieth-century heresy dreamt up by affluent Americans with gold Rolex watches, notice-me platinum rings and Armani suits to justify the materialism and greed of the developed Western world. It's as old as the hills, and not confined to those blatant charlatans who use it as an evil justification for their relentless acquisitiveness and empire-building. In a milder, more implicit form it's a part of everyday culture, evident in the grieving parent who wonders what *they've* done to 'deserve' the death of their child, or in the dot.com entrepreneur or financial whiz kid who imagines they're better than everyone else because they're faster and richer. It's even there in the complacency of our middle-class suburban churches, when we forget that 'there but for the grace of God' go we, and instead wonder why people in the poorer, more deprived areas of the country can't just pull themselves up by their own bootstraps and enjoy the 'fruits of blessing'.

The Bible has a lot to say about this ancient heresy . . . and none of it's good. The book of Job, for example, is the original anti-health-and-wealth tract. It's about a man who loses first his *wealth* (including his family) and then his *health* (suffering from a variety of ailments, including painful sores). His three best friends arrive to comfort him. In eloquent terms, they express the natural religious 'common sense' of the day: righteous and faithful people are rewarded in the here-and-now with prosperous and fortunate lives. The flip-side to this, of course, is that those – like Job – whose lives *aren't* prosperous or fortunate must be either sinful or faithless . . . or both. Seeing his desolate state, Job's friends automatically jump to the obvious conclusion: he's committed some *dreadful* sin. Job, however, doesn't agree – he firmly maintains his innocence. He doesn't claim to be perfect, but he knows that he hasn't done anything bad enough to deserve his dire fate.

To begin with, Job is angry with God. If it's true that God rewards the righteous and punishes the wicked in the here and now, then *God* must have made a mistake, and therefore stands accused of punishing an innocent man. His friends throw up their hands in horror at this suggestion. To them it's clear that God *doesn't* make mistakes, so Job *can't* be innocent. In fact, as the conversation goes on and he stubbornly continues to maintain his innocence, Job's friends gradually start to accuse him of more and more heinous crimes! Even the fact that he continues to protest his innocence in the face of the overwhelming evidence of his guilt (his poverty and illness), they feel, is enough to prove he's a dreadful sinner.

In a flash of inspiration, however, it's Job who eventually realises where the real fault lies: not actually with God, but with the dogma that always squeezes God's actions into a rigid curse-and-blessing mould. He sees that he's by no means the only innocent person suffering. In fact, many people – especially the poor – are constantly being exploited by the wicked, who seem to act with total impunity: 'Why do the wicked live on, reach old age, and grow mighty in power?' he asks. 'They spend their days in prosperity, and in peace they go down to Sheol. They say to God, "Leave us alone! We do not desire to know your ways. What is the Almighty, that we should serve him? And what profit do we get if we pray to him?" Is not their prosperity indeed their own achievement?' (Job 21:7, 13–16).

In the end, it's Job's friends – still locked in their prosperity theology and unable to see either *their* mistake or *Job's* innocence –

who stand condemned by God. Job, by contrast, is totally exonerated because, as the first two chapters of the book make clear, the reason for his suffering isn't the *lack* of his faith, but the *depth* of it.

Real faith isn't a passport to instant health or wealth. In fact, it can often prove to be a 'fast track' to pain and distress. Singer Bruce Cockburn remembers sitting alone in a hotel room one night during a tour to promote his album *Dancing in the Dragon's Jaws*. Though his career was doing well, his marriage was collapsing, in part because of his recent conversion to the Christian faith. Switching on the TV, he started watching a religious talk show. 'This guy was saying, "I was a drinker and my marriage was falling apart. I found the Lord and all of a sudden I got a higher paying job and my marriage got back together,"' he recalls. 'The irony was that I could have gone on that show and given the complete opposite story.'

And so could most of the early church leaders. Initial persecution by local Jewish leaders soon gave way to official persecution by the pagan Roman Empire. According to tradition, most of the apostles died grisly deaths, largely at the hands of the Romans. Of the initial apostles, only John lived to old age, often thought to have died on Patmos, the 'Alcatraz' of the ancient Near East. When facing execution, Peter is said to have felt so unworthy to die like Jesus that he insisted on being crucified upside down. Being a Christian, it was said, was 'exciting, challenging and short'!

All this is a very long way from the umpteen houses, cars or valuables promised by some prosperity preachers as a reward for faith and self-sacrifice, on the grounds of their reading of Jesus' words in Mark 10:29–30: 'Truly I tell you, there is no one who has left house or brothers or sisters or mother or father or children or fields, for my sake and for the sake of the good news, who will not receive a hundredfold now in this age – houses, brothers and sisters, mothers and children, and fields, with persecutions – and in the age to come eternal life.' Some have even argued that this is the theological basis for what they call 'seed giving' – the process by which, if you give away a rusty old Skoda, you can expect to receive a brand-new Mercedes in return. Others merely consider it an explanation of the kind of 'fruit' Christians can – and *should* – expect from their faith.

But the truth is, while there's plenty of evidence that Jesus' disciples received *persecutions*, none of them seems to have received the hundredfold houses or fields or mothers guaranteed by a simplistic reading. As Robert Jackson notes, 'Levi did not become phenomenally rich, nor did James and John receive a hundred fishing boats, or one worth a hundred times as much. A closer examination of the passage seems to suggest that the rewards for sacrifices made for the sake of the gospel are realised in the common life of the church.'

A dog's life

If we show partiality to the wealthy then we're not free, because we're still slaves to the mentality that says that power and riches are more important than love. If we do this, we don't have God's spirit controlling our lives.

Nicaraguan doctor and Baptist minister Gustavo Parajon

In fact, the 'common life' lies at the heart of Jesus' approach to both health and wealth. Most prosperity churches – as well as many *non*-prosperity churches – adopt a very consumerist approach to money and healing. From catholic to charismatic, and from Lourdes to Toronto, there's a real danger of overemphasising the *personal benefits* of the gospel to individuals . . . at the cost of community considerations. In the Bible, health and wealth weren't important for their own sakes – they were never prized as some kind of official indication of God's blessing in the way that believe-and-receivers advocate. Instead, health and wealth were important for the sole reason that they enabled people to play a full active role in their local community. They were at heart responsibilities to be treasured and exercised for the benefit of others, not privileges to be *selfishly* enjoyed. If you were healthy and wealthy, you were more capable of helping others in the community than if you were constantly hampered by illness and poverty.

This aspect of Jesus' understanding is clearly seen in one of his most dramatic parables, about a rich man and a beggar named Lazarus (Luke 16:19–31). The two men are popular stereotypes – the rich man of those who're 'blessed', Lazarus of those who're 'cursed'. The rich man has all the trappings of real 'faith' endorsed by 'health and wealth' advocates, both then and now. He's hugely wealthy, wears the best clothes, lives in the lap of luxury, and hosts extravagant daily banquets. By contrast, the beggar at his gate is completely destitute. He's so hungry that he longs to eat the scraps of bread (which were used as the equivalent of both cutlery, for dipping into food, and napkins, for wiping fingers) that fall from the rich man's feast-laden table. But the scavenger dogs beat him to it, and then move on to lick his painful sores. Unlike the rich man, Lazarus has neither health nor wealth. And when he dies, he doesn't even get a decent burial – the dogs that lick his sores probably make a meal of his emaciated and sickness-ridden corpse.

This situation is entirely reversed, however, when the scene cuts to the underworld: Hades. (As in many of his parables, Jesus isn't afraid to borrow from non-Jewish cultures like Greece in order to make his point.) From his place of torment, the rich man sees Lazarus feasting at a heavenly banquet, seated in the place of honour by 'Abraham's bosom'. The rich man is clearly astonished and disturbed by this turn of events, and has trouble adjusting to the total reversal of fortunes. So having previously ignored Lazarus, he now tries to exploit him, first as a personal servant and then as a messenger boy!

The rich man's problem is that he's previously interpreted his health and wealth as rewards for his faithful lifestyle. As such, he's understood them to be primarily for his own benefit. At the same time, he's seen illness and poverty as a sign of religious infidelity, and assumed that they invite God's curse rather than his active help and compassion. In other words, instead of seeing health and riches as giving him the power and responsibility to 'bless' those less fortunate, the rich man sees them as the natural rewards of his faith, to be enjoyed in full comfort and entirely guilt-free. As Craig Evans notes, 'The "religious" assumed that health and wealth evidenced God's blessing, while sickness and poverty evidenced God's cursing.' And in a glorious piece of understatement, he adds, 'As the parable indicates, such assumptions can be hazardous.'

The point of the parable, in fact, is to contrast the *rich man's* behaviour – not even giving Lazarus leftover scraps to eat – with *God's* behaviour – sitting him beside Abraham at the messianic banquet. This is the key to understanding what Jesus was teaching: the real point of comparison isn't between the rich man and Lazarus, but between the rich man and God. As 'Moses and the prophets' had insisted, God is the protector and redeemer of the poor and needy. He faithfully discharges his responsibilities toward the poor people of the community, seating them as honoured guests at his banqueting table. He helps them not because they're more *virtuous* than anyone else, but simply because they're more *needy* than anyone else – a fact even reflected in Lazarus' name, which is derived from the Hebrew *Eleazar*, meaning 'God has helped'. But the rich man, who never *has* a name in the story (the name he's often given, Dives, is just Latin for 'rich'), hasn't even realised that his health and wealth carry huge responsibilities toward the poor. Instead, he makes the dreadful mistake of seeing them as purely or primarily signs of blessing for the depth of his faith.

So what right does somebody have to assemble a $172 million empire in the name of the one who was rich but for our sakes became poor? Well, if your version of 'Moses and the prophets', like Jim Wallis' 'holey Bible', has massive chunks cut out from it, then you might manage to concoct a positive answer to this very pointed question. But if your Bible comes complete, the way it was intended, then your response would have to be, None. Invitations to 'touch the screen and be healed' – one of the slick catch-phrases of the health-and-wealth movement, cuttingly lampooned by Phil Collins in the video for Genesis' single 'Jesus, He Knows Me' – are a very long way from an authentic and orthodox biblical approach to health, wealth and community.

13

'Would you like to apply for church membership?'

It was supposed to be impregnable – 250 miles of well-equipped fortifications, strengthened by forty-five divisions of French troops armed with tanks and artillery. Built between 1929 and 1934, the famous Maginot Line ran the entire length of the French/German border, right the way from Belgium and Luxembourg to Switzerland. It was designed as the ultimate defensive line, one the Germans would never be able to break. And they *didn't* break it. They simply went around it! On 10 May 1940, Hitler's armies invaded neutral Holland and Belgium, sweeping into France from the north. Holland collapsed in five days, Belgium in a little over two weeks and France herself on 25 June, less than seven weeks after the initial German attack.

The problem was, the Maginot Line had been set up to defend the French against the kind of prolonged trench warfare attack that had characterised World War One. Nothing had prepared them for the Nazis' new lightning-fast *blitzkrieg*. As a result, the line proved useless. In fact, it was *worse* than useless, because it effectively prevented Allied troops from taking the initiative themselves and going on the offensive after Hitler's conquests of Poland, Denmark and Norway. In the end, France's own 'strong line of defence' proved to be her undoing.

Tragically, much the same is true of the Church. In an effort to defend ourselves against the 'menace' of liberalism and secularisation (or worse), those of us in the more conservative and orthodox wings of the Church have often unwittingly adopted our own brand of Maginot Line strategy. From exclusive membership to strict moral and theological codes of conformity, we've created atmospheres and attitudes which, though designed to nurture and protect faith, have in all honesty backfired. We're *not* safe from the things we've tried to protect ourselves against, which have merely found their way in through the back door. At the same time, we're seriously hampered in our efforts to evangelise and influence the society around us by our rules and regulations – rules that not only seem bewildering to people outside the Church, but send them the message that being a Christian is all about obeying a list of stern 'thou shalt nots', rather than responding to the unconditional and unmerited gift of God's love and forgiveness.

Drawing up the battle lines

Christians are a dim, ego-tripping minority which is dead set on telling everybody why they ought to become Christians, instead of finding out why they aren't.

Australian journalist Max Harris

On various occasions over the years I've been invited to speak to university Christian Unions. Most have asked me beforehand to sign their statement of faith. Though it was never treated as anything more than a formality, the implication was that if I couldn't endorse their specific creed, I couldn't address the students. I must admit, I've always found this odd. It seems totally out of keeping with the idea of a university – protecting students from potentially 'corrupting' or contrary opinions at an institution specifically designed to expose them to a wide variety of different views. No wonder some people say that 'Evangelical scholarship' is an oxymoron!

A great many of our churches, however, seem to operate an unconscious system very much like this, not just for leaders but for *anyone* who wants to join – believe or leave. As a cartoon caption I read recently goes, 'God may have accepted you already, but *our* standards are just a little bit higher!' 'Real' membership is reserved for those who can sign our creedal formulae, use the right vocabulary, fulfil their duties and obligations, respect our dress code and worship etiquette, tithe their 10 per cent, conform to our unspoken expectations and, of course, not park in someone else's space! As a result, we unwittingly come across as being suspicious of, or even downright hostile to, those who don't entirely conform to 'factory specifications'.

When Sheila's church ran its first *Alpha* course, it billed it as a 'no-holds-barred chance to explore the basics of the faith'. The course attracted both established churchgoers and people on the fringes, but it wasn't long before problems began to emerge. Not used to having their faith scrutinised and questioned, a few of the core members started giving the 'just-lookers' a hard time. 'Believe this or get out' was the impression many fringe members received, and Sheila and the other leaders needed all their persuasive powers just to get them to come back again the next week. None of the 'hardliners' *wanted* to give this impression, of course. It's just that they were so used to the church being filled with card-carrying, dotted-line-signing believers that they unintentionally gave off the vibe that if people couldn't believe all the right doctrines ('orthodoxy'), they'd never really be accepted.

This heed-the-creed approach to church life is, of course, totally understandable. Orthodoxy is important, and at certain crunch times during the Church's two-thousand-year history it has seemed *all*-important. Every community has a need to define itself in terms of what it *is* and what it's *not*, both for its own clarity of mind and also for the benefit of those outside. The Church is no exception. Occasionally – in times of profound crisis, for example – this definition will be stark and challenging: a time to nail your colours to the mast.

This is formally known as a *status confessionis*, a time to speak out, 'in which the Church,' as US theologian Robert McAfee Brown notes, 'in order to be true to itself and its message, must distinguish *as clearly as possible* between truth and error.' As a recent example, Brown cites the 1982 World Alliance of Reformed Churches decision to condemn apartheid as a heresy. 'Until 1982,' he explains, 'members of the various Reformed churches in South Africa had managed to take all sides of the issue. Some argued that apartheid was consistent with the Christian gospel, others declared that it was not, many said that the issue wasn't clear.' But in 1982, 'A clear either/or was stated: either Christ or apartheid, but not both.'

The problem is, many of us act as if *every* point of conflict and disagreement we encounter in church – moral or theological – were basically a *status confessionis*. Consciously or not, we react to differences or dissent in ways that enforce strict uniformity, forcing people to *believe* or leave. In effect, we our use own unique understanding of 'orthodoxy' like a parliamentary political party's three-line whip, where all members have to vote with the party or else risk expulsion, whatever their consciences tell them. Of course, if a political party imposed such a whip as often as some churches, it would rapidly disintegrate . . . as many churches are doing. From tongues and Toronto to women priests and worship styles, they bitterly fragment over issues that seem vital now, but will no doubt seem trivial in a few generations' time.

Ten years ago, I was involved in an ecumenical mission in a small London-area commuter-belt town. The town had one of almost every kind of church you could imagine . . . but *four* Baptist churches. Each had split off over some flashpoint issue in the past, and one of them still wasn't talking to the others. But when I asked *why* they'd balkanised in this way – what those crucially important issues were that had split them off from one another in the mid-1900s – no one could remember. They were lost in the mists of time. Only their divisive and confusing impact remained. It reminded me of a joke about a Welshman shipwrecked on a desert island who passes the years he's there building an exact replica of his home village. When rescuers finally arrive, they're amazed to find a picture perfect hamlet, complete with pub, post office, grocer, butcher . . . and two churches. When they ask the man why there are *two* churches, he points to one of the buildings and replies, 'Well, that's the one I *don't* go to!'

Dallas Willard suggests that although every local church needs to have a clearly articulated mission statement — knowing what it believes on a full range of pastoral, moral, theological, liturgical, educational, environmental and social issues — there's absolutely no reason why every member (or person who comes along, if 'membership' is restricted) should be completely *on-message* in every single area. Not only is this an *impossible* requirement, it's also an *undesirable* one. Comparing the Church to a body, Paul asked, 'If the whole body were an eye, where would the hearing be? If the whole body were hearing, where would the sense of smell be? But as it is, God has arranged the members in the body, each one of them, as he chose. If all were a single member, where would the body be?' (1 Corinthians 12:17–19). In other words, a wide amount of 'biodiversity', so long as it includes nothing specifically toxic, is far healthier for the Church than an enforced on-message uniformity.

In fact, surprisingly enough, this approach also lies at the heart of the Reformation, which wasn't so much one *status confessionis* as several. Luther, Calvin, Zwingli, Oecolampadius, Bucer, Cranmer . . . different regions had different reformers with different ideas. In 1529, the Reformation 'giants' Luther and Zwingli met in Marburg to try to iron out their differences on communion. After heated discussion, they could finally agree only to *dis*agree. This decision established theological diversity as a key principle of Protestantism. Twenty-six years later, a summit of German princes in Augsburg went a crucial stage further, enshrining in principle what was happening in practice all over the continent: *cuius regio eius religio* — region determines religion. Rather than customising their own doctrinal stance, most people followed local leaders in choosing where to site themselves on the Reformation spectrum. Together, these two decisions set in place not just a principle of biodiversity, but also an understanding that *belonging* is usually a major factor in determining *belief*.

Sign on the dotted line?

I do not seek to understand in order to believe, but rather I believe in order that I may understand.

Former Archbishop of Canterbury St Anselm

In fact, this same dynamic works in most churches today, including – perhaps *especially* – those operating a heed-the-creed mentality. I'm a Baptist because my parents (both of whom grew up Anglican) took me to a local Baptist church when I was young. It wasn't a doctrinal decision that led them to that church – they simply felt more welcome there, more accepted by people whose age and interests were closer to their own. It took them a long time to think through all the doctrinal issues. In fact, because the church reserved formal 'membership' for those 'believers' who could sign on the dotted line of the Baptist Union's doctrinal statement, it took them twenty-five years to become official 'members' . . . by which time I was a Baptist minister!

In the same way, as a boy I didn't minutely analyse the things I was being taught in Sunday school, cross-checking them exhaustively against Bible references before deciding whether or not to accept them – instead, I learnt them from other people and gradually came to refine or even perhaps question them later. As American theologian Marcus Borg notes, our doctrine is usually heavily coloured by our experience, and what we pick up as children isn't always necessarily consistent or rational. 'I knew [Jesus] was "born of the virgin Mary",' he writes, 'before I knew what a virgin was.'

Of course, I'm not suggesting that I don't believe, sincerely and intelligently, the official doctrines held by the Baptist Union. (After four years of being able to think them all through at theological college, and nearly twenty years of testing them 'in the field', I'm convinced of the soundness of . . . well, *almost* all of them!) I'm just saying that I didn't *initially* come to hold these doctrines by looking through the available options and then *choosing* them, like dishes from an *à la carte* menu. Instead, like most people, I believed them through being served up one 'dish of the day' after another over a long very period of time in church. In other words, *belonging* to a Baptist church preceded my *believing* Baptist-approved doctrine. What's more, belonging played a big part in believing. Being part of the church wasn't just a way of being with others who believed the same things, it was also an opportunity to *explore* those beliefs and see them reflected, to varying degrees, in other peoples' lives.

And I'm no exception. Most people absorb doctrines and denominational stances before they analyse and intellectually accept them. As she hit her forties and started a family, Terri found herself becoming more and more interested in spiritual things. She lived just down the road from an Anglican church, so she decided to give it a try. The welcome she received was sincere and enthusiastic, and having grown up in a C of E church she found it easy to fit in. After a year or so as a regular member of the church, she was asked to join the twenty-strong church leadership council (PCC). However, she soon realised that some church members felt her faith wasn't yet 'mature enough' for the PCC. When she drew this to the vicar's attention, wondering if she should resign, he asked rhetorically, 'How mature is "mature enough"? I honestly don't know. We're all on a journey, learning and maturing the whole time.' Terri stayed on the PCC. She felt it gave her a sense of self-worth and belonging. It was a forum in which she could contribute her artistic and business skills. And as she became more and more a *part* of the church, so her understanding of God grew and her faith deepened and matured. If the church had asked her to stand down, she'd never have had the opportunities and feeling of acceptance she needed to grow in her faith, and her sense of belonging might have become a sense of exclusion. Rather than being drawn toward God, she'd have felt pushed away.

Some church leaders defend an élitist, heed-the-creed position using Paul's strict guidelines on just what kind of people the church in Ephesus should chose as leaders (1 Timothy 3). The truth is, however, that this is a gross distortion of Paul's teaching. The Ephesian church drew its members from a truly cosmopolitan population – Ephesus wasn't just a bustling city, it was also a vibrant centre of pagan worship, especially of the Greek goddess Artemis, and people's belief and behaviour went from the sober and sensible right through to the weird and wacky. If all church members had been doctrinally and ethically 100 per cent 'pure', Paul wouldn't have had to raise the bar for leaders – *any* member would have done. So the fact that he had to set a standard – and that he encouraged Timothy and the other leaders to set a good example 'in speech and conduct, in love, in faith, in purity' for those *within the church* (1 Timothy 4:12) – suggests that the church in Ephesus was considerably more inclusive and tolerant of people's short-comings than most of our respectable, suburban churches today. Morals mattered among leaders precisely because the church *didn't* adopt an élitist, heed-the-creed approach.

So the decision not to accept people fully into membership until they've reached what we see as an acceptable level of ortho-doxy isn't just massively short-sighted, it's also unbiblical. It's far more sound and sensible to treat acceptance as a *cause* of orthodoxy than to see it as a necessary *precondition*. What's more, the decision to accept people only 'on probation' until they can sign on the dotted line involves a total misunderstanding of the Church's function.

An Anglican diocesan director of ordinands – the man or woman in each diocese charged with the task of guiding people in their sense of vocation to the priesthood – was once invited to address a group of theological students who were just about to be ordained. He was known for being forthright in his views, so a sense of hush fell over the auditorium as he shuffled his notes. 'In a few weeks' time,' he told them, 'you'll leave here and start a lifetime's work as a local minister. Before you go, I have just one piece of advice to impart to you. If you follow this advice, you'll have the satisfaction of knowing that you're doing the job for which you've been *called*. I must warn you, however, that your church will probably try to lynch you! My advice is simple: *always go after the lost sheep*. There's safety in numbers, and the ninety-nine can usually look after themselves perfectly well, but the lost sheep really needs your help. Above all, it's your job to give a lead in doing what the *whole church* is actually called to do, which is to go looking for the lost sheep.'

Very often, our churches are almost exclusively structured around meeting the needs of the people whose relationship with Jesus is well established and who're already secure members of the flock. But while meeting this need is, of course, vital, we should never allow it to be the *only* – or even the *main* – occupation of the Church. As John Drane warns, 'Effective ministry today will be shaped less by the needs of those already in the church, and more by the concerns of the millions who are not, but who are engaged on a serious spiritual search and could be reached with the Gospel.' Our task as a whole faith community is to reach out to lost sheep and welcome them (back) into the fold. And the way to accomplish this task isn't to lay down the law, but to demonstrate God's unconditional love and acceptance to people.

In Margery Williams' classic story, *The Velveteen Rabbit*, a boy's toy rabbit is made to feel unloved, unwelcome and unaccepted by all the other toys except the Skin Horse. They all feel superior to the Rabbit, who is, after all, just made of velveteen and straw. Only the Horse can see the Rabbit's potential to become *real* – something most of the nursery toys never achieve. 'Real isn't how you are made,' the Horse explains. 'It's a thing that happens to you. When a child loves you for a long, long time, not just to play with, but REALLY loves you, then you become Real . . . Generally, by the time you are Real, most of your hair has been loved off, and your eyes drop out and you get loose in the joints and very shabby. But these things don't matter at all, because once you are Real you can't be ugly, except to people who don't understand . . . Once you are Real you can't become unreal again. It lasts for always.' In the story, the boy and his Velveteen Rabbit become inseparable, and the boy's love makes the Rabbit real, first to him and then to everyone. Like the boy, our task is to help people become 'Real' by demonstrating God's grace in the way we welcome and accept them.

Letting your hair down

Who are the elect? You, if you wish.

St Augustine

In this, we're only following in Jesus' footsteps. His approach to those on the fringes of first-century Palestinian Jewish society, as well as some of those well *beyond* the fringes, was consistently one of invitation, not investigation. And rather than inviting them to *apply* for membership in the 'chosen people' of the kingdom of God – an application that most of them knew would be blackballed if their contemporaries had anything to say about the matter – Jesus welcomed them in without any of the normal entry requirements or formalities.

Nowhere is this approach better demonstrated than in his encounter with a town prostitute during a formal dinner (Luke 7:36–50). Having spoken and healed in the town and the surrounding countryside, Jesus had earned himself something of a reputation, but for most people he was still an enigma. Curiosity obviously got the better of a prominent local Pharisee called Simon, who invited Jesus to be 'guest of honour' at a little banquet. Simon was taking a big risk – Jesus was far from popular with other Pharisees, who tended not to be backward in voicing their disapproval of his *un*orthodox approach to healing, forgiveness, fasting, Sabbath rules and tax-collectors. Perhaps that's why Simon then hedged his bets, deliberately failing to extend to Jesus the customary kiss of greeting, or to have a servant wash his feet or anoint his head with oil. To withhold these courtesies to a visiting 'rabbi' ('teacher') would have been a glaring omission, but Jesus graciously let the insult go.

However, when a town prostitute gatecrashed the party and began to wash his feet with her tears, dry them with her hair, kiss them and anoint them with perfume – a tool of her trade – both Simon's attitude and Jesus' response changed. Diners at a formal meal reclined on their left side on *chaises longues* around a low table, their feet facing out behind them, so without deliberately turning his head (which Luke says he did only in verse 44), Jesus would have had no real view of what was going on at his feet. In fact, he seems to have been happy just to let the woman continue, virtually ignoring her actions. By contrast, Simon, who would have had a good view of the proceedings, suddenly came to a decision about Jesus: 'If this man *were* a prophet, he would have known who and what kind of woman this is who is touching him – she is a sinner.' It was a comment laced with irony – you didn't have to be a prophet to realise this woman was a prostitute.

Jesus responded to Simon's words by telling a story about two debtors. One owed a money-lender ten times as much as the other, and money-lenders weren't exactly renowned for their generosity. But as neither could repay the debt, both were forgiven. 'Now which of them,' Jesus asked, 'will love him more?' 'The one for whom he cancelled the greater debt,' Simon replied. It's very easy for us to miss the shocking implication of this story – *love grows out of forgiveness*. Jesus didn't absolve the woman because she was repentant. Just the opposite: she was repentant because she had already *heard* his message and *experienced* forgiveness before this encounter. Jesus' parable makes no sense unless the initiative came from *him* – unless she had somehow, somewhere, already heard his words of forgiveness and acceptance, prompting her extraordinary demonstration of gratitude. 'Her sins, which were many,' Jesus remarked, 'have been forgiven; *hence she has shown great love*' (Luke 7:47). Her sense of *belonging* led to her dramatic change of *belief* and *behaviour*.

What's more, this 'sinner' didn't immediately become a perfect 'saint' – the woman's act of devotion was extremely provocative, full of vestiges of her former profession. Most of those attending the dinner would have considered her actions highly improper. One detail in particular would have scandalised those present: drying Jesus' feet with her hair. A woman's hair was considered a valuable – and very *erotic* – asset in the ancient Near East, as it still is in many parts of the Middle East today. While a prostitute might think nothing of letting her hair down in front of a client, most women would never dream of doing something so intimate and sexually charged in the presence of anyone but their husband. In her enthusiastic response to her acceptance and forgiveness, the woman massively overstepped the bounds of propriety. But rather than setting her straight, Jesus let her continue. God's love and grace had already produced dramatic changes – they would produce more in the fullness of time.

Simon's firm stance on belief and behaviour prevented him from recognising God's spirit at work. He could see only that the woman was a notorious 'sinner' who'd not yet made a public expression of her change of heart (he didn't seem to realise that this was *it*) or purified herself and made a formal sacrifice of atonement. Then, and *only* then – and only within well-defined limits – would he accept her. By contrast, Jesus' actions and words showed that he accepted her on the spot. He interpreted her foot-washing devotion as equal to any official purification rite, and with the authority usually reserved for a priest, he granted her absolution of her sins (which defined her standing in the community). *His* acceptance enabled *her* change.

The challenge that faces our churches, therefore, is to emulate the welcome Jesus gave this unnamed woman, and she in turn gave him, rather than the lack of welcome Simon extended to them both. Rather than insisting that people conform themselves to our code of conduct and doctrine before inviting them to *apply* for membership, we need to take the initiative. As they say, the Church is a hospital for sinners, not a museum for saints. Or as Lesslie Newbigin put it, the Church is a family, not a factory. We need to go positively *out of our way* to include people in our church family.

We need to give them an authentic sense of acceptance and belonging, demonstrating the overwhelming and unconditional love that God shows them rather than letting or even making them feel inadequate or alienated.

A few years ago, I was asked to speak at a friend's wedding. Since it seemed appropriate, I talked about the need for couples to follow God's example and love with no strings attached, and about the constant need for forgiveness both in our relationships and in the whole of life. Afterwards, during the reception, a woman came up to me, agitated and upset. She thanked me for what I'd said, but I could tell there was a massive 'but' hidden among her words. As we talked, she became more and more distressed, the mascara began making tracklines down her face. 'I desperately want that forgiveness,' she explained. 'I desperately need God's love. If *only* I could have it.' I started to explain that it was hers for the asking, but she cut me off. 'No,' she replied, totally distraught, 'you don't understand. There's no forgiveness or acceptance for people like me. God *hates* me. I even hate myself. I'm beyond redemption. I'm what you people call an "abomination". I'm a lesbian.'

I tried to console her, to assure her that *no one* is beyond redemption. I wanted her to know, in a way she could understand, what Paul told the Christians of Rome: 'that neither death, nor life, nor angels, nor rulers, nor things present, nor things to come, nor powers, nor height, nor depth, nor anything else in all creation, will be able to separate us from the love of God in Christ Jesus our Lord' (Romans 8:38–9). I tried to explain to her that God's unconditional love and forgiveness were just a one-word prayer away, but she was unconvinced.

'You name the church that would accept someone like me,' she replied.

That's the challenge. Are we up to it?

14

'Pray the little prayer with me'

I watched in awe at the calm, easy way one of Britain's finest home-grown evangelists commanded his audience's attention, guiding people in a mere twenty minutes through all the troubles of humanity right up to 'the foot of the cross'. And then, as if it were the most natural thing in the world, he asked us to lower our heads and invited anyone who wanted to 'receive Jesus into their hearts' and be 'born again' quietly to raise their hand. As the pianist softly played an old hymn, he addressed those whose arms had tentatively gone up. 'I acknowledge that hand. Pray this little prayer with me . . .'

The whole evening was a precision-tooled, textbook example of how to do an evangelistic guest service. It was the late 1970s, and I was training for 'the ministry' at Spurgeon's College, a theological college founded by the great nineteenth-century preacher and evangelist Charles Spurgeon. Afterward, as we were introduced to the event organisers, one elderly man summed up the general mood. 'Now *that*, gentlemen,' he said, taking the opportunity to influence a group of future ministers, 'is THE way evangelism *should* be done!' The nods and murmurs that followed confirmed that he wasn't the only person in the room to feel like that. But I personally couldn't agree. (And I'm not sure that

Spurgeon – possibly the greatest evangelistic preacher of his generation – would have shared the old man's sentiments either.) Somehow, I can't imagine Jesus arriving at a new town or village, taking out a huge marquee and putting on a show at the end of which, to the soft strains of a harpist playing a psalm, he'd invite all those present to lower their heads as those who wanted to 'receive him in their hearts' and be 'born again' quietly raised a hand. Somehow I can't hear him saying, 'I acknowledge that hand. Pray this little prayer with me . . .'

'That old time religion'

The plodding multitudes will never be benefited by preaching which requires them to bring a dictionary to church.

Charles Haddon Spurgeon

It's not that there's anything inherently *wrong* with the 'guest service' approach to evangelism or a persuasive speaker – in our multimedia age, as Marshall McCluhan suggested, the *medium* and *message* are totally inseparable. Nor is there anything wrong with creating a conducive atmosphere – from aromatherapy to candlelit dinners, that's something we do all the time without it being seen as 'manipulative' or deceptive. And there's *certainly* nothing wrong with inviting people to make a personal commitment. The problem is, we've inherited a way of doing this that's now so far removed from our culture that it seems totally artificial.

When Billy Graham first started coming to the UK in the 1950s, people flocked to hear him in such large numbers that his 'crusades' had to be massively extended. His success rode high all through the 1960s and 1970s, and into the 1980s, with hundreds of thousands hearing and responding to his gently magnetic presentation of the Christian gospel. Graham's message and sincere style struck a note with the majority of those who heard him speak. But by the 1990s, the cultural tide had begun to turn. Graham continued to attract crowds, but more because he was a genuine twentieth-century icon than because stadium evangelism – the ultimate 'guest service' – was the most effective, 'cutting edge' tool for communicating the gospel. Other evangelists got used to playing to half-empty auditoriums, and even cancelled events.

This became all too clear when Graham's talented unofficial protégé, Luis Palau, visited the West of England in 1997. The 30,000-seater football stadium booked for the event was only a quarter full. As a friend of mine explained to me at the time, recriminations flew back and forth, with a few of the UK organisers lamenting that local churches hadn't done more to bring people along, and a number of local church leaders pointing the finger at the organisers for the mission's lack of 'success'. But the truth is, it was just a cultural mismatch. Over the years, revivals and stadium campaigns had slowly dropped out of people's cultural vocabulary and younger generations of Britons had grown up without enough basic knowledge of Christianity to make sense of Palau's message. The writing now seems to be on the wall for *that* kind of event in *this* kind of culture.

However, the truth is that this way of doing evangelism isn't set in stone . . . and never was. Not only are 'guest services', stadium crusades and their predecessors, 'tent revival meetings', far from the only way of doing '*real* evangelism', they aren't even as old as we think they are. The roots of the modern evangelistic crusade and guest service lie in the outdoor events and preaching tours of eighteenth-century evangelists like John Wesley and George Whitefield. Both men became evangelists as a reaction against the tepid interest in the gospel shown by most of their fellow Anglican clergymen, many of whom considered enthusiasm of any kind, especially in 'matters of religion', highly suspect. They started preaching in the open air when they found that the majority of church doors were shut to them. Deprived of a church pulpit, where people would have had a chance to come and listen, the two men went instead to where the people were, making a 'pulpit' in the corner of a field or a village square.

Wesley and Whitefield revolutionised the church in Britain and its colonies, deliberately trying to turn it from a mirror of middle- and upper-class respectability into something more closely resembling the kingdom of God. But as revolutionary as Wesley and Whitefield were, they still wouldn't have gently invited people to lower their heads as those who wanted to be 'born again' quietly raised a hand. Wesley wouldn't have listened to the soft strains of a hymn (written no doubt by his brother) on the accordion and uttered the words, 'I acknowledge that hand. Pray this little prayer with me ...' He *couldn't* have. Public meetings in Wesley's day were, after all, a lot more raucous, and public stands were a lot more public. His favourite time to preach was five o'clock in the morning, just as people were heading off to work, and his impromptu meetings were often far from smooth – there were no tame crowds, no stewards, no platforms, no hymn sheets, no choirs, no PA systems, no video overflow lounge and not even a great deal in terms of the all-important 'follow-up'. People just turned up and took their chances on level ground. By our standards, it was crude almost to the point of being shoddy. What's more, it wasn't always what we'd consider a resounding 'success'. Wesley was frequently heckled or pelted with rocks, and sometimes physically beaten or 'escorted' to the edge of town.

The even flow of the fully orchestrated, stage-managed, professional approach we've come to expect of guest service evangelism didn't actually begin until Charles Grandison Finney in New York in the 1820s. Though Finney had undergone 'a mighty baptism of the Holy Ghost' in 1824, he was never tempted to see his task as just reaping effortlessly what the Spirit had sown. He took very seriously the important role that human free will plays in religious 'revivals'. As a result, while he consciously tried to avoid what he saw as the 'emotional excesses' of many earlier US evangelists, he still took pains to give his audience a good show – complete with hellfire preaching, a 'sinner's bench' and a full choir musical soundtrack – in an effort to persuade them of the crucial relevance of his gospel message. He was even prepared to 'name and shame' people in order to bring them to repentance and faith. Today, most of us would question his methods, considering them exploitative and manipulative, but he considered them merely the 'right use of the constituted means'. His approach proved highly influential, not just on later big names like Dwight Moody, but on endless anonymous Evangelical ministers. It even persists today, particularly in the standard media caricature of the American televangelist and fundamentalist preacher.

As the Good Book says . . .

Evangelism is one beggar telling another beggar where to get bread.
D. T. Niles

Flipping through the pages of the New Testament, especially Acts, it's easy to think that our 'guest service' approach to evangelism follows a biblically established pattern. But the truth is, the evangelistic sermons recorded in Acts were actually very different to our own. Peter's two speeches to the people of Jerusalem, for example, were both given off the cuff in response to unexpected events – at Pentecost, and after the healing of a crippled beggar (Acts 2 and 3). Neither formed part of a well-orchestrated presentation, thematically arranged and carefully choreographed in order to work logically toward an appeal. Neither had a three-point structure or subheadings that began with the same letter of the alphabet. Neither would have passed muster on examination of their exegetical or 'expository' character. And neither had an altar call at the end. At Pentecost, the initiative to take things further came from the crowd, not Peter, and in Acts 3 Peter and John got arrested before they'd finished!

Even Paul, the great travelling evangelist, spoke in contexts that bear no real similarity to modern evangelistic events – first in synagogues, and then in the cut and thrust of debate in a public forum. We often imagine him to have been a great preacher, inspiring the crowds who flocked to hear him and persuading them to 'receive Jesus into their hearts' there and then, but Acts paints a very different picture both of his skills and of his success rate. After tremendous accomplishments in Acts 13, things rapidly started to unravel for Paul and Barnabas, and they were forced to flee for their lives from Pisidian Antioch, Iconium and Lystra. In Lystra, Paul's failure to convince the crowd that he wasn't a pagan god got him stoned half to death by the local Jewish community, while in Philippi and Thessalonica his exploits got him and Silas beaten up and thrown in prison, and trouble followed them from there to Berea. Even Wesley didn't manage to prove *so* unpopular to *so* many people in *so* short a timeframe as Paul!

But if these instances were the 'exception', the 'rule' was hardly much better. The normal response to Paul's message was a desire by just a handful of people to continue the discussion elsewhere afterwards. His 'sermon' to the Athenians in Acts 17 – a brilliant piece of cultural adaptation in which Paul referred to an altar 'to an unknown god' he'd seen in the city, and argued that this was the Judeo-Christian God by quoting two pagan poets – impressed only a tiny minority of listeners. Most sneered, and the resident philosophers, who were very skilled in the art of public speaking, dismissed him as a 'babbler' – someone who treasured away sound-bites he didn't really understand, but then liberally peppered his conversation with them in order to give the *illusion* of being well-informed!

In fact, Paul 'preached' (as we understand the word) only rarely. Most of the time, he chose to adopt the far more interactive approach seen in his 'final night rally' in Troas (Acts 20:7–12). 'Like many Western readers,' writes John Drane, 'I had always imagined that Paul must have preached a very long sermon, for the unfortunate Eutychus fell fast asleep [and then straight out the window to his death three storeys below]. But that was until I . . . began to look more closely at what Luke actually says. As elsewhere, he chose his terminology with care, and the key words describing what Paul was doing are *dialegomai* (verse 7) and *homilesas* (verse 11). The first even transliterates into English as 'dialoguing', and is the same word used to describe how the disciples "argued with one another about who was the greatest" (Mark 9:34, Luke 9:46), while the second describes regular conversation and is used in Luke 24 to describe what the couple on the road to Emmaus were doing. All of this implies clearly enough that, insofar as there are models for effective communication in the New Testament, at their heart are values of interactive sharing and community.'

These values were an integral part of life in the ancient world, and remain a vital ingredient in the Middle East even today. As Kenneth Bailey notes, 'The leading men of the village still "sit at the gate" and spend literally years talking to one another. The slightest transaction is worthy of hours of discussion.' There's no compulsion to cut to 'the bottom line' of a conversation as quickly as possible, in part because the *discussion* is as much a part of the decision-making process as the *data*.'The elder in such a community makes up his mind *in community*,' Bailey remarks. It's a way of doing things that's actually a lot closer to home than many of us realise. Very few of us make big decisions without the advice of those we trust, and without talking it all through with those closest to us.

In fact, despite our 'bottom line' culture, all of us appreciate the importance of 'interactive sharing and community'. When we meet friends for a drink in the pub, or have them round for a meal or a cup of coffee, we don't immediately 'cut to the chase' and ascertain all the salient facts about what's changed in their life since we last saw them. Nor do we cut the encounter short the moment we think we've probably heard enough. Instead, we take our time, enjoying their company. We know that far more is usually communicated non-verbally, in the pleasure we take from being with them for a few hours, than comes across in the actual content of what we say. The medium really *is* the message. If this weren't true, we'd all drink and dine alone – and send e-mails to one another – rather than bothering to waste the travelling time of actually meeting up!

Altared states

Preach the gospel. Use words if necessary.

St Francis of Assisi

But if this is true of life in general, it's doubly true of evangelism and preaching, especially when the content of our preaching is the love of a God who cares enough to become human. Interactive, dialogue-based approaches send people the message that we're interested in them, that we enjoy their company, that we're prepared to spend time with them and accept them on their own terms, and that what we've got to say is relevant to their life as it stands. By contrast, our extra-biblical face-the-front approaches – while very effective in their time – now tend to send people the message that if they can't adequately adapt and conform to our institutional, one-size-fits-all way of living the Christian faith, then they'd better forget it.

A friend of mine recently bought a new computer. After visiting several shops and websites to find the right machine at the right price, she explained, 'It's so bewildering. There are so many firms offering so many deals that, even when you've got a pretty good idea what you're looking for, it's hard to decide where to go.' In the end, the company she bought from wasn't the cheapest, but it was the only one that took the time to find out what she *needed* before suggesting what she should buy. 'They didn't push me to make a decision, but were keen to discuss my requirements and find a suitable match,' she added. 'They were the only firm that treated me like a human being rather than a walking dollar sign. I liked that.'

In *Finding Faith Today*, his 1992 report into just how and why people become Christians, Bishop of Pontefract John Finney reveals that much the same thing is true when it comes to evangelism. 'For most people the corporate life of the church is a vital element in the process of becoming a Christian, and for about a quarter it is *the* vital factor . . . Forms of evangelism which fail to recognise this are doomed.' Our 'outreach' may be painstakingly prepared and thought through, carefully planned right down to the tiniest detail; it may be well orchestrated and stage-managed, with the appropriate message, music and mood; it may be imaginatively and effectively advertised, and thoroughly 'covered in prayer'; it may even be tied in with a variety of different follow-up options and events; but if it doesn't allow for genuine human 'interactive sharing and community', and if it's not self-evidently honest and loving, then it's no more than a 'noisy gong or a clanging cymbal' (1 Corinthians 13:1).

The reason is simple: what people understand about the *content* of what we say depends entirely on the *context* and *manner* in which we say it. If our words aren't backed up by real care and consideration, and a genuine interest and involvement, people can even conclude that the truth is, in fact, the exact opposite of what we tell them. In Scott Turow's bestselling novel *Presumed Innocent*, murder suspect Rusty Sabich finally reacts to the state prosecutor's taunts that he killed the victim with the words, 'Yeah, you're right.' The prosecutor is overjoyed at what he sees as a blatant admission of guilt, but when the case finally comes to trial, the judge refuses to accept the supposed 'confession' as evidence. Instead, assuming that Sabich's tone of voice *must* have been sarcastic, Judge Lyttle acknowledges what we all know to be true – words themselves aren't enough. As the old adage goes, 'it's not what you say but the way that you say it' that counts.

And that's why *interactive* ways of teaching and evangelising are so important. Rather than giving people the impression that all they're really expected and allowed to do is tick the box and respond, interactive approaches underline the fact that we (and therefore by implication God) are genuinely interested in them, their questions and their views. Tragically, all too often our evangelistic overtures come across to those outside the Church as little better than high-pressure selling techniques – 'respond now, before it's too late' – more focussed on meeting seasonal quotas than on meeting real needs.

Warning that sermons, whether evangelistic or not, 'are more popular with ministers than with other people', John Drane suggests that the Church urgently needs to rethink its strategy and tactics, taking its lead from Jesus rather than mindless tradition. 'Jesus himself typically did two things: he asked questions, and he told stories. He also began where people were at – both literally and metaphorically – and also challenged and moved them on effectively. We seem to have lost the ability to do either of these things very effectively. 'Very occasionally,' he adds, 'Jesus used the Jewish scriptures, but there is no evidence at all that he ever used a text as a basis for what might be regarded as expository sermons.'

In fact, a good illustration of all these things can be seen in Jesus' encounter with two of the disciples (Cleopas and possibly his wife, Mary) on the road to Emmaus after his resurrection. Rather than barging in, halo glowing and all guns blazing, Jesus accompanied the two of them incognito, and began the conversation by asking them questions about themselves. 'What are you discussing [literally, 'What words are you *exchanging*'] with each other?' Only then did Jesus begin to explain *from their own experience and questions* what they'd failed to grasp, enabling them to see how the Bible's story and his own interacted. And rather than force-feeding them with an everything-you-never-wanted-to-know kind of approach, he left them instead with a cliff-hanger ending, preparing to go his own way before the full impact of what he'd taught them had hit home. Luke records that he 'walked ahead' when they reached their destination 'as if he were going on' and the disciples pressed him to stay with them. It's a tiny detail, but it's pregnant with meaning. Etiquette in the Middle East was well defined – the first time an invitation was given, it was *expected* to be declined, giving both host and guest a chance to walk away with their honour intact. Only if a host was persistent, like Cleopas, was the offer seen as serious rather than merely polite (which is why people had to be 'compelled' to come in the parable of the great banquet, Luke 14:23 – no thumbscrews, just a persistent assurance that the offer was sincere). In fact, in the end, it wasn't even a *verbal* message that enabled the two disciples to fit all the pieces of the jigsaw puzzle together – it was a familiar mealtime gesture: the breaking of bread which Jesus, as their rabbi, would have done not only during the 'last supper', but at the start of every formal and semi-formal meal like this one.

The same technique is demonstrated in Acts 8, where Philip met an Ethiopian official on the road to Gaza. Rather than launching headlong into a fully-illustrated, NICAM digital stereo explanation of the gospel, he asked a simple question: 'Do you understand what you are reading?' Only when the official asked for help did Philip talk about his faith. And rather than taking him back to some theoretical ideal starting point, he used the passage of Isaiah that the Ethiopian had been reading to explain the Christian message. In other words, he used the official's own deep questions and exploration as a starting point, and steered him from there *naturally* to a real understanding of Jesus. We, too, as John Drane suggests, need to let people explore at their own pace, beginning where they're at, both literally and metaphorically. We need to supplement our 'come and see' approach – exemplified by services and campaigns – with a more dangerous, risky and unscripted approach that responds to people on *their* terms, on *their* turf, about *their* perceived needs – what we might call a 'go' approach.

I recently took a 'service of blessing' for the baby boy of a friend of mine called Annie. Her husband, Jeff, is uncomfortable in church, as are most of their friends, so she'd asked if the service could be held in their own home. I said, 'Why not?' I knew that the change of location would inevitably cause a few eyebrows to be raised in concern among their few Christian friends, one or two of whom even asked me if it was actually proper and 'official' in a private house (though that's where churches started in the New Testament era). We began the afternoon with a barbecue in their back garden, and we didn't move on to the 'formal' bit until after lunch, by which time people were very relaxed and comfortable with one another. What's more, we didn't change venue or vestments, or whip out a guitar and start singing hymns. Instead, I tried to make the move from 'informal' to 'formal' as seamless as possible in order to underscore the fact that the 'spiritual' side of life isn't removed or separate from the rest. It's not an artificial bolt-on extra, but a natural element of everyday reality and relationships. I hope that what Jeff and Annie and their friends took away from the occasion was an impression that God is an integral part of their lives, constantly and easily accessible wherever they are, literally or metaphorically, and only a one-word prayer away.

After the 'formal' bit was over and we returned to the food, one or two of the guests asked me questions about the meaning of what we'd just done and about the Christian faith. I hope they'll continue to ask lots of questions in the months and years ahead. I hope they'll even find one or two answers. After all, underneath all the hype and the hymns, isn't that what evangelism is really about?

15

'My country, right or wrong'

In August 1945, George Zabelka was stationed on Tinian Island as Catholic chaplain to the 509th Composite Group, the B29 bomber unit charged with dropping the two atomic bombs ('Little Boy' and 'Fat Man') on Hiroshima and Nagasaki, as well as 'conventional' bombs on other Japanese cities. 'Little Boy', which instantly incinerated everyone within half a mile of the fireball, killed 140,000 people before the year was out. 'Fat Man' resulted in the deaths of 70,000 before the end of 1945. A high proportion of these deaths – as well as those caused by the 'conventional' fire-bombing of cities like Tokyo, where 100,000 people were killed – were women and children.

After the war, George Zabelka began to wonder why he'd never questioned the morality of US bombers inflicting what military strategists now euphemistically call 'collateral damage'. As he told an interviewer many years later, 'The destruction of civilians in war was always forbidden by the Church, and if a soldier came to me and asked if he could put a bullet through a child's head, I would have told him absolutely not. That would be mortally sinful. But in 1945, Tinian Island was the largest airfield in the world. Three planes a minute could take off from it around the clock. Many of these planes went to Japan with the express purpose of killing not one child or one civilian but of slaughtering hundreds and thousands and tens of thousands of children and civilians – and I said nothing. I was certain that this mass destruction was right,' he explained. 'The secular, religious and military society told me clearly that it was all right to "let the Japs have it". God was on the side of my country.' *Us* and *them*.

Love it or leave it?

I should like to love my country and still love justice.
French novelist Albert Camus

National identities are immensely powerful. They help bind us together. They help create a real community out of an otherwise disparate group of people. They help us define ourselves. Nationality is about more than just where we were born. It's also about who we are – our language, our literature, our culture, our colour, our music, our media, our fashion, our food, our weather, our wit, our politics, our pets, our houses, our hobbies, our history . . . in fact, *all* our preoccupations, great and small.

Sometimes our 'differentiators' – those things that bind us together as a people, acting as symbolic rallying points to mark us out from others – seem in themselves to be rather trivial. In the book of Judges, for example, the Gileadites distinguished between themselves and their enemies, the Ephraimites, by the latter's inability to pronounce the word *shibboleth*. Those who failed the test were killed – a staggering 42,000, according to Judges 12:6. A similar sort of measure was proposed more recently and much closer to home by the hard-right former Tory frontbencher Norman Tebbit. His so-called 'cricket test' was aimed at probing the loyalties of immigrants living in the UK by determining which nation they'd support in a cricket match between England and their root country. (Lord Tebbit didn't elaborate on what should happen to those who failed his test, but it's probably safe to say that he *wouldn't* have favoured execution!) However, the true tests of UK nationality, of course, as we all know, are our appreciation of a 'decent cup of tea' and our passion for Marmite! Most of the world finds our strange love of this yeast-extract concoction totally baffling. It's a true UK *shibboleth*.

Understanding where we've come from can be a vitally important part of knowing who we are now. For example, after the publication of Alex Haley's novel *Roots* in 1976 – America's bicentennial year – hundreds of thousands of US citizens began tracing their ancestry back in the 'old country' their forefathers had left to settle in the 'New World'. *Roots*, a fictionalised account of Haley's own family history dating back six generations to the ancestor brought from Africa as a slave, provoked more than just curiosity. For the first time, many Americans began to understand that some of their peculiar 'family traditions', preserved for generations and pivotal in their understanding of themselves, actually had an origin in the national and 'tribal' identity of their ancestors. Standing in a Glasgow street or a Warsaw market, they gained a far greater understanding of themselves, their family and their own US culture.

The past plays a big part in our national consciousness. The year 2000 saw the very last official remembrance of the British evacuation of Dunkirk by a ragtag flotilla of 'little ships' in 1940. With the gradual death or disablement of increasing numbers of Dunkirk veterans, their heroic endeavour is slowly passing from living memory into the pages of history. Many of those still alive, however, see it as a foundational experience, playing a significant part in determining the kind of men they became in later life. They remember vividly all the horrors of that period – the danger, the deprivation and, at times, the despair. But most also look back to it with a great deal of fondness. 'The whole nation pulled together,' they explain. 'There was a real sense of camaraderie and community that just doesn't exist any more.'

Sometimes it takes a crisis like this to firm up a nation's spirit and mould together a national identity. In his bestselling book on American life and language, *Made in America*, Bill Bryson recalls how one particular historical incident helped to galvanise the population of the various British colonies in North America until 'out of this inchoate mass a country began to emerge'. Almost 250 years after John Cabot sailed from Bristol to discover Newfoundland, the citizens of Britain's American colonies still thought of themselves as essentially *British*, despite their grievances. But in 1739, Spanish sailors cut off the ear of English smuggler Edward Jenkins. Britain responded by launching what Bryson calls 'the only interesting-sounding conflict in history': the War of Jenkins' Ear. It began twenty-five years of on-off conflict with France, Spain's ally, over its colonies in America, leading to their eventual withdrawal from the continent. Crucially, however, in the process of this quarter-century of 'armed struggle' for land and liberty, the American colonists gradually stopped seeing themselves as 'British' and began to understand that they were, instead, something unique and distinct: 'American'.

What this demonstrates, of course, is that the things that bind us together as 'us' also tend to be the things that mark us apart from everyone else ('them'). And that's *bad* news as well as *good*, especially when it comes to issues and areas where fear is a big motivator. It could be argued that the fierce debate over 'surrendering the pound' in favour of the Euro, for example, has less to do with the potential pitfalls of the new currency than with fears over the loss of 'sovereignty' and UK identity in a 'pan-European melting pot'. Legitimate concerns over losing what makes the British 'tribe' ('us') special and unique are being used to fuel xenophobia against continental Europeans ('them'). Similarly, Orange Day Parades in Northern Ireland are now less about remembering William III's famous victory at the Battle of the Boyne in 1690 than about fears of losing Ulster's majority 'British' and 'Protestant' identity in the face of the perceived threat of a 'United' and 'Catholic' Ireland.

In a sense, it's Marmite gone mad: the things that bring us together also have the power to tear us apart. When we pin our understanding of our identity too firmly on a very rigid set of national symbols, we lose our ability to cope with cultural change and begin to fear the future. Our desire to safeguard what makes us 'us' prompts us to lash out at what makes other people 'them'. It's a terror that can strike across the board, from those at one end who worry that the English language is falling apart because the *Oxford English Dictionary* now accepts split infinitives ('to *boldly* go . . .') to those at the other who firmly resisted the dismantling of US segregation in the 1960s or South African apartheid in the 1990s because they were frightened by the unpredictable and less exalted place they'd have in the 'new world order'. (As Gene Hackman's father says in the film *Mississippi Burning*, 'If you ain't better than a nigger, son, who are you better than?') It doesn't even have to be consistent – many of the most ardent supporters of tough UK immigration policies, for example, have no trouble accepting curry as the new 'national dish'!

A word of revelation

Nationalism as an ideology is in conflict with biblical norms because it assigns more worth and importance to one people and nation over others.
American church and Sojourners Community leader Jim Wallis

'Nationalism is not, one could argue, an unmitigated evil. It provides a bonding force to unite highly diverse tribes and peoples. It furnishes a sense of collective identity capable of drawing people out of themselves and their family groupings into a larger whole,' writes US biblical scholar Walter Wink. However, 'what makes nationalism so pernicious, so death-dealing, so blasphemous, is its seemingly irresistible tendency toward idolatry.' Sooner or later, what makes us 'us' becomes so all-important that it more or less takes the place of God – 'God and country' become virtually synonymous.

In George Orwell's celebrated 'fairy story', *Animal Farm*, the mistreated animals of Manor Farm join forces to oust cruel farmer Jones in what amounts to a revolution. With Jones gone, they set up a human-free state based on the premise that 'all animals are equal'.

To begin with, 'Animal Farm' runs smoothly and all the animals contribute to its welfare and do their share of the work. But it isn't long before things go badly wrong. The pigs – the intellectual leaders – squabble among themselves, and the good-hearted Snowball is exiled by the self-serving dictator Napoleon. From there, things rapidly get worse. Freedom is curtailed, and all dissent and disagreement are swiftly crushed. In the end, the pigs become every bit as cruel and abusive as Jones had been, and even the farm's guiding principle is changed: 'All animals are equal, but some animals are more equal than others.'

Orwell wrote *Animal Farm* in the early 1940s as a savage critique of the Russian revolution. Although he was a passionate left-winger, he was also a political realist and knew that even governments that start off with the best intentions – committed to peace, justice, freedom and equality – eventually degenerate, believing their own publicity. As historian Lord Acton so famously remarked, 'Power tends to corrupt, and absolute power corrupts absolutely.' The pigs in *Animal Farm* begin to believe in their own superiority, and that in turn leads them to take steps to increase their grip on power and their excessive demands on the other animals. In modern politics, this kind of megalomania often accompanies what's called a national security state, where government power becomes total and all opposition is crushed on the pretext of it potentially helping external aggression ('them' against 'us'). Like the USSR, the nation state hijacks people's *positive* national identity and uses it negatively, enabling its rulers to take the place of God and demand *absolute* loyalty. Idolatry.

But it's not only when a country's leaders abuse national senti-ment that nationalism can be destructive and idolatrous. As Walter Wink explains, nationalist ideas and feelings can take on a life of their own, stoking the fires of racial hatred or cultural superiority without the need for evil rulers. 'When a nation is made a god *it becomes a god*, not just as the inner conviction of individuals, but as the actual spirituality of the nation itself.' World War One was a case in point. At no point before the outbreak of hostilities in August

1914 was war inevitable, but the national pride and feelings of superiority displayed by *all* sides made it a certainty. No tyrant like Hitler or Stalin dominated the major players – they were governed on the whole by good men who simply failed to realise that some things are not worth fighting for. National pride and fervour swept them along the path to four years of death and destruction. Nationalism was an integral part of the spirituality of all the major European powers.

'The Bible sees an inevitable drift toward the demonic inherent in the state, which always and irresistibly demands for itself more than it should,' writes Jim Wallis, 'demanding what is God's alone.' Nowhere is this insight more visible in the New Testament than in the book of Revelation. Most of us are used to seeing the book as a list of predictions about the 'end of the world', but the truth is that very little of it primarily deals with the future. Its vivid, other-worldly language often seems totally baffling to us, with the result that we consign it firmly to the realm of the not-yet, but its rich and complex imagery would actually have been far more straight-forward and understandable for people living in first-century Palestine. It belongs to a style of writing well known at the time John wrote the book – a style now called 'apocalyptic' after the Greek word that begins the book, literally meaning 'unveiling' or 'revelation'.

In fact, there are good examples of apocalyptic literature in the Old Testament (especially in Ezekiel, Daniel and Zechariah) and elsewhere in the New Testament (such as Mark 13 and its equiv-alents), as well as in a number of non-biblical Jewish books from around the same time. It was a way of writing that concentrated on *meaning* rather than *action*. Just as the famous Cubist painter Pablo Picasso controversially attempted to paint what he *felt* when he looked at something rather than merely what he *saw*, so John avoided merely narrating and commenting on what was going on around him like a journalist, and instead used extraordinary pictures and images to describe the *meaning* of those otherwise 'ordinary' people and events. 'It is not another world,' writes Revelation expert

Richard Bauckham. 'It is John's readers' concrete, day-to-day world seen in heavenly . . . perspective.' John's intention in writing Revelation was to provide a counterblast to Rome's official propaganda, attacking the imperial worldview 'which was the dominant ideological perception . . . John's readers naturally tended to share'.

By around AD 100, when Revelation was written, the Romans had built one of the biggest and most powerful empires the world has ever seen, stretching from England across to Egypt and encompassing the entire Mediterranean. They maintained order through a combination of brutal military repression and clever cultural imperialism. Although they were rightly famous for their military prowess, their success owed as much to their skill as propaganda merchants. Surrounding their iron fist was a velvet glove – they were clever and sophisticated, and they marketed their vicious totalitarian ideology with all the artistry and brand-awareness of a modern multinational corporation. They borrowed heavily from classical Greek culture and religion, but made them uniquely their own. In their national epic, Virgil's *The Aeneid* – a kind of 'sequel' to Homer's famous Greek epic *The Iliad* – it's the Romans, not the Greeks, who come out on top. But behind the chic cosmopolitan culture of amphorae and aqueducts was a cut-throat, pagan, violence-backed, 'might is right', ultra-nationalist philosophy. Rome was a powerful 'us', conquering any kind of 'them' with breathtaking brutality and efficiency.

Revelation attacks this idolatrous thinking head-on. As Jim Wallis explains, it's 'a political-religious manifesto against the Roman Empire, a Christian tract against the brutal iniquities, arrogant injustice, and blasphemous nationalism of the world's most powerful state'. Both the style and the substance of 'the beast' (Rome) are sharply contrasted with that of God and 'the Lamb' (Jesus). 'Revelation portrays the Roman Empire as a system of violent oppression, founded on conquest,' Bauckham concludes. 'Either one shares . . . the view of the Empire promoted by Roman propaganda, or one sees it from the perspective of heaven, which unmasks the pretensions of Rome.'

Praise God and pass the ammunition

Whoever takes up the sword shall perish by the sword. And whoever does not take up the sword . . . shall perish on the cross.

French philosopher and writer Simone Weil

The roots of Revelation's staunch anti-Roman and anti-nationalist stance, of course, lie in the life and teachings of Jesus. We're not used to seeing Jesus as 'anti-Roman' – after all, there are only one or two occasions recorded in the Gospels where he even had any contact with the Romans. But as strange as it seems, that actually tells us a lot. Jesus chose to spend his time in the Jewish countryside, living and working among the kind of simple rural Jewish peasants who counted for almost nothing in the grand Roman scheme of things. Though he grew up just a few miles from the Greek city of Sepphoris, then in the process of being rebuilt in grand scale by the Romans, the Gospels behave as if these Roman centres of excellence didn't even exist. Roman culture was dominant and seductive, but the only hard evidence that Jesus was even aware of it – as he must have been, living so close – is his occasional choice of words. For example, he calls the Pharisees and others a bunch of masked play actors (the Greek gives us our word 'hypocrite'), who say their lines correctly but never really enter into the spirit of their 'dramatic performance'. Given the influence and importance of Roman culture, Jesus' almost total lack of interest in it tells us as much as an outright condemnation. It's like someone today showing their dislike of corporate giants such as Coke or Sony by studiously boycotting everything American or Japanese.

Most of Jesus' passionately anti-nationalistic teaching, however, was reserved not for Rome but for his fellow Jews. It's hard to exaggerate just how important nationalism was for Jews in first-century Palestine. Their whole way of life was based around their national identity as God's chosen people in his Holy Land. Far from being a rural idyll, Palestine was a hotbed of revolutionary fervour. The vast majority of Jews saw the Roman occupying forces not just as a *political* insult, but as a *religious* one as well, challenging their ideas about the sovereignty ('kingdom') of God. For them, national liberation was an integral part of God's 'redemption'. After all, what good is a 'promised land' if it now belongs to someone else? As Tom Wright says, 'If someone had offered a first-century Palestinian Jew the consolation of pie in the sky, it would have been refused, no matter how kosher the pie.' Like the Romans, and umpteen empires since, first-century Palestinian Jews saw themselves as God's 'us', while the Gentiles, and especially the Romans, were very definitely a second-rate or even despised 'them'.

In fact, the first century was witness to a growing level of nationalist revolutionary activity among Jews. In AD 6, around the time Luke tells us that Jesus' family went to the Temple for Passover and he failed to return with them (Luke 2:41–52), the Romans deposed their unpopular Jewish puppet ruler Archelaus, son of Herod the Great, and put Judea under the direct control of a Roman military governor. To determine the level of its tax burden, they held a census (similar to the one Luke tells us about in Luke 2:1) which provoked a bitter rebellion led by a Galilean named Judas. The revolt failed, but it saw the founding of the movement later known as the 'Zealots'. A decade after Jesus' execution, a revolt sprang up under the leadership of a would-be Moses figure called Theudas, who led people to the Jordan with promises that he'd part the waters to allow them to cross over on dry land to 'liberation' on the other side. Unlike Moses, however, Theudas and his followers were caught, captured and killed by the 'chariots and horsemen' of Roman governor Cuspius Fadus. Ten years on, another revolutionary, this time a would-be Joshua known only as 'the Egyptian', led people out to the Mount of Olives where he promised to bring down the walls of Jerusalem. Again the Roman governor, this time Felix, savagely crushed the rebellion. Another decade later, a full-scale revolutionary war against the Romans broke out, again unsuccessful, leading to the tragic destruction of the Jerusalem Temple in AD 70 and ending with the infamous siege of Masada in AD 74.

It's this 'Judea for the Jews', them–and–us nationalism – and the frequent outbreaks of bitter revolt and brutal repression that accompanied it – that forms the backdrop to Jesus' career as a prophet. (He was, of course, far *more* than this, but certainly no *less*.) He had the insight to see that war with Rome was a disastrous policy. His logic was simple: most of the time, the Romans kept 'order' in Palestine without the need for a single legion (the much-feared five-thousand-strong units of professional Roman soldiers). The nearest legion was based in Syria. Instead, Judea was controlled by a cohort of 'auxiliaries' (professional *non-Roman* soldiers recruited from Rome's occupied territories), who were less feared, less disciplined and less well paid, but still a force to be reckoned with. If revolt could normally be suppressed by less than a thousand auxiliaries, what chance did Jewish nationalist revolutionaries have against the full weight of Rome's twenty-eight legions? (It was this reality that lay behind Jesus' comments in Luke 14:31–3 about a king with 10,000 soldiers asking for peace terms from a king with 20,000.) As it was, the Jewish army was easily wiped out by just three legions in the AD 66–74 Revolutionary War.

So while Jesus was no 'wannabe' Roman, he could see that violence wasn't an answer. 'Put your sword back in its place,' he told his disciples when he was arrested, 'for all who take the sword die by the sword' (Matthew 26:52). It was a position that was open to misunderstanding. In a tense, hot-house environment, opposing the use of force against the enemy more or less invited the accusation of covert collaboration – as many pacifists and conscientious objectors have found over the years. Tom Wright explains, 'To a nation bent on violence, anyone who claims to be speaking for God's kingdom and who advocates non-violent means . . . is likely to be caught in the crossfire. That, in a sense, is what happened.'

But his desire to avoid a catastrophic showdown with Rome wasn't the only reason Jesus mounted a full-on challenge to Jewish nationalism. It wasn't just the 'means' he objected to – it was the 'end' as well. The reason why so many of Jesus' parables begin with the words 'the kingdom of heaven/God is like . . .' is that *his* view of the kingdom of God stood in marked contrast to other people's. Most of those who listened to his stories were sure in their own minds that the kingdom of God would be a renewed, revitalised, nationalist, political and firmly *this*-worldly kingdom of Israel. To most Jews living under the jackboot of Roman oppression in occupied Palestine, it was a term that symbolised the chosen people's rise as *the* new and final global superpower.

But Jesus saw things very differently. Just as he rejected the idea that God (or the gods) had chosen Rome to rule the world, so he rejected the idea that God had chosen Judea to rule the world. He not only saw himself as a 'servant king' – an idea rooted in Isaiah 53 with which we're all familiar – but he also saw the kingdom of God as a 'servant kingdom'. This was key to his understanding of the Jewish nation's 'magna carta', the covenant struck between God and Abraham: 'I will make of you a great nation, and I will bless you, and make your name great, so that you will be a blessing' (Genesis 12:2). For Jesus, the true spirit of the nation was to be righteous, not self-righteous; responsible, not repressive. Its focus was to be justice, not 'just us'. Israel was to be 'a covenant to the people, a light to the nations' (Isaiah 42:6).

In fact, this more or less summarises Jesus' approach to nation and nationalism. He was a passionate believer in the nation of Israel, but he saw it as God's instrument of blessing for the entire world. Its task was to invite the Gentile nations to come into the heavenly banquet, not act as their lord and master. Jesus' national manifesto was drawn from the book of Isaiah (42:1): 'Here is my servant, whom I uphold, my chosen, in whom my soul delights; I have put my spirit upon him; he will bring forth justice to the nations.' The Jewish nation was to be an 'us' *in service of* 'them', not just another tin-pot dictatorship. The things that marked it out – its differentiators or *shibboleths* – were to be its love, justice, holiness and mercy, not its might, mastery or materialism. It was to be a 'breed apart', not a 'breed above'.

Jesus loved his nation, but he wasn't a nationalist. In fact, it was precisely *because* he loved his nation that he wasn't a nationalist. He *loved* his country 'right or wrong' – weeping over Jerusalem in anticipation of its brutal destruction in AD 70 (Luke 19:41–4) – but he couldn't *support* his country 'right or wrong'. He couldn't remain silent or inactive while it pursued a set of self-righteous policies that would inevitably lead to its demise. He couldn't allow it to neglect its God-given responsibility to be a 'light to the nations' and a peacemaker.

And neither can we. In 1967, at the height of the Vietnam War, the Canadian Broadcasting Corporation aired a 'Christmas sermon on peace' by Martin Luther King. The Nobel peace prizewinner had lost a considerable amount of popular support because of his insistence on speaking out against America's involvement in what he considered an unjust and unwinnable war. In his sermon, he urged his fellow Christians, 'Our loyalties must transcend our race, our tribe, our class, and our nation; and this means we must develop a world perspective.' His words are as true now as they were when he first spoke them. Our obligation as Christians, as the Church and as citizens is clear: to love our country (whatever it may be) but love God more, and to work and pray to shape it into God's instrument of blessing for the entire world. To modify the words of former US President John F. Kennedy, 'Ask not what your country can do for you – ask what your country can do for the world.'

16

'You can't teach an old dog new tricks'

A few years ago, my friend Michael 'swapped' from being a Baptist minister to being an 'Anglo-Catholic' Church of England priest. Friends who didn't know him well were taken aback by what they saw as an abrupt and dramatic change, but for Michael it was the culmination of a long process and, at the same time, the next step in a lifetime journey of spiritual growth. Having been raised a self-confessed 'Bible-thumping' Evangelical, he'd first encountered smells-and-bells Christianity as a student, singing in the choir in his Cambridge college chapel – a place he'd have entirely written off as a 'den of liberal iniquity' if it weren't for his love of music.

When he finally made the switch some two decades later, it was because by then he'd come to see it as more in tune with his life as a whole. Not only did it fit his middle-age personality like a glove, it also made more of a unity between the needs and concerns he had in church and the needs and concerns he had in every other area of his life. 'I haven't really changed my core theology,' he explained. 'It's more a change of emphasis. Some of the things I thought were totally vital twenty years ago now seem less important, while some of the things I pushed to the background twenty years ago now occupy centre stage in my thinking.'

As Michael shows, in spite of the legendary inability of anyone over forty-five to set a video timer, the sixteenth-century adage, 'You can't teach an old dog new tricks,' is far from true. In fact, Michael is living proof that an 'old dog' can not only *learn* new tricks, but *discover new depths to themselves* in the process. All of us are changing and learning, all of the time. The truth is, if you're beyond learning new tricks, you're not an *old* dog, you're a *dead* one!

Rock of ages

Everybody wants to **be** *somebody; nobody wants to* **grow.**

German novelist and philosopher Johann von Goethe

Throughout our lives we're constantly growing and developing, both as people generally and in our Christian faith. We're *all* learning new tricks. Some of us, especially as we get older, actively try to resist this learning curve, attempting like the apocryphal story of King Canute to turn back an inevitable tide. 'Can't change, won't change'. We let our stubbornness and fear push us into pretending that we can continue doing what we've always done, the way we've always done it, without becoming out of touch, out of date and finally out of time. But the truth is that the world is in a constant state of change, and all of us – young and old – are running just to keep up. As the Red Queen tells Alice in Lewis Carroll's *Through the Looking Glass*, 'Now *here*, you see, it takes all the running *you* can do, to keep in the same place.'

Body and mind, we're all in a state of continual development. In areas where we see that change as *negative* or frightening – from the bewildering social and work practices that are arriving in the wake of the Internet revolution, for example, to the more mundane problem of the 'middle-age spread' – we tend ardently to resist change. However, where we see that change as more *positive* or exciting – in terms of our moral or spiritual development, perhaps

– most of us have the opposite problem: we want change to be *instant*.

As a parent, I've watched all four of my children make the huge transition from toddler to teenager. With each passing stage I've had mixed emotions, mourning some elements of their now-gone childhood, but at the same time looking forward with great excitement to the developments to come. The time has flown past and, as clichéd as it is to say it, it still seems like only yesterday that I was holding them in my arms in the maternity ward. But while it seems like a zip of a trip to me, none of my children actually seems to have appreciated the brevity of their childhood. For them, maturity is something they can't get to fast enough. The whole business of growing up seems painfully slow, especially when it comes to all the awkward physical transitions that inevitably accompany puberty.

The strange thing is, many of us adopt the same kind of impatient, headlong-rush approach when it comes to our spiritual growth and maturity: we want it to be instant. Mark Twain famously described a literary 'classic' as a book that everyone wants to have read, but no one actually wants to *read*. Much the same is true about maturity – we want to *be* mature without having to go through the slow, often agonising process of *becoming* mature. We want *instant* knowledge, *instant* wisdom and *instant* emotional assurance. Immersed in a quick-fix culture, we tend to focus on those episodes of dramatic, fast-paced transformation that seem to offer us a model of instant perfection, underplaying the slow-but-sure way in which the Holy Spirit habitually works. But behind the scenes, the truth is that even the most flash-in-the-pan transformations are really far more slow and steady than they initially seem. Take the two undisputed 'giants' of the New Testament Church, for instance: Peter and Paul.

Peter's Pentecost transformation is often cited as an example of the breathtaking speed with which the Spirit sometimes operates. After all, not only did he and the others develop instant language skills, but – having denied even *knowing* Jesus only a few short weeks before – he preached a brave and stunning off-the-cuff sermon about Jesus being the messiah to a crowd of over three thousand loyal Jews assembled in Jerusalem for one of the three big religious festivals of the year. All this seems pretty instant . . . until you remember that he'd already spent three full years as Jesus' disciple, making almost every conceivable mistake! The Gospels don't paint a flattering picture of Peter's learning skills. And even *that* catalogue of errors isn't the end of the story, for Paul recalls a subsequent run-in with Peter (Galatians 2) in which the 'rock' had gone back to his 'old tricks' and was back-pedalling from the decision to include Gentiles in the Church that he himself had pioneered (Acts 10).

Similarly, after an initial burst of activity following his conversion on the road to Damascus, Paul disappeared off the scene for several years. When he finally emerged from his 'cocoon' as Barnabas' junior partner, his entire way of understanding the world had changed. His old Pharisaic beliefs had undergone a thorough shake-up, with many of the more positive aspects retained but the negative ones purged. It was a transformation that took several years – hardly quick as a flash. And again, even then his maturing process was far from over: his bitter bust-up with Barnabas (Acts 15:36–41) demonstrates a lack of maturity and understanding that even he, with his headstrong nature, came to see as misguided in the fullness of time.

The truth is, instant change is a modern myth, a product of our 'makeover madness' culture. Just as nothing stays exactly the same, so nothing changes in an instant. Old dogs *learn* new tricks, slowly and often painfully – they don't suddenly wake up automatically knowing how to do them. Most rapid changes, like new year resolutions, 'take' for a while, but then we gradually slide back to our old ways. By contrast, the really permanent and effective changes in people's lives, whether they initially happen quickly or not, tend to require a lot of time and effort to be *consolidated*. Perhaps that's why, when Jesus spoke about the need for dramatic change and spiritual development, he used the powerful image of birth and childhood. When Nicodemus, a leading Pharisee, came to see him one night, Jesus remarked that 'no one can see the kingdom of God without being born from above' (John 3:3), or, as we often translate it, without being 'born again'.

What makes this image so special is that it not only suggests that we have the ability to start again – like a new year resolution – as if we were starting out on a brand-new life, but that it also takes full account of the fact that this new start is the beginning of a *growing* experience. Being 'born again' is the start of a journey, not the end. Spiritual transformation doesn't happen overnight, in one easy instalment. Just as no one emerges from their mother's womb fully grown, designer-dressed and clutching a copy of the *Daily Telegraph*, so no one emerges into what Jesus and others called 'eternal life' as a mature adult. However much we might want to be catapulted into instant spiritual adulthood, we actually enter on a very steep learning curve.

As new Christians, we make a mess and we're massively dependent on others for the things we need to grow and survive – just like newborn babies. And we continue to make a mess and to be dependent on others for a great many years, long after we've been weaned off milk and progressed onto 'solid food' (1 Corinthians 3:1–3 and Hebrews 5:11–13). In fact, to one extent or another, we continue to make mistakes and be dependent on others for the rest of our lives! Developing into maturity is a long process, full of setbacks and successes. None of us, no matter how 'old' we are, ever learns all our 'new tricks' straight away, trouble-free.

'Life is like a butterfly'

Caring is an interaction in areas of life where helper and helped are both vulnerable ... At the simplest level we need to learn genuinely to listen to others. This is surprisingly difficult, because of our natural tendency to try to formulate an interpretation of what we hear as quickly as possible to prepare for rapid action.'

Christian ethicist and pastoralist Alastair Campbell

In *Ordering Your Private World*, Gordon MacDonald recounts the experience his family had when they bought an abandoned farmhouse in New Hampshire. The first challenge they faced was clearing the land around the house in order to turn it into a lawn. Having lain unused for quite a while, it was littered with rocks and stones, some of them quite large. They set about the task of clearing the big rocks first, before turning their attention to the smaller ones. Eventually, having cleared the whole ground of rocks, stones and pebbles, they were ready to seed the grass. It grew well, and with surprising speed they found they had a lawn to be proud of. However, the next year they noticed that, thanks to the feverish activity of worms and ants and other bugs, *new* tiny rocks and stones had begun to appear among the blades of grass, surfacing from beneath ground level. The MacDonalds discovered that clearing the ground of little stones wasn't a one-off event: it needed to be done year after year. In the same way, writes MacDonald, the things that need transforming in our lives can't be dealt with all in one go – they have to be dealt with in stages, and some of them don't rise to the surface until after quite a few years have passed.

A friend of mine prayed intently as a teenager to be given the gift of an instant 'word of knowledge' to help people with their emotional problems. Now in his late forties, he admits that God *did* give him a kind of 'gift of knowledge' . . . but it took a couple of decades to acquire, and wasn't quite what he expected. 'I prayed for instant insider information – dramatic stuff,' he explains. 'Instead, God in his wisdom painstakingly taught me to *listen* to people. I've slowly learnt to pay close attention to their words and gestures, and what they *don't* say, in order to work out the meaning of what they *do* say. As a teenager, I wanted to know what the problem was as quickly as possible so I could help people *recover* as quickly as possible, but I now realise that kind of thinking was foolish. People change slowly, and even on those rare occasions when you *do* get to the "cancer" of the problem fast, and cut it out, they still take a very long time to recover from the "operation". I'm actually glad I never did get any instant "words of knowledge" – I might have known things *about* someone, but I wouldn't have known *them,* and it's that human relationship and trust that really helps them overcome their problems. Most of the time you can't short-cut that – it takes time and effort to establish it.'

The truth of this became clear to me a few years ago at a Christian conference. As a speaker, I was invited to take part in a time of 'prayer ministry'. The conference organisers gave out strict guidelines: don't ask people for their name, don't ask what the problem is, don't get too specific, and don't spend too long on any one person. I broke all four rules. I just didn't feel at all comfortable with the organisers' rapid-turnover assembly-line approach. 'Look,' I told the twentysomething man who presented himself to me for prayer, 'I can pray for you as we're supposed to, anonymously and impersonally, or we can go and get a cup of coffee and talk it over. It's your choice.' He chose the coffee. In the conversation that followed, two things became apparent. First, his problem – which had racked him with guilt for months – wasn't moral but medical, and could be solved over time with the involvement of a GP. Second, in all the months he'd been seeking help for his problem – at conferences, house groups and in 'prayer ministry' at a well-known charismatic church – no one had ever thought to ask him what his problem was, or talk to him about solving it. Instead, they'd opted for the inefficient, unbiblical and superstitious approach of trying to *zap* the problem. When I saw him again the following year, the man explained that things had gradually improved a lot. As a result of our chat, he'd got over his feelings of guilt, and that had paved the way for real transformation.

In fact, Paul provides us with the model for this gradual transformation in Romans 12:2: 'Do not be conformed to this world, but be transformed by the renewing of your minds, so that you may discern what is the will of God – what is good and acceptable and perfect.' He's clearly not talking about a one-off instance of renewal. As Leon Morris points out, 'The force of the present tense should not be overlooked; Paul envisages a continuing process of renewal.' When he says 'be transformed' – the Greek gives us our word 'metamorphosis', which we normally apply to the total transformation of a caterpillar into a butterfly – he's actually talking about a gradual, ongoing, continuous, *life-long experience*, not a flash-in-the-pan moment of splendour.

Of course, anyone who's ever tried to keep a new year resolution knows just how tough it can be. More often than not, it proves to be all but impossible, even when we're geared up to see it as the start of a long process that will need consolidation. But that's why it's so vital for us to understand that the transformation Paul talks about isn't really something *we* do – it's more a process we allow God's *Spirit* to do in us. In fact, for Paul this is the essence of the gospel: God saves us gratuitously through Jesus' death and resurrection, which we accept in faith, and then gradually renews us by his Holy Spirit in the boiling pot we call the Church. (It's no coincidence that the remainder of Romans 12 is concerned with the way individual Christians are members of the whole body of Christ.) In other words, unsurprisingly, spiritual transformation isn't something we accomplish without the leading and guidance of the Spirit.

This is, in fact, all part and parcel of being 'born from above'. In translating Jesus' Aramaic into Greek, John deliberately used a word that could mean either 'again' or 'from above'. In the encounter in John 3, Nicodemus understands it to mean 'again', prompting him to ask, 'How can anyone be born after having grown old? Can anyone enter a second time into the mother's womb and be born?' (John 3:4). However, Jesus – in line with all the other occasions John uses the word in his Gospel (3:31; 19:11, 23) – clearly intends it to convey the sense of 'from above', reflecting God's integral and intimate involvement in the whole process. The 'presence of God' that Nicodemus suggests surrounds Jesus (John 3:2) isn't reserved for a select few 'holy' people with special knowledge and miraculous powers. Instead, it's all around us, available to and active in *everyone* who's open to its possibilities, gradually transforming them . . . and, through them, the entire world that God loves so much.

Joining the master-class

If your morals make you dreary, depend on it, they are wrong.
Robert Louis Stevenson

Of course, the fact that God's Spirit is at the heart of the trans-formation process has some big implications for us, not only as individuals, but also as the Church. When people start coming to church, it's tempting for us to place great expectations on them, especially in terms of what they believe and how they act. We often feel, and sometimes even let them know, that their transformation is going just a bit too leisurely for our liking. These 'old dogs' are rather slow in grasping what we see as some of the core aspects of the 'new trick'. However, if God is in charge of the transformation, then *we* don't set the timescale. The Holy Spirit does.

John Newton earned his living at sea as a slave-trader. One day, caught in a particularly violent storm, he became totally convinced he'd drown. His mother had been very religious, and she'd made sure that some of that faith rubbed off on him, so he cried out to God to save him . . . and there and then he became a Christian. But although he accepted God's gift of 'new life' – being 'born again' – Newton initially continued to sell slaves! In fact, it took him quite a long time to see that selling other people for money really wasn't compatible with being a Christian. It may seem obvious to us now, but at the time many Christians were supporters of slavery. However, while the Holy Spirit's gradual transformation of his character may have seemed slow to arrive, it was nevertheless powerful and permanent. Though he's now best known for having written the hymn 'Amazing grace', Newton became a leading figure in the early years of the Evangelical movement – smoothing the transition between such people as John Wesley and William Wilberforce – and a major player in the fight to end the slave trade, which was finally abolished in Britain in 1807, the year he died.

Many of us would, if we're honest, have written Newton off as stillborn at an early stage in his very gradual Christian transformation. But the truth is that not everyone is at a point where they're ready to make as fresh a start as we personally might want, and not everything that will eventually be transformed in their life has to be – or ever *is* – dealt with at one and the same time. As the Church, we need to understand that maturity doesn't happen overnight, and we need to build that into the way we deal both with core members and with those on the fringe. Whatever stage they're at, we must resist the temptation to hurry people along – the 'spiritual' equivalent of a parent telling their child to 'act your age' – or, worse, condemn them out of hand. Instead, we need to give them the generous support, encouragement, opportunity, freedom and space they need to change slowly, trusting that God is at work in their lives and will get around to dealing with those issues that seem so important to *us* in good time.

Sharon and Derek lived together with their two young children on a council estate. Through Sharon's involvement with the local church-run community centre, she and Derek slowly got to know some of the people from the church. After a while, they decided to go along to a family service, to see what it was like. Feeling welcome, they kept going. Their kids loved the Sunday school, and when Derek and Sharon were invited to join the 'just looking' Christian basics course the church was running, they felt confident enough to give it a try. It helped them understand a bit more about God and the church, although they didn't feel ready to make any firm commitments.

After a couple of years of being part of the church, and of having been well supported, both spiritually and practically, Sharon and Derek reached the point where they felt they trusted God enough to become Christians. Quietly, they made a commitment of faith. And as that faith grew, and they learnt more and more about the depth of God's love for them, they found that they were learning to love and trust each other more as well. Though their relationship had always been good, they both sensed that it was reaching new levels. After about eighteen months, they felt they wanted to get married. This was a big step: they'd always shied away from it before, because it had seemed to be the kiss of death for their friends' relationships. But now it felt like the *right* thing to do – the most natural and obvious step to take.

Looking back, they were grateful that people in the church hadn't made it an issue for them, pushing them into marriage before *they* felt ready for it. No one had ever seemed to mind the fact that they were just living together, they said, and *that* alone had spoken volumes to them about God's unconditional love. 'We just figured we'd cross that bridge when we came to it,' the minister replied when they finally raised the subject with him. 'I admit, one of the churchwardens *did* suggest I had a "quiet word" with you at one stage, but I felt you had a lot on your plates just coming to grips with some of the basic bits of your new-found faith. I trusted the Holy Spirit would get round to the marriage thing eventually.'

It is, of course, extremely difficult for us to trust God for the timing. We rightly worry about maintaining moral and theological standards. We're genuinely concerned about the erosion of Christian values in society, and keen for the Church to model an alternative approach rather than becoming indistinguishable from its surroundings. But 'ends' don't justify 'means', and not approving of someone's behaviour, or the slowness of their rate of change, never makes it right to burst in on them with all guns blazing. That isn't God's chosen approach – he chooses to transform us gradually through the graciousness of his love, not at 'makeover' speed with the iron rod of discipline and judgment. And if that's true, what gives us the right to be so judgmental and impatient?

A few weeks ago, I was involved in filming a programme for the BBC as part of a moral issues series. The programme took the form of a panel discussion, hosted by a well-known news presenter. I wasn't the only Christian on the panel, but I was the token clergyman, invited – I soon discovered – to help kick-start a heated debate. Among the other panellists were two women who couldn't have been more different from one another if they tried. One, Carol, was an extremely reactionary Christian lady, well known for her outspoken and often unpopular views; the other, Jan, was an atheist lesbian politician. From the word go I found myself being expected to agree whole-heartedly with Carol and to attack Jan, expressing views on a whole range of moral issues with all the tolerance, compassion and self-humbling love of Genghis Khan. So when I failed to take what both the presenter and Carol considered to be the appropriate 'moral high ground', they began to accuse me of 'prevaricating'.

Jan, however, kept reacting positively to my comments. Having steeled herself against what she thought would be my attacks on her lifestyle and ethics, she found my acceptance of her at first bewildering, and then encouraging. Tragically, I began to realise that the number of Christians she'd met who were willing to accept her as she was, as God accepts her, rather than jumping to instant judgment and condemnation, was very small indeed. (As Mohandas Gandhi said, 'All the world would be Christian, were not Christians so unlike their Christ.') 'God grants us freedom, even when some of our actions are out of line with his wishes,' I explained. 'So who am I to complain that his morality is too lax? Who am I to condemn anyone when God refuses to write them off? When, from all I know of him, he keeps the door very firmly open?' My views, born of my belief that we should trust God for the timing of people's transformation, incensed Carol, but hopefully made Jan think that, perhaps, God might just love her after all.

Throughout his career as a wandering rabbi, Jesus consistently incensed the religious and moral conservatives of his day – those who, for all the right reasons, insisted on maintaining and tirelessly promoting a morally 'pure' lifestyle. They strongly disapproved of his mixing with the 'wrong sort of people', and especially of his refusal to speak out and solidly condemn moral laxity. They branded him 'a glutton and a drunkard, a *friend* of tax-collectors and sinners' (Matthew 11:19). The implication was clear enough: as a friend of 'sinners', he was therefore no friend of God. In essence, they were accusing him not just of 'going soft' or 'going liberal' – or even 'prevaricating – but of 'going pagan'. It was a charge of nothing less than idolatry. So I knew that, whatever Carol and others might say to the contrary, I was in the very best of company in be*friend*ing Jan, accepting her unconditionally just as God does – just as Jesus would have, and *does* – and then trusting the Holy Spirit in terms of her gradual journey of faith and transformation.

As Gerald Coates urges, 'Treat everyone as winnable. Never write them off.' The problem is that when we refuse to trust God for the timing, in reality we deny that he's able to touch someone's life. We effectively set ourselves up as sole judge and jury of both them and God, taking it upon ourselves to decide that a person is beyond redemption. In essence, we assert that this particular 'dog' is too old or slow to be capable of being taught any 'new tricks', even by such a master of the impossible as God.

17

'If you're a nice guy, nice things happen to you'

Paul Schindler was worried. When Dorothy and Jean hadn't returned home to La Libertad the night before, he'd assumed they'd spent the night at one of the Cleveland Diocese mission team's other bases. They'd done so before. But when they didn't show up for the weekly staff meeting, he knew something was wrong.

Paul had reason to fear for their safety. El Salvador wasn't a safe place, and even though the two were both blonde, blue-eyed Americans – and Dorothy was a nun – the killing of Oscar Romero, San Salvador's Archbishop, in March of that year had proved that absolutely no one was beyond reach of the country's military-backed death squads. So as Cleveland team leader Paul made some phone calls, two other team members drove back over the route Dorothy and Jean had taken the previous day on their way from collecting two American nuns from the airport. What they found multiplied their concerns: there, by the side of the road, was the burnt-out wreck of Dorothy's white Toyota van. All four women were missing.

The next day, Thursday 4 December 1980, US Ambassador to El Salvador Robert White was informed that four bodies had been found sprawled along the roadside and had been quickly buried, for health reasons, in an unmarked grave in a nearby field, an hour's drive from the airport. As the bodies were lifted to the surface using ropes, the full scale of the tragedy began to emerge. Dorothy's jeans were on back-to-front. A local man explained that the bodies of all four women had been found naked from the waist down, and those burying them had tried to restore some dignity by dressing them. The underwear of three was found separately. At least two of them had been raped, and all of them had been beaten before being shot in the head. The impact of the bullet had crushed Jean's face. Photos of Robert White and Paul Schindler standing by the graveside graced US papers and TV screens the following day.

Ambassador White advised outgoing US President Jimmy Carter to suspend all economic and military aid to El Salvador until adequate steps had been taken to apprehend the killers – strongly suspected of being members of the nation's security forces – but no one ever stood trial for the killings. In fact, the Salvadoran authorities even intimated that the four American women had been 'communist subversives'. But the truth is, they'd done nothing more than try to help and support El Salvador's poor. Dorothy and Jean had even had a friendly dinner with Robert White and his wife at the US Embassy the night before their deaths. They weren't political activists – they were just missionaries. And like so many other missionaries before them, they became martyrs. Nuns Dorothy Kazel, Ita Ford and Maura Clarke, and lay worker Jean Donovan, died because they followed God's call to put their faith into action in a small and desperately poor Central American country torn apart by the brutality of what US military strategists rather quaintly called 'low-intensity conflict'.

'If you're a nice guy, nice things happen to you?' In this case, at least, it didn't work out that way.

A mother's request

Several times I have decided to leave El Salvador. I almost could except for the children, the poor, bruised victims of this insanity.

Who would care for them? Whose heart could be so staunch as to favour the reasonable thing in a sea of their tears and helplessness? Not mine.

Murdered American lay worker Jean Donovan

The twentieth century saw more Christian martyrs than ever before. El Salvador alone saw an estimated 75,000 civilians murdered or 'disappeared' during the 1980s, mostly for the 'crime' of taking seriously their faith commitment to 'love thy neighbour'. Archbishop Oscar Romero was the most prominent of those killed for daring to put their faith into action – gunned down just after finishing his sermon during a 6 p.m. communion service in the small chapel of Divine Providence Hospital in San Salvador on Monday 24 March 1980. And the decade ended as violently as it had begun, with the brutal slaying of six Jesuit priests, together with their cook and her fifteen-year-old daughter (who had, ironically, taken temporary residence with the Jesuits because they believed it would be safer than their home), in the grounds of San Salvador's University of Central America at around 1 a.m. on Thursday 16 November 1989.

Christianity has had a very long history of martyrdom. Though the word 'martyr' comes from a Greek term that literally just means 'witness', it's taken on all kind of overtones down through the ages – especially that of dying as a result of refusing to renounce the faith. Though the first martyrdoms – including that of the first ever Christian martyr, Stephen (Acts 7) – were carried out at a local level, often as a disciplinary measure against the Christian movement *within* Judaism, they began in earnest with Emperor Nero.

In an effort to dispel the rumours that he'd personally ordered the burning of Rome in AD 64, Nero 'fabricated scapegoats', wrote the ancient Roman historian Tacitus, 'and punished with every refinement the notoriously depraved Christians' whose 'deadly superstition had broken out afresh, not only in Judaea (where the mischief had started) but even in Rome . . . Their deaths were made farcical. Dressed in wild animals' skins, they were torn to pieces by

177

dogs, or crucified, or made into torches to be ignited after dark as substitutes for daylight.' These savage persecutions only stopped when Nero was deposed and committed suicide in AD 68.

They began again, however, with the Emperor Domitian in AD 95, and from then until the legalisation of Christianity by Emperor Constantine's famous Edict of Milan in AD 313, martyrdom was an expected fact of life for a great many Christians. Those who weren't exiled or forced to work in the Roman mines could look forward to being crucified, burnt, decapitated, tortured to death or thrown to wild beasts such as lions, leopards, bears, boars or bulls. (And anyone who somehow managed to survive this mauling in the arena was promptly beheaded.) Nice things happen to nice guys? Hardly. Christian faith was at times nothing less than a walking death sentence.

It was a state of affairs that Jesus had worked hard to prepare his followers for, though not always with much success. When the mother of James and John approached him in the run-up to their final entry into Jerusalem, she asked for her two boys to be given the best jobs when – as they imagined – he stormed Jerusalem and established his independent and newly powerful 'kingdom of God' in place of the Roman occupation. Jesus' unexpected response was to warn both her and her sons of just what lay ahead. 'Are you able to drink the cup that I am about to drink?' he asked, reminding them of his imminent death (Matthew 20:20–8). It was a timely warning, though their desertion of him at the cross suggests that they'd failed to understand it at the time. Nevertheless, according to Luke, James was the first of Jesus' disciples to die for his faith, and only the second martyr in the Church's history (after Stephen; Acts 12:2).

Martyrdom and rejection were also outcomes that Jesus hinted at to those even *thinking* about becoming his followers. Someone approached him as he and his disciples were on the road and rashly promised, 'I will follow you wherever you go.' Jesus' response was to suggest that 'foxes have holes, and birds of the air have nests; but the Son of Man has nowhere to lay his head' (Luke 9:58). Though on the face of it, this was simply a warning to would-be disciples that even the *animals* had a more certain and comfortable future than Jesus could guarantee, what he was saying actually went a lot deeper than that.

For one thing, a visiting, respected rabbi could expect to have offers of hospitality coming out of his ears at every town and village he came to – hospitality was, after all, a key feature of Jewish life in first-century Palestine. But Jesus was warning potential disciples that their having a comfortable place to sleep wouldn't always be a foregone conclusion. In other words, he was making it clear to them that a large number of people saw him as *persona non grata*, and they could expect the same treatment. But added to this, the fact that Jesus had already dubbed Galilee's ruler, Herod Antipas, 'that fox' (Luke 13:32), and that the phrase 'birds of the air' was sometimes used as a way of referring to the Gentiles, suggests that he was keen to highlight the contrast between himself and the 'powers that be'. As Kenneth Bailey notes, 'Jesus in a veiled fashion may well be saying: Look, if you want power and influence, go to the "birds" who "feather their nests" everywhere. Follow the "fox" who manages his own affairs with considerable cunning. For, in spite of your expectations, the Son of man stands powerless and alone. Are you serious in wanting to follow a rejected Son of man?' Bailey then adds, 'The point is not only, "You, too, may have to suffer privation, and have you considered this?" but also, "Whatever your motives, keep in mind that you are offering to follow a *rejected leader*." '

'When the going gets tough . . . the tough get gone!'

We must somehow believe that unearned suffering is redemptive.

Martin Luther King

The ultimate symbol of Jesus' rejection, of course, is the cross – something Paul describes as 'a [deeply offensive] stumbling block to Jews and [sheer] foolishness to Gentiles, but to those who are the called, both Jews and Greeks, Christ the power of God and the wisdom of God' (1 Corinthians 1:23–4). The ultimate 'nice guy', the one entirely 'without sin' (Hebrews 4:15), Jesus nevertheless died by the most painful and demeaning form of execution the Romans could devise – considered even more shameful and humiliating than being set alight or fed to dogs – in order to 'deal with sin' (Romans 8:3). For his followers, especially Paul, the cross – an instrument of violent and, in Jesus' case, undeserved death – became the central and defining image of the Christian faith. So those who followed Jesus had to be prepared to 'take up their cross' because martyrdom was the example Jesus himself had set.

That's why, for example, when the disciples left prison after having been given the statutory thirty-nine lashes (one less than forty to ensure the limitations of Deuteronomy 25:3 weren't accidentally exceeded) for teaching unauthorised doctrine in Jerusalem's Temple, 'they rejoiced that they were considered worthy to suffer dishonour for the sake of the name' of Jesus (Acts 5:41). They weren't masochists, secretly enjoying the pain they suffered – their joy stemmed from their realisation that their fate was, to a lesser extent, the same as that of Jesus (who was given thirty-nine lashes before his crucifixion). Martyrdom wasn't something to be sought after, but neither was it something to be avoided at all costs.

Following in Jesus' footsteps is, of course, far from easy. There's an old poster caption that reads: 'If Christianity were illegal, would there be enough evidence to convict you?' For many of us, the answer could be no. But in some parts of the world, Christianity effectively *is* illegal, and the 'evidence' of commitment to Christ is used not only to convict, but also to kill. How many of us – whatever our intentions here and now – would actually have the courage and moral strength to stand tall and affirm our Christian faith if it meant certain death?

In his bestselling novel *Silence*, Japanese author Shusaku Endo tells the story of Sebastian Rodrigues, a Portuguese priest who undertakes the dangerous job of being a missionary pastor to rural Christians in seventeenth-century Japan. In 1614, Christianity was outlawed in Japan, and Christians were banned from practising their faith on pain of death. Priests were moving targets, especially missionary priests like Rodrigues. But in travelling from village to village, Rodrigues finds large numbers of Christians – whole villages, in fact – willing to take massive risks just to have him with them. His guide around the countryside, however – Kichijiro – is less committed. As Rodrigues learns, Kichijiro has a simple way of dealing with persecution: he renounces his faith . . . and then takes it up again later, as if nothing has happened. At first Rodrigues is appalled by what he sees as Kichijiro's total lack of courage and faith. But he slowly realises that, in another time and place where active persecution wasn't a factor, Kichijiro would most likely be a pillar of his local church and a great support to those around him.

The practice of apostasy – of ditching your faith when the going gets tough – was one of *the* major problems of the early Church, from the start of Domitian's persecutions to the Edict of Milan. The different attitudes taken to 'apostates' (those who'd renounced their faith under torture or persecution) frequently split the Church, both at a local and at a diocesan level. The hardliners held to their strict understanding of the view that 'it is impossible to restore again to repentance those who have once been enlightened, and have tasted the heavenly gift, and have shared in the Holy Spirit, and have tasted the goodness of the word of God and the powers of the age to come, and then have fallen away, since on their own they are crucifying again the Son of God and are holding him up to contempt' (Hebrews 6:4–6). But the majority took a far softer approach – while they didn't reject the view held by the author of Hebrews that a 'second repentance' was impossible, they doubted that what happened in those whose courage failed them at the critical moment was the *total* rejection of Jesus discussed in the book. Their inspiration came in part from the example of Peter, who (with the other disciples) abandoned Jesus at the critical moment of his arrest, trial and crucifixion . . . but who was subsequently reinstated not just as a disciple but as the Church's supreme leader.

Fit to live

I have frequently been threatened with death. I must say that, as a

Christian, I do not believe in death but in the resurrection.
Assassinated Archbishop of San Salvador Oscar Romero

Thankfully, most of us will probably never have to face the threat of active persecution. We'll never be called on to make the 'ultimate sacrifice' and lay down our life for our friends . . . or enemies. We'll never be forced to make the tough choice between our faith and the immediate future. Like the vast majority of Christians down through the ages, the only real dilemma we'll have to grapple with is the choice between *faith* and *face*. But in spite of that – or perhaps because of it – it's actually no less vital for us to have come to terms with the fact that simply having a Christian faith and a 'living relationship with the Lord Jesus Christ' isn't a kind of foolproof insurance policy against harm. We're not immune from the ill effects of a sinful world. Tragedy can strike even 'the best of us'. The real question, therefore, is how we deal with it when it comes. Is our faith robust enough to cope with our walking through what Psalm 23:4 calls 'the valley of the shadow of death'? Is our doctrine not only 'biblical' but also practical? Is the theology we learn in our churches – and teach to new Christians – an applied theology that really works, or just a vacuum-packed imitation that falls apart the moment it comes into contact with the harsh, cold air of trouble, hardship and failure?

There's something about facing the stark reality of one's own death that often brings an astonishing level of clarity. In a moment, we see our lives in a new perspective, evaluating with real vision and insight just what matters to us and what doesn't. 'The report of my death was an exaggeration' was how Mark Twain responded to the *New York Journal* on 2 June 1897, after reading an account of his own tragic demise. A decade earlier, explosives genius Alfred Nobel had had exactly the same experience, but while his own response was nothing like as funny, it was in the long term far more profound. Shocked at the way he was characterised as a millionaire merchant of death by a hapless journalist who'd mistaken him for his recently deceased brother, Nobel resolved to set about changing his will to ensure that, when he died, the bulk of his vast fortune would go to found the world-famous prizes that now bear his name. His brush with death – albeit only in the morning paper – spurred on the dramatic transformation of his life.

Addressing a civil rights rally in Detroit in June 1963, Martin Luther King suggested, 'If a man hasn't discovered something he will die for, he isn't fit to live.' Few of us actively think of our lives as being lived in the service of something – or some*one* – greater than ourselves. But the truth is, from faith to family, there really *are* some things worth dying for. Existence at any price is too expensive. Over the last few years, I've had the opportunity to interview a number of celebrities in the worlds of politics, sport, music, religion, entertainment, charity and the media. Inspired by Martin Luther King, one of the questions that I've asked many of them is, 'What are you prepared to die for?' The responses have been far more varied that I could ever have imagined, but the majority of those I've asked have admitted that it's not something they've ever really thought about before. We don't tend to dwell on death. In fact, if possible we tend to ignore it, even though we know it's inevitable. However, one reply stood out from the others – that of Chief Rabbi Jonathan Sacks. 'Martin Luther King was quite right,' he explained, 'if you know what you're prepared to die for, you know all the more what you're prepared to *live* for. And that's why Judaism, despite its tragedies, remains a religion of life.'

As Christians, of course, we affirm the same thing. Without attempting to deny the reality or the starkness of death, we believe and trust in the ultimate triumph of life over death. After all, that's the *real* message of the cross – not divine protection against all kinds of evil, like some kind of magic talisman, but the knowledge that whatever evil does befall us is *not* the final word. As Tony Campolo puts it, we acknowledge in the spirit of Easter that 'it's Friday, but Sunday's coming'. Death has lost its sting, and its final victory (cf. 1 Corinthians 15:54–7). We accept death, but like Oscar Romero, we also believe in the power of the resurrection.

18

'The Lord laid this on my heart'

Biblical scholar Don Carson, renowned for his ability to make sense of hard-to-understand passages in the New Testament, once had a conversation with an enthusiastic fellow Christian who relayed what God had 'told' him about the meaning of a particular Bible verse in his quiet time that morning. It was an odd interpretation, and one based, Carson realised, on a total misunderstanding of the Author-ised Version's archaic English. Aware that the Greek text couldn't support this interpretation, Carson suggested as humbly as he could that perhaps his companion might be mistaken. The man's reaction was blunt – he *couldn't* be wrong, because the Holy Spirit, who doesn't lie, had informed him personally about its meaning.

Try as he might, Carson couldn't persuade him that it was grammatically and textually quite impossible for the verse to mean what he imagined. Finally, both exasperated and intrigued, Carson asked what the man would have said if he'd put forward his interpretation, not on the basis of a logical approach to the text, but on the basis that the Holy Spirit had given it to *him* personally in his *own* quiet time. The man was silent for a long time and then replied, 'I guess that would mean that the Spirit says the Bible means different things to different people.'

You don't have to be Einstein to realise that this kind of approach makes a mockery of the Bible. Of course, on the one hand it's ridiculous to suggest that even a scholar and Christian of Carson's calibre and maturity can fully grasp all the ins and outs, breadth and depth of the whole biblical text. As J. C. Ryle said, 'The Bible would not be the book of God if it had not deep places here and there which man has no line to fathom.' But by the same token, it's clearly ludicrous to believe that absolutely *any* way of understanding a verse or passage is legitimate, regardless of how much or how little sense it makes in context, just so long as we're personally convinced that 'the Lord laid this on my heart'. Though this blinkered kind of approach is popular with some Christians, and may even sound 'spiritual' to the naïve, it is in reality nothing more than a secularisation of the bankrupt secular maxim, 'It doesn't matter what you believe, as long as you're sincere.' It's essentially a triumph of style over substance.

Shoot first, ask questions later

If God intended us to pickle our brains and put them aside, if he hadn't wanted us to struggle with the great issues of human history and culture, then he wouldn't have sent us a Middle Eastern book spanning many centuries and cultures – he'd have sent us a small tract.

Australian biker minister John Smith

'In terms of a Christian mind, we evangelicals characteristically pit "heart" versus "head" and opt for the heart as the more spiritual choice,' writes Os Guinness in his book *Fit Bodies, Fat Minds*. 'We are like the Tin Woodman, in L. Frank Baum's *The Wonderful Wizard of Oz*, who chooses a heart rather than a head . . . "for brains do not make one happy, and happiness is the best thing in the world."' Most of the time, the short-term effects of this heart-over-head option are fairly innocuous, like the Pentecostal minister who announced to his congregation one Sunday how the Lord had clearly revealed to him that 'Sister Lucy will lead us in our informal time of communion this morning' . . . only to be informed by another member of the congregation that Sister Lucy wasn't there that day! Stupid, but harmless. Occasionally, however, the effects of not thinking things through properly, but merely relying on what we think God is saying to us, can be significantly more dangerous.

Arthur Miller's play *The Crucible* is based on the true story of the infamous witch-hunt in Salem, Massachusetts. In 1692, when a group of young girls began to scream, convulse and bark like dogs, three women were arrested for witchcraft – a capital offence – and brought before a special court. Terrible accusations flew back and forth, and others were arrested. The court pursued a tough policy of 'zero tolerance' in an attempt to stem what it perceived as the demonic tide sweeping the area. But the lack of clear and objective thinking in its decisions can be seen in its sentencing policy: those who 'confessed their guilt' were jailed, but those who protested their innocence were treated more severely. In less than a year, twenty people were executed and two died in prison. However, when all the panic finally died down, the townsfolk began to express strong doubts about the safety of the convictions, and the remaining suspects were eventually acquitted. Historians now seriously doubt the existence of *any* real witches in Salem at the time.

Miller wrote the play in 1953, the same year Senator Joseph McCarthy's witch-hunt against supposed communists in the USA reached fever pitch. Once again, the accusations flew back and forth, and the central government House Un-American Activities Committee (set up in 1938 to counter a perceived threat of Nazi infiltration) tried to root out all suspected communist insurgents in an effort to protect the US from what President Reagan, addressing the National Association of Evangelicals years later, in 1983, characterised as 'the aggressive impulses of an evil empire'. In a kind of shoot-first-ask-questions-later replay of the Salem incident, Arthur Miller himself was investigated by the HUAC three years after the play's opening, in 1956.

Tragically, this heart-over-head approach to life and faith persists, even within the Church. For example, the sense of hysteria that often surrounded 'baptism in the Holy Spirit' in the 1970s, clapping and dancing in worship in the 1980s and the 'Toronto Blessing' in the 1990s caused deep divisions in many congregations and denominations. Rather than adopting a balanced, rational attitude, committed to thinking very carefully through all the potential pros and cons of such phenomena, and trying to see the bigger picture – or even adopting the kind of 'wait and see' attitude taken by Rabbi Gamaliel toward the Christians in Acts 5 – most churches either jumped uncritically on the bandwagon or reacted just as uncritically in vehement condemnation. In the cool light of day, all these issues now seem like a series of storms in a teacup, but the continued impact of many Christians basically giving themselves a head bypass operation – leaping to judgment, one way or another, without real thought – has left a number of churches up and down the country still licking the wounds of bitter division.

One of the most famous incidents of this kind of shoot-first-ask-questions-later policy, of course, was the Catholic Church's reaction to the writings of the famous Italian astronomer and mathematician Galileo Galilei. In 1632, aged sixty-eight, Galileo published *Dialogue on the Two Principal Systems of the World*, in which he tentatively put forward and defended the banned theory of Nicholas Copernicus that the earth orbited the sun, rather than vice versa. Galileo was personally convinced of the truth of Copernicus' idea, having tested it by observations made with his state-of-the-art refracting telescope. But after taking advice from bishops and theologians, he chose to adopt the more cautious approach of proposing the idea not as 'fact' but as 'fancy'. However, even this caution wasn't enough. The Vatican, which had applauded all his previous work, reacted by letting its heart silence its head. Faced with the prospect of giving tacit approval to an idea that would totally change the way people saw God's creation and humanity's place within it, it opted instead to bury its head in the sand, indicting Galileo for heresy (and only retracting this indictment in 1992, 350 years after Galileo's death).

In fact, Martin Luther had reacted in a very similar way when Copernicus himself had first voiced his ideas. Luther was convinced that heliocentrism – the idea that the sun is at the centre of a solar system, with the earth in orbit around it – was totally incompatible with the Bible's view of the world, a position very few of us would take today. He struck out at what he saw as a dangerous error, and attempted to nip it in the bud. In the process, he opted firmly for heart over head. Like a parent fighting a bitter pitched battle with their teenage son or daughter over issues that seem all-important at the time but are really inconsequential – such as hem lengths, hairstyles or nose piercing – he strained out a gnat but swallowed a camel (Matthew 23:24). To use John Stott's categories in explaining this still all-too-common problem, he was 'dogmatic' where he actually should have been humble and 'agnostic', but 'agnostic' where he should have been firm and 'dogmatic'!

Check your brain cells at the door

An Englishman should never think, sire. It's bad for his health.
French playwright Jean Anouilh

There are three main reasons why we tend to react by opting for the heart at the expense of the head. The first basically has to do with *familiarity*. In essence, we become so used to certain ways of seeing the world, or a particular doctrine or Bible passage, that we rarely if ever re-examine them. They become part of the theological furniture – comfortable and unquestioned.

Bill Bryson notes how a traveller to a small island situated between Denmark and Sweden in 1940 came across some local children singing a nonsense song that went, 'Jeck og Jill vent op de hill og Jell kom tombling after.' If it sounds familiar, that's because it *is*. This famous British nursery rhyme had come to the island from English troops stationed there during the Napoleonic wars, 130 years before. The strange thing is, 'Jack and Jill' makes even less sense in Danish than it does in English! None of the children actually *understood* the words – they just sang them because they were taught them by their parents, who were taught them by *their* parents, who . . . well, you get the idea. In the same way, a lot of what we believe as Christians has come to us from tradition – ancient or modern – passed on like the children's rhyme. But tragically, we often take on this tradition entirely without question, repeating it almost parrot-fashion. We never understand its meaning, let alone check either its biblical authenticity or the sell-by date of its cultural baggage. And then, of course, like all comfortable things, we become so used to it being there that we react instinctively – and negatively – whenever someone dares to question it. Right or wrong, it's part of who we are.

The second main reason why we so often leave our brain cells at the outer door of our faith has to do with our idea of what is, and isn't, true *spirituality*. There's often a basic assumption that theology in particular – and a well thought-out approach to the Christian faith in general – is, at the very best, just plain unnecessary. Os Guinness cites the example of Dwight Moody, the famous US preacher and evangelist, who responded to comments about his theology by exclaiming, 'My theology? I didn't know I had any!' Guinness notes that whenever Christians 'have an experience of direct, personal access to God, we are tempted to think or act as if we can dispense with doctrine, sacraments, history and all the other "superfluous paraphernalia" of the Church – and make our experience the sum and soul of our faith'. I came across this attitude first-hand when, as a young assistant minister fresh out of theological college, I gave what I thought was a brilliant expository sermon only to be shot down in flames by a pillar of the local church community. Not only did he object to my use of the text (on the grounds of what I still think was a highly *suspect*, if not totally impossible, interpretation), but when I finally admitted that I'd stolen my best points from the almost unimpeachable F. F. Bruce, he replied, 'I don't need theologians with their worldly degrees to hear the Lord speaking to me. If it's not in the Good Book itself, I don't want to know.'

The third main reason for our open-mouth-before-engaging-brain approach has to do with our suspicion that a questioning attitude is a hallmark of *hostility* to the faith. A few years ago, two Evangelical theological college lecturers gave a late-night Spring Harvest seminar entitled 'What have the theologians done to us?' They intended the title to be tongue-in-cheek – as theologians themselves, they believed that the title 'What have the theologians done *for* us' would have been far more appropriate. But to their surprise, the seminar was jam-packed . . . and most of the people there were keen to know what they could do to protect both themselves and their churches against what they saw as the potentially harmful effects of theologians. Put off by various bad apples – especially some of the liberal theologians of the nineteenth and twentieth centuries – many in the audience seemed to consider theologians as a breed as being a bit like the evil child-catcher in the film *Chitty Chitty Bang Bang* – basically dubious and 'unspiritual' people dead set on eroding and stealing away Christian faith by questioning and gradually undermining things that should be, and generally *are*, simply taken for granted. Yet as Jim Packer explains, *all* Christians are theologians to some extent – the only question is, is our theology good or bad?

'At root,' writes Os Guinness, 'anti-intellectualism is both a scandal and a sin. It is a scandal in the sense of being an offence and a stumbling block that needlessly hinders serious people from considering the Christian faith and coming to Christ. It is a sin because it is a refusal, contrary to the first of Jesus' two great commandments, to love the Lord our God *with our minds*.' This is a stark challenge for most of us. We've become used to a kind of 'soundbite Christianity', in which everything has been reduced to its simplest terms and all of the rough edges have been smoothed away. 'Biblical faith' is presented in easy-to-manage bite-sized chunks that fail to disturb us. For many Christians, what G. K. Chesterton said of the 'Christian ideal' is equally true of serious, thought-out faith: '[It] has not been tried and found wanting. It has been found difficult; and left untried.'

The problem isn't an either/or one – *either* head *or* heart. God gave us both and expects us to *use* both. Opting for the head over the heart would be just as contrary to the commandment of Deuteronomy 6:5 as the anti-intellectualism that Guinness rightly condemns. It's just that, in most churches, it's the head that gets neglected. Gordon MacDonald recalls the time he and his wife were browsing in an antique bookshop and found an old book – one whose cover was so worn and beaten that it looked as if it must have been very well thumbed over the years – only to find that none of its pages had ever been cut. Despite its well-worn appearance, the book had never actually been read. 'The Christian who is not growing intellectually is like a book whose many pages remain unopened and unread,' he suggests. 'Like the book, [they] may be of some value, but not nearly as much as if [they] had chosen to sharpen and develop [their] mind.'

One of the barriers many of us face to sharpening and developing our minds is that we tend to surround ourselves very heavily with those whose opinions mirror our own. Labels and *shibboleths* help us to determine between 'friend' and 'foe', but while we happily listen to our 'friends', we rarely if ever actually listen to our 'foes'. Instead, we either imagine that we know in advance exactly what they're going to say (and so assume it isn't worth listening), or take on board only snippets of their arguments – often only the buzzwords that galvanise our opposition – and spend the rest of the time they're speaking planning our next move.

Out of curiosity, I recently asked a theologian friend what book he'd take to a desert island if he could take just one from his impressive collection. His choice surprised me. Written by a scholar whose views are far from orthodox, it's not what you'd call light reading. Instead, it's demanding, hugely technical, and virtually unintelligible to anyone who's not a professional New Testament scholar. My friend admitted it had taken him several months to read it all through the first time around, on what he jokingly called an 'instalment plan'.

'Is that why you'd choose it?' I asked. 'Because it would take so long to read?'

'No,' he replied, 'I just think it's one of the best books I've ever read.'

'I'm surprised you agree with what it says,' I continued.

'Oh, I *don't*,' he answered. 'That just it. I disagree with *most* of it, but I've never read a book that's made me *think* more about my faith and helped me clarify so many issues in my own theology.'

Winston Churchill is credited with having suggested that we should always listen to our best friends *and* our worst enemies, as they both tell us the truth, but from different angles. In his controversial book *Wolf in the Sheepfold*, Old Testament theologian Robert Carroll remarks, 'The bits which interest me in [the Bible] are those which get under your fingernails and cause great pain – those irritating sayings and sections which disturb the mind and rob you of sleep at night; the parts which sit uneasily with doctrine and dogma and which mock the domesticities of religions which swear by the Bible.' The truth is, every Christian should be able to put their hand on their heart and say the same. Tragically, however, we tend either to ignore the bits we don't like or find very difficult to understand, or else we run very fast in the opposite direction, embracing experience and joy of the 'heart' over an ache in the 'head'.

'Go on, you know you want to . . .'

Jesus does not want me for a cabbage. Church is not the ecclesiastical equivalent of the Red Army or Hitler Youth, where lots of unthinking clones do what they're told and, when asked to jump, ask only 'How high?' We need to bring all our critical faculties to bear on our belonging. It is this that has the potential to make church such a rewarding experience.

Baptist minister Simon Jones

Unlike us, Jesus' thinking was sharp because he didn't mentally shut himself away. Instead, he made a point of carefully listening to his opponents' ideas before dialoguing and debating with them. Not only was his 'career' filled with run-ins with scribes, Pharisees, Sadducees and political powers-that-be, but it began in a dramatic confrontation with views that severely challenged and tested his own. Immediately after his baptism in the River Jordan by John, complete with God's voice of endorsement, Matthew tells us that Jesus was 'led up by the Spirit into the wilderness to be tempted by the devil' (Matthew 4:1).

'All temptation is to do what is attractive, and the subtlest and strongest temptation is to do what appears to be good. The strength of a temptation is in proportion to the attractiveness of the goal,' writes George Caird. We tend to assume that the devil put in a personal appearance for Jesus's temptations, but if we take seriously the claim of Hebrews 4:15 that Jesus 'in every respect has been tempted as we are, yet without sin', then perhaps his temptations were more like our own – trying to work out if the voice we hear on our shoulder telling us what we *want* to hear is really God 'laying this on our hearts' or if its origin is altogether less wholesome. 'Conscious of a unique vocation,' continues Caird, 'and endowed with exceptional powers, he must set aside all unworthy interpretations of his recent [baptismal] experience. He has heard a voice saying, "Thou art my Son"; now he hears another voice, "If you are the Son of God . . .", and he must decide whether or not it comes from the same source. Three times he makes up his mind that the voice which prompts him to action is that of the devil.'

The three temptations in the wilderness (without doubt just the first of many more) tested both Jesus's faithfulness and his intelligence. All three were very real and extremely agonising. It's all too easy for us to fall into the trap of imagining him giving glib and somewhat quick-fire answers rather than wrestling with a real dilemma in each case. But what kind of temptation would it be, enabling him totally to 'sympathise with our weaknesses' (Hebrews 4:15), if he could brush it off that quickly? Just like us, Jesus was stretched to the limits, but with great strength and spiritual determination resisted everything that was thrown at him.

In fact, the answers he gave suggest that he'd thought very carefully about his situation, and was fully aware of the precedents from the Israelites' history. It's often pointed out that the verses he quotes from the book of Deuteronomy were close together on the same scroll, prompting some people to imagine that he merely replied with the last thing he'd heard at the synagogue before going off into the wilderness. But in fact, this part of Deuteronomy – which includes the beginning of the regular daily Jewish prayer known as the *she'ma* (6:4–9) – was one of the most important passages of the Hebrew Bible. It looked back to the mistakes of the past in order to find the way forward for the future. Jesus would probably have known it as well as he knew his own name, but he recited it now not out of empty habit, but out of personal, passionate, well-thought-through conviction.

In other words, by using this section of Deuteronomy as his yardstick (the word often used for the content of both the Old and New Testaments – 'canon' – literally means 'yardstick' or 'measure'), he was applying brain, bowels (then seen as the seat of emotion) and Bible to the problem of whether or not God really had 'laid this on his heart'. Head, heart and Holy Writ. It was a habit *he* appears to have cherished. It's one *we'd* do well to acquire.

19

'When in Rome, do as the Romans do'

In 1582, a thirty-year-old Italian priest named Matteo Ricci arrived in China. Newly 'reopened' to Western visitors, Ming dynasty China had an ancient and sophisticated culture, but it was still extremely isolationist and xenophobic. At the heart of Chinese culture was Confucianism, a blend of philosophy and tradition stretching back to Confucius some two thousand years before. Ricci, a very intelligent man with a real gift for languages and a passionate commitment to authentic incarnational mission and evangelism, gradually intended to plant a thoroughly indigenous branch of the Catholic Church. But as Europeans, he and his team of Jesuit missionaries found it an uphill struggle just to be accepted. They soon realised that, to make any impact, they'd have to immerse themselves in Chinese culture to a far greater extent than they'd initially thought.

Eventually Ricci decided to target China's intellectuals and adopted the role of a Confucian scholar. Changing his name to Ma Dou (as near as he could get to Matteo) and donning traditional clothes, he slowly worked his way into the emperor's court at Peking, making himself indispensable. Then, in 1595, in a further effort to blend in, he authorised his team of missionaries to participate in the so-called 'Chinese rites'. These included using the traditional Chinese title 'Lord of Heaven' for God, as well as being involved in rituals to honour Confucius, together with burning incense and offering libations linked to the time-honoured cult of the family ancestors.

By allowing these rites Ricci, was taking a calculated risk. He knew that many Christians would very strongly disapprove of his decision and accuse him of idolatry. But personally convinced that the rites were at heart about nothing more than respect and tradition, he could see no reason for Christians to steer clear. However, after his death in 1610, Rome took the opposite view. Condemning the rites as blasphemous superstition, it banned all Chinese Christians from taking part in them. This ensured that the Chinese Church's distinctiveness was undoubtedly safeguarded. But at the same time, its appeal to most Chinese people was significantly reduced, and its censure and persecution as a 'foreign influence' in Chairman Mao's post-war 'Cultural Revolution' was virtually guaranteed.

Was Ricci's 'When in Rome . . .' approach an example of divinely inspired genius, or pure missiological madness? In essence, the Catholic Church's Chinese dilemma demonstrates the knife-edge on which Christian mission – *anywhere* in the world, 'home' or 'away' – is very delicately balanced. On the one hand, we want to remove as many needless obstacles as we can to people under-standing and accepting the gospel. We want them to hear it expressed, like the crowd of Jewish pilgrims at the Pentecost festival, in their 'own native language' (Acts 2:8), culturally as well as linguistically. On the other hand, we know that when the Church behaves like a chameleon and becomes totally indistinguishable from the rest of society, it not only fails to offer people anything life-changing or uniquely valuable, but it also ends up steering perilously close to idolatry . . . if not actually crossing over its borders.

So the big question the Church has had to face from Day One

is, when in Rome, should we do as the Romans do? Or should we keep ourselves 'pure' and detached? How can we be both relevant and effective, and at the same time holy and distinctive?

An impossible combination

All conservatism is based upon the idea that if you leave things alone you leave them as they are. But you do not. If you leave a thing alone you leave it to a torrent of change.

G. K. Chesterton

The same question was very much a live issue in the first century, not only for Jesus and his disciples but for *all* Jews. Both in the so-called 'diaspora' – the Jewish settlements and districts throughout the Roman Empire – and in Palestine itself, God's 'holy nation' (Exodus 19:6) was surrounded by the religion, politics, culture and morality of pagan nations. Roman and Greek culture were as dominant and 'seductive' then as US culture, with its Coke and commercialism, is today. The big problem was how to deal with it. As Tom Wright explains, 'Greek culture had been a fact of life in Palestine for a couple of centuries at least by the time of Jesus, and many had learnt to live with it, while others, though still resenting it, were nevertheless influenced by it in a variety of ways. There was no invisible checkpoint at the borders of the Holy Land, confiscating "Hellenistic" ideas or exchanging them for "Palestinian" ones.'

There were five basic approaches taken by Jews toward the pagan and idolatrous culture of the Empire: isolation, rejection, accommodation, adoption and adaptation.

Isolation was the option taken up by the loose collection of groups known as the Essenes, who broke away from mainstream society to live in self-contained compounds, often in remote locations. One Essene group, for example, based itself in Qumran, and its now-famous library – first discovered in 1947 – is known as the Dead Sea Scrolls. Dismissing the world as so impure that it was little more than a source of contamination, and seeing even Jewish society as being largely for the chop, they withdrew to their isolated retreats and waited for God to act decisively in vengeance and judgment. Their lives were well ordered and regimented, designed to be as pure and faithful to God as possible. As one of the Dead Sea Scrolls, the so-called Community Rule, states, 'They should keep apart from men of sin in order to constitute a Community in law and possessions.' Later Christian communities, such as the Mennonites and the Amish, would take the same strategy and form their own societies of saints, drawing their inspiration from their understanding of Paul's advice to the church in Corinth, ' "Come out from them, and be separate from them," says the Lord' (2 Corinthians 6:17, quoting Isaiah 52:11).

Rejection was the preferred option of the various resistance movements, including both the shady group of assassins known as the *Sicarii* or 'dagger-men' – who specialised in killing those Jews they considered too chummy with the Romans – and the more organised political resistance movements such as the Zealots. Given a free hand, they'd probably have 'ethnically cleansed' every Roman and Roman sympathiser from the country, and rid it of everything Roman. They'd probably also have identified strongly with the motto attributed to eighteenth-century American Revolutionary leader Patrick Henry, 'Give me liberty or give me death!'

Accommodation was the policy of the Sadducees, who were convinced of the rule that 'God helps those who help themselves', but still realistic enough to know that victory against the Romans on the battlefield was nothing more than a pipe dream. As a result, they took what they could get, collaborating with the Romans in the same way that the defeated Vichy French government collaborated with the Nazis when Hitler overran France in 1940. The Sadducees justified this accommodation policy theologically by dividing the world up into 'secular' and 'sacred', politics and religion (see Chapter 8), and though they resigned themselves to the fact that they'd never rule the roost politically, they did everything in their power to ensure they had control of religious life. In fact, they exploited an 'opt-out' clause that Julius Caesar had given the Jewish people in gratitude for their help in the military *coup d'état* that brought him to power: Caesar had exempted all Jews from military service, and safeguarded their religious freedoms (such as keeping the Sabbath day work-free) throughout the Empire. In effect, this gave the Sadducees a fair amount of 'home rule', and they opposed anything and anyone who looked like rocking the boat.

Adoption – throwing holiness out of the window and swallowing pagan culture hook, line and sinker – was the approach taken by 'tax-collectors and sinners', and all those who found the 'sophisticated' Roman way of doing things so attractive that they simply copied it and made it uncritically their own. To some extent, however, it was also the approach taken by two of the towering Jewish intellectuals of the era: Philo and Josephus. Philo was an exact contemporary of Jesus, a philosopher who lived in the cultural metropolis of Alexandria and whose life's work was an effort to interpret the Jewish Bible in the light of pagan Greek philosophy. Josephus, by contrast, was a Jewish general in the disastrous war of AD 66–74 who not only went over to the Romans' side himself after being defeated, but insisted that *God* had done so as well. His books on Jewish life and history, and on the war itself, provide us with a lot of (not altogether unbiased) information about life in the first century.

Adaptation, however, was the rule of thumb taken by most Jews – especially those living in the major trading cities of the Empire, where pagan culture surrounded them every day. They tried to steer a middle course between *totally rejecting* Roman morals, beliefs and behaviour on the one hand, and *totally embracing* them on the other. It was a difficult balance to strike and maintain, and one that wasn't so much an *individual* problem as a *communal* one. Synagogues provided Jews outside easy reach of Jerusalem with far more than just a place to worship – they also acted as a surrogate extended family and as a basis of moral support and theological reflection. They were an oasis of faith in a desert of idolatry, where Jews could discuss together how to get the balance right between being 'in' and 'of' the Roman world. They could then come to collective decisions about how to proceed as a community.

It was this approach of adaptation – of making careful and thought-through decisions about what was acceptable and unacceptable in Roman culture, with the aim of not only surviving in it but also transforming it – that lay beneath the ethical views both of Jesus and his followers (and subsequently of the Church) and also of the Jewish group with whom he had the most run-ins: the Pharisees.

Clear blue water?

Every country is home to one man and exile to another.
T. S. Eliot, 'To the Indians who died in Africa'

Within the broad confines of an adaptationist position, however, there was still considerable room for doubt and debate. Even among the Pharisees themselves, there were huge disagreements about how to understand the Bible's teaching and remain faithful to God in a Roman world. In fact, the Mishnah – a sort of 'collected works' of the great Jewish rabbis, compiled in about AD 200 – is jam-packed with heated debate, including the famous clashes between the two great rabbis of the period just before Jesus' birth, the 'lenient' Hillel and the 'hardline' Shammai, who took totally opposite views on almost everything. But if their disputes among themselves were sometimes fierce, the Pharisees' disputes with Jesus were even more heated and hard-nosed.

We're used to seeing Jesus and the Pharisees as bitter opponents, and in a sense they were. But the truth is that the Pharisees were also the closest of all the various Jewish movements to the teaching and tactics of Jesus. They *agreed* far more than they *disagreed*. They were united in their enthusiasm for evangelism, for example, and in their insistence that 'salvation' was a gift from God that made way for a subsequently faithful lifestyle. They were joined in their belief that the 'kingdom of God' had to reign in every area of life, not just the purely 'sacred', and in their passion for justice. They shared a belief in resurrection and the full authority of the entire 'Old Testament'. They were equally determined that 'holiness' was neither an unattainable goal nor the preserve of an élite, but was a potential way of life for everyone, and they both firmly believed that the nation had a God-given task to be a 'light to the Gentiles'.

They came to serious blows, however, on just how to achieve all that. The Pharisees held a 'clear blue water' approach to holiness. They felt the way to attract 'the nations' to God was to live such pure, clean, uncontaminated lives that they'd be a shining example to all around. In fact, faithfully keeping the whole of the Jewish law was so important to them that they adopted a 'belt and braces' approach, adding a whole tier of extra rules and regulations to ensure that they never even came close to breaking the law itself. They were, in essence, squeaky-clean. And that's why they had a problem with Jesus. His associations with the 'wrong kind of people' seemed to muddy the clear blue water they'd carefully established. For instance, they more than doubted his ability to make friends with 'tax-collectors and sinners' without some of that sin rubbing off on him and his disciples, and were especially concerned that onlookers would be confused as to just what made God's 'chosen people' special, distinct and worth joining.

By contrast, Jesus adopted a revolutionary, 'incarnational' approach to holiness. Fully aware of what made him and his followers distinct, he could see that the Pharisees' strategy was disastrously backfiring. They came across as being 'holier than thou'. Instead of role-modelling a clear, easy-to-copy 'holy' lifestyle, they made God seem unapproachable and remote to those who most needed to come close to him. That's why Jesus deliberately sought out those on the fringes of Judaism who didn't quite make the moral grade. He wanted them to know that a new life and a right relationship with God was theirs for the asking. What's more, he knew that the best way to demonstrate the appeal of that new life was to live it in and among the people who needed it the most, letting them see at close quarters what a difference it could make.

One of the bitterest flashpoints between Jesus and the Pharisees was the issue of just what could be done on the Sabbath. The Pharisees were real sticklers for keeping the Sabbath. It was one of the things that most clearly distinguished Jews from everyone else. No other race or religion in the ancient world had a regular weekly holiday (literally 'holy day'). Some pagans felt it was ridiculous; most thought it was just lazy. But for Jews it was an essential way of honouring God, and the most important day of the week. It ran from sundown on Friday to sundown on Saturday, kicking off with a celebratory meal (often with friends or neighbours) and usually including a synagogue service. Anything that could be seen as 'work' was forbidden. But the problem was, of course, that while Jewish Law (Exodus 20:8–11, Deuteronomy 5:12–15) was clear that 'work' was off-limits, it didn't give hard-and-fast guidelines about just what counted as 'work' and what didn't. And this was where Jesus and the Pharisees came to blows.

When Jesus arrived in a Galilean synagogue one Sabbath and healed a man with a withered hand, he immediately found himself the subject of a judicial enquiry: 'Is it lawful to cure on the Sabbath?' the local Pharisees asked him, angry at what he'd done (Matthew 12:10). Giving medical attention was classed as 'work' unless it was a matter of life and death, in which case 'exceptional circumstances' applied. Since a withered hand wasn't exactly a life-threatening condition, the Pharisees felt Jesus could – and *should* – have waited until the following day to cure the man. As a result, they accused him of being a Sabbath-breaker – a serious offence, especially for a rabbi, and one that carried the death penalty (Numbers 15:32–6).

It's easy for us to play down just how important the Sabbath was to the Pharisees, imagining that their motives were less than honourable. However, the story of Eric Liddell – hero of the film *Chariots of Fire* – may help us put their feelings in perspective. Liddell, clear favourite to win gold in the 100 yards at the 1924 Paris Olympic games, shocked the British public and the establishment by refusing to run in the qualifying heats because they fell on a Sunday, the Christian 'Sabbath'. He knew he'd be disqualified from the final, but some things were more important to him than winning, and his religious convictions wouldn't let him compete on a Sunday. His superiors, including the future Edward VIII, tried to get him to change his mind, but Liddell was resolute. He ran to honour God, and couldn't bring himself to see competitive running on a Sunday as honouring to God. It wasn't exactly life or death. His decision made him Public Enemy Number One . . . until, of course, he unexpectedly won the 400 yards (a distance he'd never run competitively before) by a full 5 yards, smashing the existing world record with a time of 47.6 seconds.

The Pharisees similarly saw the Sabbath as a day to honour God and display their distinctive holiness. That's why they ring-fenced it so firmly, keeping it sacrosanct. But for Jesus, this was an approach that came perilously close to missing the point of the whole thing. According to Deuteronomy 5:15, the Sabbath day was a celebration of the Exodus, when God rescued the Israelites from slavery in Egypt. What better day, Jesus reasoned, to heal someone's withered hand – a condition that would have severely limited his ability to participate in the life of the community and would also probably have been seen (wrongly) as a result of his own sin.

'Which of you,' Jesus asked, 'if you had a sheep that fell into a pit on the Sabbath, wouldn't get hold of it and lift it out?' (Matthew 12:11). It was a heavily loaded question. While most sheep owners (whose livelihood could have depended on it) would have wasted no time at all in lifting out a sheep, whatever day it was, the Damascus Document – one of the Dead Sea Scrolls – explicitly prohibits this kind of action. 'No one should help an animal give birth on the Sabbath day,' it insists, 'and if he makes it fall into a well or a pit, he should not take it out on the Sabbath.' However, the Pharisees were very concerned about cruelty to animals, and would have insisted that the sheep be rescued immediately. They'd happily have made just the kind of exception to the Sabbath rules they *weren't* prepared to make for the man with the withered hand. 'If you'd do that for a sheep,' Jesus challenged them, 'how much more should you do it for a human being! Clearly, then, it's lawful to do good deeds on the Sabbath.'

Romans worked on the Sabbath. Jews didn't. So for the Pharisees, what they saw as Jesus' cavalier attitude to one of the key distinguishing marks of Judaism wasn't just steering close to the borders of law-breaking, it was also running the risk that onlookers would see no basic difference between pagans and Jews. For Jesus, however, there was no point in being distinct for its own sake – if it was just a case of reinforcing a 'them' and 'us' mentality, with 'them' having to swim across an exhausting and perilous ocean of clear blue water to get to 'us'.

Pushing out the boundaries

Panic among the angels.
Hundreds of thousands
Of principalities, dominions and powers
Are taking crash courses in Zulu.

Leo Aylen, *Zulu Eucharist*

Jesus believed in holiness. He lived it. But what he *didn't* believe in was the effectiveness of a holier-than-thou approach. As far as he was concerned, it didn't work, and as a principle it was out of line with God's character. 'In this is love,' wrote Jesus' disciple John, following his master's teaching: 'not that we loved God but that he loved us and sent his Son to be the atoning sacrifice for our sins' (1 John 4:10). Rather than expecting people to pull themselves up by their own moral bootstraps before they could be fully accepted, Jesus took the initiative – and the risk – and accepted them anyway. He saw repentance as a *consequence* of forgiveness, not a *precondition* for it. He saw 'believing' as a consequence of 'belonging', not vice versa.

It was an attitude that left him open to the accusation of his being 'soft' on sin, just as his approach to the Sabbath had left him open to the accusation of his being a 'Sabbath-breaker'. 'It was one thing to eat with outcasts,' notes US theologian Walter Brueggemann, 'but it was far more radical to announce that the distinctions between insiders and outsiders were null and void.' And this is effectively what Jesus did by consistently breaking down the harsh barriers that distinguished Jews and Gentiles, holy and unholy, clean and unclean, saints and sinners.

To test their hypothesis that he was 'soft' on sin, a group of scribes and Pharisees brought a woman to him who'd been caught red-handed committing adultery. 'Now in the law Moses commanded us to stone such women,' they suggested, referring to Deuteronomy 22:22. 'What do *you* say?' (John 7:53–8:11). It was clearly a trap. As F. F. Bruce notes, 'By the first century AD the full rigour of the law was no longer applied as a general rule, in urban communities at any rate.' In other words, though the 'law of Moses' clearly commanded the death penalty, it was intended as a *maximum* sentence, and one that was rarely enforced in practice. By bringing the woman to Jesus for judgment, therefore – rather than quietly reprimanding both her and the man and then letting them go – the scribes and Pharisees were deliberately trying to exploit an in-built biblical tension between 'law' and 'mercy' in order to catch Jesus out. If he urged her release, they'd accuse him of being opposed to the law of Moses, while if he called for her stoning, they'd accuse him of being an unforgiving and uncompromising hardliner, opposed to God's mercy.

Jesus said nothing. He calmly remained seated, as any good rabbi would, but rather than pronouncing judgment he merely drew on the ground with his finger. When finally pushed for an answer, his reply was crisp, clean and conclusive. Aware that Deuteronomy 17:7 demanded that the first stone be cast by one of the two male eyewitnesses required by the law (Deuteronomy 19:15) to testify that they'd actually seen her committing adultery, he challenged them, 'Let *anyone* among you who is without sin be the first to throw a stone against her.'

Hardline holiness would have insisted that an example be set and a stretch of clear blue water be visible between the pure perfection of God's way and the moral morass of the pagans' way. Jesus's approach, however, while not belittling the woman's sin – he refused to condemn her for her sin, rather than suggesting that there was really nothing to be condemned — demonstrated that holiness isn't really about *our* conduct but about *God's* love. At the end of the day, our holiness and moral behaviour is no more than a response to and reflection of God's holiness and moral behaviour. And the best way to communicate *that* is rarely across a stretch of clear blue water.

This is often hard teaching for us to follow. It's easier to enforce a black-and-white policy than to have to grapple with shades of grey and the realities of God's boundless compassion and 'amazing grace'. Interestingly, the early Church seems to have had just the same problem as we do. While few scholars doubt its authenticity, *no* early manuscript includes this story of the woman caught in adultery *anywhere* in the Gospels. This has led to the reasonable suggestion that it was deliberately removed from manuscripts of one of the Gospels — probably Luke — by later Christian leaders who, ironically, feared that it blurred the distinction between 'holy' and 'not holy'. As Ben Witherington puts it, 'It may have called into question the early Church's strict disciplinary measures when sexual sin was committed.'

A friend of mine, Colin, is a leader in his local church. A decade ago, in his late thirties, he played a major role in taking steps to 'discipline' a church member who'd admitted having had an affair. Colin was adamant: the rot needed to stop. 'We've got to send a clear message to everyone in the church and the surrounding community that this kind of thing is wrong,' he explained. 'It's just not acceptable behaviour for a believer. Marriage is a sacred institution, and taking marriage seriously is one of the things that marks us out as Christians.' Since that time, Colin's marriage has, tragically, fallen apart (though not through an affair). Today, he's far less dogmatic about 'taking decisive action', and far less concerned about keeping up appearances. He's as clear as he ever was about moral absolutes — it's just that he's also a lot clearer about God's love, forgiveness and grace. He's come to realise that, as far as the New Testament is concerned, all disciplinary action is geared toward restoration not retribution. And the funny thing is, I've noticed that people are not only less keen to describe him as 'arrogant' these days, some of them – including those who aren't Christians – are even starting to remark on how 'holy' and 'Christ-like' he is.

'When in Rome, do as the Romans do'? Not entirely. But having said that, there's no excuse for throwing stones at the Romans, either. We're called to imitate the incarnational approach to holiness modelled by Jesus, the 'Word [who] became flesh and lived among us' (John 1:14). Though Jesus is the judge of all humanity, he walked among us humbly and faithfully, filled not only with righteousness but also with God's overwhelming mercy and compassion. The truth is, incarnational holiness makes it necessary, when in Rome, to be critically accepting of Roman customs. As they say, you don't have to speak Italian to enjoy pasta!

20

'If you've got it, flaunt it!'

In 1216, Innocent III – arguably the most powerful Pope in history – died after eighteen years in office. Under his leadership, the Church had gained unrivalled influence over Europe's kings and emperors. In world terms, it was an unprecedented 'success'. As Innocent III lay in state – swamped in jewels, furs, gold, silver and other trappings of worldly wealth – kings, princes, cardinals and monks processed past his body to pay their respects. But as night fell, a band of local thieves broke into the cathedral and stole every piece of treasure and finery they could find ... including the Pope's clothes! It was July in central Italy. The heat had already caused his body to start decomposing. But the story goes that a small, poor young man, wearing only a dirty tunic, had hidden in the shadows to pray. When the thieves left, he approached the dead Pope, removed his own tunic, and used it to cover the old man's naked corpse.

Even in his lifetime, Innocent III was known as the 'new Solomon'. His court was lavish, and a tone-setter for all around. Everything about it, from the buildings and furnishings to the trinkets and uniforms, telegraphed Rome's importance and authority. Innocent III used the trappings of success to breed more success, and the accoutrements of power to increase the Church's power. By contrast, the young man whose self-sacrificial act of kindness covered the dead Pope's deficiencies had no wealth, no power and no clear signs of success. He was known affectionately as *il poverello*, 'the poor one'. If Innocent's maxim was, 'If you've got it, flaunt it,' *his* creed was, 'If you've got it, give it away.' His name? St Francis of Assisi.

First impressions

Nothing is enough for the person for whom enough is too little.
Ancient Greek philosopher Epicurus

'Image,' they say 'is everything.' In my work I get to see a large number of different company offices. You can tell a lot about the kind of firm you're dealing with just by seeing how they've arranged their lobby and reception area, let alone the offices and conference rooms themselves. Some make a point of decorating and furnishing very lavishly, one or two even splashing out on expensive works of art in order to make an impression on you as you wait for a meeting. It's all intended to communicate just one thing: success. The more successful a company appears, the more seriously they think you'll take them. And that, it seems, is good for business.

A few years ago, I went to an important business meeting in one of these office buildings in the City of London. As I got into the half-full lift, I noticed that I was the only person casually dressed and not wearing an expensive suit. Just as the doors of the lift were closing, an anxious-looking man rushed in. Hastily eyeing me up and down, he enquired, 'Are you the lift engineer?' I was actually there to attend the same meeting as he was, but since I wasn't wearing Armani, he had me marked down in a different category altogether. *Kleide machen leute*, as the Germans say – clothes make people.

It's easy for us to criticise this kind of judgment by appearance, but the truth is that we all do it. What's more, we take steps that all but *encourage* other people to do it to us. Whether it's cleaning the house before the in-laws come to visit, wearing a smart suit for a crucial job interview, adopting a special 'telephone manner' when speaking to clients, wearing perfect make-up on a date, or baking bread and brewing a fresh pot of coffee when potential buyers come to see our house, we all do things to spruce up our image. After all, we want to look and sound our best. It's only natural.

It's something we do with our churches, as well. We often tend to show off our buildings (something churches managed perfectly well *without* until around AD 300), or apologise for them if we think they're not really 'up to scratch'. But at a deeper level, we also tend to enjoy boasting about our 'successes' every bit as much as anyone else. We frequently judge the 'success' of everything from missions to membership, services to staff, prayer to projects, and youth groups to house groups in terms of their size, numbers, growth rate, income, budget, busyness or organisational effectiveness. But are these really the *right* criteria?

Top of the league

'It has always seemed strange to me,' said Doc. 'The things we admire in men – kindness and generosity, openness, honesty, under-standing and feeling – are the concomitants of failure in our system. And those traits we detest – sharpness, greed, acquisitiveness, meanness, egotism and self-interest – are the traits of success. And while men admire the quality of the first, they love the produce of the second.'

John Steinbeck, *Cannery Row*

One of the great dangers of our churches flaunting what we've got in this way is that we run the risk of ending up with the ecclesiastical equivalent of school 'league tables'. When league tables were introduced in the early 1990s, very few experts or teachers opposed the idea *in principle* – parents had a right to know how good their local schools were and to send their child to the best one, and the schools themselves could benefit from healthy competition. But at the same time, very few experts or teachers agreed with the idea *in practice*. As they say, 'In theory, there's no difference between theory and practice, but in practice there is.'

The problem was, the sole criterion used to evaluate a school's 'success' and its league table place was exam results. And this, critics argued, was the *wrong* criterion. It wasn't what some teachers called 'value added' – it took no account of what a school could actually achieve. How could a run-down comprehensive in a poor urban area – with high crime, unemployment and illiteracy levels, and with little cash or informed parental support – possibly compete with a well-equipped selective-entry school in a well-to-do suburb, where the teachers' hard work in the classroom was complemented by the pupils' home environment? Schools that were making a massive difference in their pupils' lives were losing out because the lone criterion for success was bogus. At the same time, schools that had a significant head-start and a raft of social and educational advantages were winning considerable acclaim for themselves merely by making do. Schools at the top of the table could trumpet their success – flaunt what they'd got – but it wouldn't give a true picture. And, many educationalists believed, their success anyway had little to do with *real* education.

In exactly the same way, there's a huge danger that the successes and strengths we flaunt as churches are the wrong kinds of success and strength. Of course, no one wants the Church to be 'amateur hour', but at the same time we don't want it to be an 'e-fit' of a multinational company. Neatness and efficiency can be important. So can *not* hiding your light under a bushel. But it's vital to ensure that what you choose to highlight to people about yourself and your church are the *right* things.

Size, shape, space, staff, style, situation, surroundings, savings, sophistication, soundness, skill-base, stability, sermon quality, singing, social life . . . these are all important elements of church life, but by biblical standards none of them are in the end what determines whether we're 'successful' or not. As far as the Bible is concerned, real success boils down to just one basic characteristic – *service*. If we're busy chasing all the trappings that seem to accompany 'success' in mainstream society, rather than focussing on serving people in the way that Jesus did, then we're likely to come across as being less than entirely genuine. There's a lot of truth in the old adage, 'The first Bible people read is *you*.' If our style doesn't match our substance, if our rhetoric is out of alignment with our reality, then our 'success' will actually act as a hindrance to God's kingdom, not a help. As one thoughtful critic put it, 'The world has no problem believing in a poor carpenter's son who gave his life for others. What it can't stomach is rich preachers who get fat telling the world about a poor carpenter's son who gave his life for others.'

This is a situation Paul knew only too well from his experiences in Corinth. Situated near Athens, Corinth was a major shipping and trade centre. Having been totally destroyed by the Romans in 146 BC, it had been rebuilt as a Roman city, with a new breed of citizen and a hard-nosed business culture. 'Only the strong and ruthless could survive the intense competitiveness of a wide-open boom town,' explains Irish biblical scholar Jerome Murphy-O'Connor. 'Corinth had no hereditary patrician class to give it the stately dignity that an ancient university city such as Athens enjoyed. Its prominent citizens were all *nouveaux riches*. The only Corinthian tradition which the new colony respected was commercial success.'

Paul arrived in Corinth in AD 50, and together with his fellow Jewish Christians Priscilla and Aquila founded a church that managed not only to grow, but to span the social classes. Some members of the church were poor and ranked low on the social scale, while others were, it seems, tremendously wealthy. Guessing that the city's cut-and-thrust commercialism would eventually lead to problems (see 1 Corinthians 11, for instance), Paul felt the need to pay his own way, earning his living by making tents rather than accepting financial support from some of the church's wealthier members. He supplemented this income by accepting funds from other churches, so he couldn't be accused of sponging off the Corinthians. He also deliberately played down his often-considerable debating skills, and his natural sense of authority. In fact, in a city of style-conscious, wealthy whiz kids, Paul set out to be Mr Counterculture. He strongly advocated humility, 'foolishness', 'weakness' and service to a city that treasured the opposite values of self-importance, intelligence, strength and power.

But despite this, after he left the city in late AD 51, Corinth's Christians sank back into their old image-driven ways. Egged on by those Paul sarcastically dubbed 'super-apostles', the Christian community soon became proud of its wealth, proud of its influence, proud of its wisdom, proud of its liberty and proud of the diversity of its 'spiritual gifts'. The Corinthian Christians respected only flash and cash. So writing to set them straight, Paul pitched in full-blast with a savage and comprehensive attack on their if-you've-got-it-flaunt-it approach to both individual and church life.

The Corinthians were proud of their generosity and their ability to keep the super-apostles in the style to which they'd become accustomed; but Paul accused the super-apostles of being leeches and played up the fact that he'd never taken money from the Corinthians. 'I "robbed" other churches by accepting support from them in order to serve you' (2 Corinthians 11:8), he admitted. The Corinthians were proud of the erudite style and high standard of their teaching; but Paul warned them about heresy, dismissed the super-apostles as phoneys and made a virtue out of his 'untrained' and unsophisticated speech. In fact, his second letter to them shows him to be anything *but* untrained and unsophisticated. His decision not to present himself as a flashy speaker in Corinth was deliberate (1 Corinthians 2:1–5). But when he then found himself being dismissed as 'untrained' – the Greek gives us our word 'idiot' – and therefore not as doctrinally sound as the super-apostles, he hit back very sarcastically in 2 Corinthians 11:6. 'Training', which he'd *had* but hadn't *shown off*, wasn't what mattered, he argued. He may have been (deliberately) short on style, but he was long on substance. He couldn't say the same for the Corinthians, and said just the opposite about the super-apostles.

'With ruthless irony, he turns the convention upside down and parodies the self-display of his opponents by highlighting what he should hide and minimising what should be accentuated,' notes Murphy-O'Connor. 'Are they ministers [servants] of Christ?' Paul himself asked, making his own set of mocking 'boasts'. 'I am talking like a madman – I am a better one: with far greater labours, far more imprisonments, with countless floggings, and often near death . . . Who is weak, and I am not weak? Who is made to stumble, and I am not indignant?' (2 Corinthians 11:23–30).

'Empty as a pocket, with nothing to lose'

Look at me: I worked my way up from nothing to a state of extreme poverty.

US comedian Julius Henry 'Groucho' Marx

It was an attitude that Paul had caught from Jesus himself who, he told the church in Philippi, 'did not regard [his] equality with God as something to be exploited, but emptied himself, taking the form of a slave, being born in human likeness. And being found in human form, he humbled himself and became obedient to the point of death – even death on a cross' (Philippians 2:6–8).

Jesus wasn't one to blow his own trumpet. According to the Gospels, his overwhelming topic of conversation, and the content of the vast majority of his teaching, was the kingdom of God. In fact, he said so little about himself that some scholars down through the ages have reached the conclusion (helped by Paul's relative silence on the biographical details of what Jesus said and did during his life) that he was really little more than a wandering rabbi wrongly convicted and executed. Paul, they argue, 'invented' Christianity around him, distorting his real message and importance along the way. Of course, this view doesn't fit the New Testament evidence. It doesn't even fit the evidence from Paul himself. But then, neither does our automatic assumption that Jesus highlighted his own supreme importance.

The truth is, even when Jesus *did* talk about himself, he tended to use ambiguous expressions that emphasised what he was saying rather than his own personal significance. 'Son of Man', for example, was a coded reference to the messiah (as in Daniel 7:13), but it could equally be a way of speaking of a representative of God's 'chosen people' (as in Ezekiel 2:1), a poetic way of saying 'human being' (as in Psalm 8:4), or simply an ancient equivalent of 'I'. In the same way, 'Son of God' didn't mean 'God the Son' until the New Testament writers deliberately gave it this meaning in the light of Jesus' resurrection. Before Jesus, it was basically a way of referring to the whole nation of Israel, and therefore by extension it was a term used for *any* Israelite, or sometimes even the *ultimate* Israelite, the messiah. What these terms meant depended largely on how they were used and in what context – and Jesus generally took full advantage of their ambiguity. He amazed people not so much by any grand claims he made for himself as by the staggering things he said about God and his 'chosen people'.

Above all, Jesus attacked the way his fellow Jews presumed on their 'special relationship' with God. He attacked their superior, holier-than-thou attitude, warning that they'd void their special covenant deal with God if they were more focussed on what God could do *for* them than on what he wanted to do *through* them. The whole idea of a chosen people was essentially to be a nation through whom God would save the world, not a nation whom God would save instead of the world. It was as much a responsibility as a privilege. The chosen people's status was therefore to be God's servant, not the world's master.

This was a point Jesus made very markedly during a formal dinner at a Pharisee's house, when he told a joke about guests and the seating plan. 'When you are invited by someone to a wedding banquet, do not sit down at the place of honour, in case someone more distinguished than you has been invited by your host; and the host who invited both of you may come and say to you, "Give this person your place," and then in disgrace you would start to take the lowest place. But when you are invited, go and sit down at the lowest place, so that when your host comes, he may say to you, "Friend, move up higher;" then you will be honoured in the presence of all who sit at the table with you. For all who exalt themselves will be humbled, and those who humble themselves will be exalted' (Luke 14:8–11).

Part of the humour in this story stems from the fact that rural Jews, like everyone else in the first century, were acutely aware of precisely where they stood in society's pecking order. The idea that one of them would accidentally take too exalted a seat – or that an important guest would seat themselves rather than wait to be fussed over by the host – was totally farcical. But this, Jesus warned, was just what they were in danger of doing. It's a story that was aimed primarily at the entire nation rather than specific individuals. And it's a story that's as relevant and challenging to us today as it was when it first tripped off Jesus' tongue two millennia ago. If we think too highly of ourselves, someone will always be there to set us straight . . . and it may not be a pleasant experience.

In Hans Christian Andersen's famous story 'The Emperor's New Clothes', a pompous ruler is duped by two con men who arrive in his town and pass themselves off as weavers. Their cloth, they inform him, is of such high quality, and its colour and pattern are so beautiful, that only the very wise can see it. It's totally invisible to anyone who's stupid. A fashion victim, but not a genius, the emperor orders an expensive set of clothes made from the wonder cloth. As a precaution, however, he sends round two of his most trusted officials to inspect the work. But even though both men fail to see anything at all of the cloth, neither wants to come clean and admit it – after all, who wants to acknowledge they're stupid? Eventually, the suit is ready. But though even the emperor himself can see nothing, by this stage he knows he'll lose all authority and credibility with his subjects, and demonstrate his stupidity, if he's honest about it. So instead, he ends up allowing himself to be paraded through the town wearing clothes so subtle and refined 'you'd think you had nothing on'. Until, that is, a little child dares to shout out what everyone else is secretly thinking: 'He *has* got nothing on!'

This was a lesson that perhaps Pope Innocent III should have learnt – one even Jesus' vulnerable teenage mother Mary could have taught him. 'My soul magnifies the Lord, and my spirit rejoices in God my Saviour, for he has looked with favour on the lowliness of his servant,' she said. 'He has . . . brought down the powerful from their thrones, and lifted up the lowly; he has filled the hungry with good things, and sent the rich away empty' (Luke 1:46–53). For all his triumph and treasure, Innocent III ended up as publicly naked as the newly clothed emperor. Why? Because unlike the everlasting benefits of love and service, the trappings of success have a habit of turning to nothing at critical moments. Flash and cash, size and sophistication, have none of the long-term staying power of love and compassion. As the future cardinal Jacques de Vitry lamented on seeing Innocent III's naked body (in words that were incorporated into the service of papal coronation two centuries later), '*sic transit gloria mundi*' – 'this is what happens to the glories of the world'.

But the truth is, whether we realise it or not, we *too* have frequently followed the example of Innocent III rather than St Francis of Assisi – both as individuals and as the Church. Rather than allowing God to clothe us with 'the garments of salvation' and cover us with 'the robes of righteousness' (Isaiah 61:10), we've gone willingly to the emperor's tailors, and left the premises stark naked. God told the prophet Samuel, 'the LORD does not see as mortals see; they look on the outward appearance, but the LORD looks on the heart' (1 Samuel 16:7). But rather than trying to develop this kind of Godlike vision, we've generally opted for the mortal approach, judging and expecting to be accurately judged by 'outward appearance'. In exactly the same way as the rest of the world, we've loudly flaunted what we've got in terms of the accoutrements of 'success'. The challenge ahead of us is, instead, one of humility – showing what should be our true colours in Christ-like service.

As Paul reminded the Philippians, Jesus gave up his power to express his love. He preferred the way of humble meekness rather than self-promoting, self-evident majesty. 'He humbled himself and became obedient to the point of death – even death on a cross' (Philippians 2:8). There's nothing in Jesus of the 'macho messiah' –

for that, you'd need to look to the Greek myths of Hercules. Instead, Jesus reveals a vulnerable God – one whose glory is inextricably bound up with his grace. He became a fragile baby, and died naked and abandoned. The example he set us to follow isn't 'if you've got it, flaunt it', but what the Brazilian theologian Leonardo Boff calls being 'weak in power but strong in love'.

Conclusion

It caused a scandal. In order to mark the millennium, the two thousandth anniversary of Jesus' birth, a statue of Jesus was temporarily installed on the fourth plinth in London's Trafalgar Square. In 1843, when the square had first been opened, four enormous plinths had been built around the centrepiece of Nelson's Column to hold statues of George IV, William IV and two heroes of the British Raj, Sir Henry Havelock and General Sir Charles James Napier. William IV, however, had failed to provide the funds for his own statue, so the plinth had stood empty for 156 years. The figure of Jesus, *Ecce Homo*, was installed in July 1999, the first of three statues designed to spark a public debate about what should go on the final plinth. It worked.

Cast in synthetic resin and white marble dust from a life-size mould of a bald-headed, clean-shaven art student, Mark Wallinger's statue was a mere fraction of the size of the plinth itself. Naked except for a loin cloth, with his hands tied behind his back and a gold-plated barbed wire 'crown of thorns' on his head, Jesus looked tiny and inconsequential by comparison with the grand scale of the rest of the square. Most passers-by were amazed by the image – it was so totally different to the usual, triumphalist images of Christ that adorn buildings and famous works of art. Where, people asked, were his beard, his long hair, his cross, his fine robes? And why was he so tiny and vulnerable? Many objected strongly. As one man commented, 'You couldn't put your faith in someone like that, he's as weak as a kitten.'

In the same way, Jesus himself amazed most of those people he encountered two thousand years ago, and many strongly objected to him. Neither he nor his teaching fitted the stereotype, the popular image Jews had in their minds of the messiah. Nor was he like a normal rabbi – his teaching wasn't just a rehash of everyone else's. It had an authority and insight all of its own. Jesus challenged people, disturbed them, incensed them, amused them, upset them, provoked them, inspired them, encouraged them and turned their world upside down, allowing them to see things from a whole new perspective – God's perspective. His followers, and many of those he encountered along the way, loved him for it. His enemies loathed and eventually killed him for it.

But in the intervening years, we've domesticated him. There was something fundamentally radical and extraordinary about the historical Jesus; there's something fundamentally comfortable and unremarkable about his modern-day followers. We've somehow managed to remould and remake him in our own image, turning him from a 'failed' and shamefully executed first-century Palestinian Jewish 'revolutionary' leader – and Lord of the whole world – into no more than a common expletive and a rubber stamp for some of our worst values. We've frequently allowed ourselves to put words and maxims into his mouth, and then proceeded to *live* them as modern-day creeds, without ever even bothering to check back and see how they compare with his *real* teachings.

But the Jesus barely contained in the pages of the Gospels still has the ability to surprise and disturb us, if we're willing to spend long enough listening to him. Initially we may react with scepticism, even hostility, because he doesn't fit our stereotype. But having broken through that immediate response, his difference and intimacy will open up far greater possibilities than we dare to imagine.

Prepare to be *disturbed*.

Further reading

Christoph Arnold, *The Lost Art of Forgiving: Stories of Healing from the Cancer of Bitterness,* Plough, Robertsbridge, 1998. A challenging look at the power and potential of forgiveness, told through real-life stories.

Robert McAfee Brown, *Spirituality and Liberation: Overcoming the Great Fallacy,* Westminster, Philadelphia, 1988. A firm challenge to the idea that God is only interested in the 'spiritual' side of our lives.

Frederick F. Bruce, *The Hard Sayings of Jesus,* Hodder & Stoughton, London, 1983. A clear and concise look at seventy of the more puzzling things Jesus *did* say, by one of the most influential and well-respected British theologians of the twentieth century.

Richard Burridge, *Four Gospels, One Jesus? A Symbolic Reading,* SPCK, London, 1994. An introduction to the different pictures of Jesus given by each of the four Gospels, using the early Church's Revelation-inspired symbols: man (Matthew), lion (Mark), ox (Luke) and eagle (John).

Steve Chalke and Sue Radford, *New Era, New Church?* HarperCollins, London, 1999. A practical guide to Fanfare for a

New Generation's ten-point 'New Millennium Challenge to the Churches', encouraging local churches to make themselves more 'user-friendly'.

Robert Davidson, *A Beginner's Guide to the Old Testament*, Saint Andrew Press, Edinburgh, 1992. The best non-technical Old Testament introduction on the market, by one of Scotland's most readable and respected biblical scholars.

Richard France, *Jesus the Radical: A Portrait of the Man They Crucified*, IVP, Leicester, 1989. A bit dated (first published in the 1970s), this is still a great introduction to Jesus and first-century Palestine, by a former Principal of Wycliffe Hall theological college, Oxford.

Michael Frost, *Jesus the Fool*, Albatross, Sutherland, 1994. A lively and imaginative book focussing on Jesus' ability to surprise the people he encountered during his life, both through his unpredictable actions and his dramatic shock-ending parables.

Os Guinness, *Fit Bodies, Fat Minds: Why Evangelicals Don't Think and What to Do About It,* Hodder & Stoughton, London, 1995. A insightful examination into why Evangelicals avoid theological reflection, by an Evangelical committed to helping others think about their faith.

Simon Jones, *Struggling to Belong: What Is the Church for Anyway?* IVP, Leicester, 1998. Packed with stories, this is a practical and sometimes disturbing look at what it means to be a Christian in a local church *without* surrendering either intelligence or compassion.

J. Richard Middleton and Brian J. Walsh, *Truth Is Stranger Than It Used To Be: Biblical Faith in a Postmodern Age*, SPCK, London, 1995. A look at the challenges posed to faith by postmodernism's patchwork-quilt approach, helping Christians work through the issues.

Graham Stanton, *Gospel Truth? New Light on Jesus and the Gospels*, HarperCollins, London, 1995. A challenging and informative look at Jesus, and the Gospel accounts of his life, by a leading traditionalist Cambridge theologian.

David Wenham, *The Parables of Jesus: Pictures of Revolution*, Hodder & Stoughton, London, 1989. An insightful, informed look at both the individual parables of Jesus and also the message they were designed to communicate as a whole.

N. Thomas Wright, *The Challenge of Jesus*, SPCK, London, 2000. A brief but highly rewarding look at Jesus in his first-century historical context by the Canon Theologian of Westminster Abbey and the leading Jesus scholar of his generation.

Nigel Wright, *The Radical Evangelical: Seeking a Place to Stand*, SPCK, London, 1996. A far better attempt than Tomlinson's *The Post-Evangelical* to come to terms with the tough challenges now facing Evangelicals, by the Principal of Spurgeon's College, London.

Philip Yancey, *The Jesus I Never Knew*, Zondervan, Grand Rapids, 1995. One of America's finest and most influential Christian writers takes a fresh look at the life of Jesus.

Works cited

Quotations from the Bible are generally from the New Revised Standard Version, copyright, 1989 by the Division of Christian Education of the National Council of the Churches of Christ in the USA. Those quotations *not* from the NRSV are the authors' own translations.

Other quotations in the main body of the text, and some of the stand-alone quotations, are taken from the following:

Leo Aylen, *Return to Zululand,* Sidgwick and Jackson, London, 1980.

Kenneth Bailey, *Poet & Peasant/Through Peasant Eyes: A Literary Critical Approach to the Parables in Luke*, Eerdmans, Grand Rapids, 1983.

Baptist Union, *Orders and Prayers for Church Worship*, compiled by Ernest A. Payne and Stephen F. Winward, Baptist Union, London, 1960. Fourth Edition, 1967.

Baptist Union, *Patterns and Prayers for Christian Worship*, compiled by Bernard Green, Christopher Ellis, Rachel Harrison, Stuart Jenkins, Michael Nicholls and Tony Turner, Oxford University Press, Oxford, 1991.

Richard Bauckham, *The Theology of the Book of Revelation*, Cambridge University Press, Cambridge, 1993.

Leonardo Boff, *Jesus Christ Liberator: A Critical Christology of Our Time*, SPCK, London, 1980.

Marcus Borg, *Meeting Jesus Again for the First Time*, HarperCollins, New York, 1994.

Robert McAfee Brown, *Saying Yes and Saying No: On Rendering to God and Caesar*, Westminster Press, Philadelphia, 1986.

Craig Broyles, *Psalms*, New International Bible Commentary, Paternoster, Carlisle, 1999.

Frederick F. Bruce, *The Gospel of John*, Eerdmans, Grand Rapids, 1983.

Walter Brueggemann, *The Prophetic Imagination*, Fortress Press, Philadelphia, 1978.

Bill Bryson, *Made in America*, Black Swan, London, 1998.

George Caird, *Saint Luke*, Penguin, London, 1963.

George Caird, *The Language and Imagery of the Bible*, Duckworth, London, 1980.

Mark Carnes and John Garraty with Patrick Williams, *Mapping America's Past: A Historical Atlas*, Henry Holt, New York, 1996.

Lewis Carroll, *Through the Looking Glass*, Penguin, London, 1994.

Robert Carroll, *Wolf in the Sheepfold: The Bible as a Problem for Christianity*, SPCK, London, 1991.

Donald A. Carson, *Exegetical Fallacies*, Baker, Grand Rapids, 1996.

Owen Chadwick, *The Reformation*, Penguin, London, 1964.

John Cornwell, *Hitler's Pope: The Secret History of Pius XII*, Viking, London, 1999.

Robert Davidson, *A Beginner's Guide to the Old Testament*, Saint Andrew Press, Edinburgh, 1992.

John Drane, 'Sermons – Again!' *Ministry Today*, Issue 19, June 2000.

James Dunn and Alan Suggate, *The Justice of God: A Fresh Look at the Old Doctrine of Justification by Faith*, Paternoster, Carlisle, 1993.

Thomas S. Eliot, *Collected Poems, 1909–1962*, Faber and Faber, London, 1974.

Craig Evans, *Luke*, New International Biblical Commentary, Hendrickson, Peabody, 1990.

Richard France, *Matthew*, New Tyndale Commentaries, IVP, Leicester, 1985.

Lawrence Friedman, *Crime and Punishment in American History*, HarperCollins, New York, 1993.

Florentino Garcia Martinez, *The Dead Sea Scrolls Translated: The Qumran Texts in English*, E. J. Brill, Leiden, 1996.

Joel Green, *The Gospel of Luke*, New International Commentary on the New Testament, Eerdmans, Grand Rapids, 1997.

Os Guinness, *Fit Bodies, Fat Minds: Why Evangelicals Don't Think and What to Do About It,* Hodder & Stoughton, London, 1995.

Nicky Gumbel, *Questions of Life*, Kingsway, Eastbourne, 1993.

Larry Hurtado, *At the Origins of Christian Worship: The Context and Character of Earliest Christian Devotion,* The 1999 Didsbury Lectures, Paternoster, Carlisle, 1999.

Robert Jackson, 'Prosperity Theology and the Faith Movement', *Themelios,* Vol. 15, No. 1.

David Jenkins, *God, Miracle and the Church of England*, SCM, London, 1987.

Simon Jones, *Struggling to Belong: What Is the Church for Anyway?* IVP, Leicester, 1998.

Martin Luther King, *A Testament of Hope: The Essential Writings and Speeches of Martin Luther King, Jr,* ed. James M. Washington, HarperCollins, New York, 1986.

Clive S. Lewis, *The Lion, the Witch and the Wardrobe,* Penguin, London, 1959.

Martin Luther, *Martin Luther: Selections from His Writings,* ed. and introduced by John Dillenberger, Anchor/Doubleday, New York, 1962.

Gordon MacDonald, *Ordering Your Private World,* Highland Books, Guildford, 1985.

Gordon MacDonald, *Rebuilding Your Broken World,* Highland Books, Guildford, 1988.

Neil MacGregor with Erika Langmuir, *Seeing Salvation: Images of Christ in Art,* BBC, London 2000.

Scot McKnight, *A New Vision: The Teachings of Jesus in National Context,* Eerdmans, Grand Rapids, 1999.

Leon Morris, *The Epistle to the Romans,* Pillar Commentary Series, IVP, Leicester, 1988.

Jerome Murphy-O'Connor, *The Theology of the Second Letter to the Corinthians,* Cambridge University Press, Cambridge, 1991.

Reinhold Niebuhr, *The Essential Reinhold Niebuhr: Selected Essays and Addresses,* ed. and introduced by Robert McAfee Brown, Yale, New Haven, 1986.

George Orwell, *Animal Farm,* Penguin, London, 1989.

George Orwell, *Nineteen Eighty-Four,* Penguin, London, 1989.

John Stott, *The Message of Romans*, The Bible Speaks Today, IVP, Leicester, 1994.

Gaius Cornelius Tacitus, *The Annals of Imperial Rome*, trans. Michael Grant, Guild/Penguin, London, 1990.

Richard H. Tawney, *Religion and the Rise of Capitalism*, Penguin, London, 1938.

Scott Turow, *Presumed Innocent*, Penguin, London, 1988.

Jim Wallis, *Agenda for Biblical People*, SPCK, London, 1986.

Jim Wallis, *The Soul of Politics: A Practical and Prophetic Vision for Change*, Fount, London, 1994.

Jim Wallis and Joyce Hollyday (eds.), *Cloud of Witnesses*, Orbis, New York/Sojourners, Washington DC, 1991.

Margery Williams, *The Velveteen Rabbit, or How Toys Become Real*, Mammoth, London, 1989 (first published 1922).

Walter Wink, *Unmasking the Powers: The Invisible Forces that Determine Human Existence*, Fortress, Philadelphia, 1986.

Ben Witherington III, *Women in the Ministry of Jesus*, Cambridge University Press, Cambridge, 1984.

Christopher Wright, *Living as the People of God: The Relevance of Old Testament Ethics*, IVP, Leicester, 1983.

Christopher Wright, *Deuteronomy*, New International Biblical Commentary, Paternoster, Carlisle, 1996.

N. Thomas Wright, 'The New Testament and the "State" ', *Themelios*, Vol. 16, No. 1.

N. Thomas Wright, *What Saint Paul Really Said: Was Paul of Tarsus the Real Founder of Christianity?* Lion, Oxford, 1997.

N. Thomas Wright, *The Challenge of Jesus*, SPCK, London, 2000.

Nigel Wright, *The Radical Evangelical: Seeking a Place to Stand*, SPCK, London, 1996.

Philip Yancey, *What's So Amazing About Grace?* Zondervan, Grand Rapids, 1997.

This book is dedicated to the late David McGavin, Managing Director and driving force behind Xalt.co.uk, a free internet service provider and supersite launched as an initiative by the Oasis Group.

Xalt.co.uk combines UK and world news, sport, shopping and entertainment with unique Christian content, resources, interviews . . . and a whole lot more. It also offers email and web-browsing facilities, together with web space, regular updates from your chosen church or charity and optional safe-surfing. And for every minute spent online with Xalt.co.uk, funds are raised for Christian causes.

The David McGavin Scholarship Fund

In memory of David, and his passion for both the internet and world mission, Xalt and the Oasis initiative Wire the World have joined forces to create THE DAVID MCGAVIN SCHOLARSHIP FUND. Wire the World aims to provide education in IT skills to some of the poorest people in the world, enabling them to break out of the cycle of poverty. THE DAVID MCGAVIN SCHOLARSHIP FUND will provide resources for some of these young people to go on to further education and fulfil their potential.

To find out how to give a donation to THE DAVID MCGAVIN SCHOLARSHIP FUND, log on to www.Xalt.co.uk or write to Oasis, 115 Southwark Bridge Road, London SE1 0AX . . . and change lives today.